FLORIDA STATE
UNIVERSITY LIBRARIES

JUL 1 1 2001

TALLAHASSEE, FLORIDA

NATION, IDENTITY AND SOCIAL THEORY

Nation, Identity AND Social Theory

PERSPECTIVES FROM WALES

Edited by RALPH FEVRE and ANDREW THOMPSON

*Published on behalf of
the Board of Celtic Studies of the University of Wales*

UNIVERSITY OF WALES PRESS
CARDIFF
1999

© The Contributors, 1999

British Library Cataloguing-in-Publication Data.
A catalogue record for this book is available from the British Library.

ISBN 0-7083-1545-3

All rights reserved. No part of this book may be reproduced, stored in a retrieval system, or transmitted, in any form or by any means, electronic, mechanical, photocopying, recording or otherwise, without clearance from the University of Wales Press, 6 Gwennyth Street, Cardiff, CF2 4YD.

Typeset at University of Wales Press
Printed in Great Britain by Dinefwr Press, Llandybïe

Contents

List of Contributors	vii
Acknowledgements	x
Introduction	1
1 Social Theory and Welsh Identities *Ralph Fevre and Andrew Thompson*	3
Part I: Nation	**25**
2 Situating Welshness: 'Local' Experience and National Identity *Andrew Thompson and Graham Day*	27
3 The Intellectual and the National Movement in Wales *David Adamson*	48
4 Passports to Wales? Race, Nation and Identity *Charlotte Williams*	69
5 Nationalism, Feminism and Welsh Women: Conflicts and Accommodations *Charlotte Aull Davies*	90
Part II: Place	**109**
6 Welsh Identity in a Former Mining Valley: Social Images and Imagined Communities *Brian Roberts*	111
7 Nation, Community and Conflict: Housing Policy and Immigration in North Wales *Ralph Fevre, John Borland and David Denney*	129

8	Prospects of Wales: Contested Geographical Imaginations *Pyrs Gruffudd*	149
9	Spatial Restructuring in the Capital: Struggles to Shape Cardiff's Built Environment *Huw Thomas*	168

Part III: Heritage — 189

10	Great Little Trains? The Role of Heritage Railways in North Wales in the Denial of Welsh Identity, Culture and Working-Class History *Dave Marks*	191
11	Territoriality and Heritage in South Wales: Space, Time and Imagined Communities *Bella Dicks and Joost van Loon*	207

Conclusion — 233

12	Nation, Identity and Social Theory *Andrew Thompson*	233

Bibliography — 250

Index — 270

The Contributors

David Adamson is Principal Lecturer in Sociology and Director of the Regional Research Programme at the University of Glamorgan. He has researched widely on issues of social and economic change in Wales, the sociology of nationalism and social exclusion. He is the author of *Class, Ideology and Nation: A Theory of Welsh Nationalism* (University of Wales, Press, 1991). He is currently involved in a number of research projects on social exclusion in the south Wales Valleys.

John Borland is Senior Lecturer in Sociology at the University of Wales, Bangor, where he is also Director of the Centre of Applied Community Studies. His wide-ranging academic interests are in the area of Welsh, Irish and European nationalism, the social history of Kuwait, the Irish experience in Britain, and disability.

Charlotte Aull Davies is Lecturer in Sociology and Anthropology at the University of Wales, Swansea. She has carried out ethnographic research and published on topics as varied as ethnic nationalism, feminism and cultural identities, and learning disabilities. Her publications include *Welsh Nationalism in the Twentieth Century: The Ethnic Option and the Modern State* and *Reflexive Ethnography: A Guide to Researching Selves and Others*.

Graham Day is Senior Lecturer in Sociology and Head of School in the School of Sociology and Social Policy, at University of Wales, Bangor, and a founding editor of the journal *Contemporary Wales*. He has published widely on aspects of economic and social change in Wales and has a particular interest in national, regional and local identities. Currently he is researching forms of community development and participation.

David Denney has held lectureships at the University of Kent and the

University of Wales, Bangor. He is currently Reader in Social and Public Policy at Royal Holloway, University of London. He has written and researched in a number of areas including the impact of discrimination on social and legal services, nationalism and citizenship. He is currently researching the impact of violence on professionals in the community as part of the ESRC Violence Research Project.

Bella Dicks is Research Fellow in the School of Social Science at University of Wales, Cardiff. She is working on an ESRC project investigating the potential of hypermedia for ethnographic research. Her Ph.D. examined the encoding and decoding of heritage texts, focusing on the representation of coal-mining communities at the Rhondda Heritage Park in south Wales. Prior to this, she worked on another ESRC project at Sheffield Hallam University on the responses of coalfield communities to pit closures in the 1990s.

Ralph Fevre is Professor of Social Research at University of Wales, Cardiff. His recent work includes *The Sociology of Labour Markets* (1992) and studies of the theoretical significance of Welsh nationalism. He is perhaps best known within Wales for his study of the effects of industrial restructuring in south Wales in the 1980s, *Wales is Closed* (1989). He is currently a partner in ESRC research on participation in post-compulsory education and training in the same region.

Pyrs Gruffudd is Lecturer in Human Geography at University of Wales Swansea. He completed a Ph.D. at Loughborough University on landscape and rural identities in inter-war Wales and was a post-doctoral researcher at Nottingham University on John Constable, landscape and English identity before taking up his current post at Swansea. He recently undertook a Leverhulme Trust-funded project on the 'moral geographies' of industrial south Wales between the wars.

Joost Van Loon obtained a Ph.D. from Lancaster University in 1996. He now works as a Senior Lecturer in Social Theory at the Nottingham Trent University and is associated with the Theory, Culture and Society Centre. He has published extensively on issues of risk, technology and culture, is co-editor of *Repositioning Risk: Critical Issues for Social Theory* (Sage, 1999) and the journal *Space and Culture* and is currently working on epidemiology and newly emerging viruses.

Dave Marks has been a Sessional Lecturer at the Liverpool John Moores University since 1991 in the School of Social Science. Prior to this he worked in a variety of occupations, including the engineering and railway industries, and in market gardening. He has a long-standing interest in the industrial history and culture of north Wales and has recently submitted his Ph.D. thesis on representations in the north Wales slate heritage industry.

Brian Roberts lectures in Sociology at the University of Huddersfield. His research interests include biography, community studies, national identity and Welsh labour history. He is on the editorial boards of *Auto/Biography and Family and Community History* and is active within research committees on biography within the European Sociological Association and the International Sociological Association. He is co-author (with S. Hall *et al.*) of *Policing the Crisis* (1978).

Huw Thomas is a Senior Lecturer in the Department of City and Regional Planning, University of Wales, Cardiff. He has also taught at Oxford Brookes University, and prior to that was a planner at Cardiff City Council. His current research interests include evaluating urban policy (where he has a special interest in urban development corporations), and analysing the place of town planning in a racialized society.

Andrew Thompson is Principal Lecturer in Sociology at the University of Glamorgan. He was awarded a Ph.D. in sociology from the University of Wales, Bangor in 1995. His current research interests are in the sociology of Wales, nationalism, European integration and globalization. He is the co-editor, with David Dunkerley, of *Wales Today* (University of Wales Press, 1999).

Charlotte Williams is a lecturer in Social Work and Social Policy at the University of Wales, Bangor. She has been researching, publishing, practising and training in the field of anti-racism for over fifteen years. She has a particular interest in issues of 'race', language, identity and culture in Wales and in Europe and is co-editor of the book *Social Work and Minorities: European Perspectives*.

Acknowledgements

The editors would like to acknowledge the support and guidance of the Board of Celtic Studies of the University of Wales in the production of this volume, and of Ceinwen Jones at the University of Wales Press in the preparation of the manuscript for publication. We would also like to thank those who have offered critical commentary on various drafts of the volume, especially the three anonymous reviewers. Ralph Fevre would like to thank his long-suffering family for their patience, and Andrew Thompson would particularly like to thank Cerys Davies for her help, advice and high levels of endurance.

INTRODUCTION

1 Social Theory and Welsh Identities

Ralph Fevre and Andrew Thompson

At the twilight of the twentieth century, the end of the nation and nationalism continues to seem so near and yet so far. The looming spectre of a new century, indeed of a new millennium, has encouraged speculation and introspection about the possibilities and potential which the future holds; central to this debate has been the role which nation-states and nationalisms will occupy in this new world. For some the prospect that the future will only bring more of the same seems a bleak scenario, particularly in relation to the issue of nationalism. Nationalism has been held up as one of the most destructive, if not *the* most destructive force of the twentieth century; the 'resurgence' of nationalisms in the late twentieth century has only served to confirm such views. For others, with an eye on the rise of global traders, the creation of supranational trading blocs and the evolution of new communicative technologies, the demise of nations and nationalisms seems certain, if still ahead of us. Here, nationalisms, like many of the 'ancient' traditions and rituals which are integral to them, are redolent of a bygone era and thus have little place in the (post)modern world which is unfolding. Nevertheless, the enduring potency of notions of nationhood and national differences is still evident in many aspects of our lives, from debates on education and foreign policy to questions of 'culture' and 'heritage'. Even those who wish to curb the excesses of nationalistic chauvinism and xenophobia, such as the Labour Party in Britain, dare not suggest that the vestiges of 'our' nation be removed; nations will merely adapt, not die. Moreover, as the struggle for resources, markets and privileges intensifies, the question of borders and who they include will also become more prominent, not less so. In this environment nationalisms, with their emphasis on the 'authenticity' of roots and attachment to place, provide a rich source of legitimation. How, then, are we to respond to the question of the place of nations and nationalism within the twenty-first century?

Until relatively recently, considerations of nations and nationalism have occupied a largely marginal status within 'mainstream' social theory. In the writings of some of the pioneering figures in sociology during the late nineteenth and early twentieth centuries, there is scant discussion of nationalism, a force which nevertheless had a tremendous impact on their personal lives. Indeed, this neglect is manifest in the work of many of the main figures in twentieth-century social theory. There is, of course, a legacy of important studies in this field of research, notably in history, but it is only in very recent decades that social theorists have begun to express greater interest in these questions. The period since the early 1980s has been particularly fruitful, with the exchange of ideas across disciplinary boundaries. The studies which have emerged during this time have contributed much to our understanding of nationalism and national identity, especially with respect to explorations of the 'subjective' experience of these phenomena. There is, however, much work still to be done. Within social theory this challenge is peculiarly important, as it necessitates an investigation into how issues of 'nation' and the 'national' are embedded within academic discourses on 'society'. Such a course of action will, we believe, prompt further consideration of how certain representations of the nation (and who is incorporated within it) come to be accorded public status and what the consequences of these representations are for particular groups in 'national' societies.

In the United Kingdom, the issue of national identity has in recent years also become a matter of growing public concern. Televised debates on the future of the monarchy, on the issue of European Union as well as on devolution have each exposed differing responses to the significance of the 'British nation'. In the lead-up to the 1997 General Election, the issue of 'national sovereignty' was a major source of conflict between each of the main political parties, with regard to both the external process of European integration and internal processes of change between the constituent parts of the UK. In academic debates, too, there has been intense discussion about the current 'crisis of national identity' in the UK. The issue of devolution, for example, has often been reduced to a quite simple proposition: if Scotland and Wales constitute distinct nations, then they require distinct forms of representation. Yet, it must be asked to what extent the prevailing notions of Welsh or Scottish nationhood are themselves broad enough to accommodate the diverse forms of social life which are contained within their territorial borders. It is also necessary to ask what it means to claim a Welsh or Scottish identity and through what kinds of channels the differing experiences of Welshness and Scottishness are represented. Given the discussions about the need to forge a more democratic polity in Wales, and the questions concerning the role which the National Assembly will play in this future, it is important that we ask how these changes will be reflected in the need to open a more inclusive debate on the 'Welsh nation'. Responding to these questions means that we must begin to consider how public representations of 'Wales' and 'Welshness' are reproduced as well as to explore what the consequences of these practices are for how people understand what it is to be 'Welsh'.

This volume brings together writers who are placing such questions at the heart of their research on Wales. Each of the chapters explores differing dimensions of representations of Wales and Welshness, yet a common theme which binds them together is the desire to point to the diversity of Welsh experiences. This collection, then, seeks to draw out the multifarious, competing and changing national identities of the people who live (and have lived) in Wales. By drawing on some of the most recent developments in social theory the chapters in this volume bring a fresh element to existing debates on national identity. Debates on national identity in Wales, particularly within sociological theory, emerged in the mid-1970s and were stimulated by the work of two writers from outside Wales: Tom Nairn and Michael Hechter. In order to establish the context for the subsequent chapters we begin by turning our attention towards a consideration of some of this earlier work.

Social Theory and the 'National' Question in Wales

In many respects the growth of sociological research on Wales during the mid-1970s (principally under the auspices of the British Sociological Association Sociology of Wales Study Group) was itself a necessary response to what one participant (G. Williams, 1978) described as the 'centralist ethnocentricity' of mainstream British sociology. The collective work of the BSA Group was, then, directed towards filling some of the many gaps in knowledge concerning the social structure of Wales and the impact of economic restructuring.[1] There were, in addition, a number of other internal and external factors which influenced the early development of a sociology of Wales. Another early contributor to this debate (Day, 1979) argued that one of the key aims of the generation of sociologists working in this period was to come to terms with the legacy of the work of earlier indigenous sociologists (A. D. Rees, 1950; E. Davies and A. D. Rees, 1960), who, through their rural 'community studies', had developed something approaching a 'dominant account' of Welsh society. As Day stressed: '[t]here is a necessity for demythologizing Welsh society . . . We need an historically informed sociology of Welsh *ways* of life, and the transformations of communities' (1979: 452–3). Similarly, other sociologists have argued that some of the early social anthropological research on Wales, as developed, for example, in the writings of Frankenberg (1957) and Emmet (1964), portrayed Welsh rural society as a 'somewhat endangered, primitive form of social organisation which must yield to the larger, more complex forms of British society' (G. Williams, 1980: 169).

If, then, part of the driving inspiration behind some of the sociological research of the 1970s and early 1980s grew out of the desire to provide a corrective to earlier treatments of the 'Welsh way of life' (Day, 1979), another important influence was more directly connected to the growth in support for the nationalist movement in Wales. Electoral victories for Plaid Cymru in the 1970s, the rise and fall of the 1970s devolution programme and the campaign for a Welsh Fourth Channel (realized in 1982 with the launch of Sianel Pedwar Cymru) combined to heighten public awareness of questions of national identity. Moreover, studies by scholars from outside of Wales (Hechter, 1975; Nairn, 1977) which sought to locate the rise of nationalism in Wales (as well as in Ireland and Scotland) within the broader framework of the internal dynamics of the British state, also had the effect of intensifying the debate among sociologists of Wales. The cumulative impact of these developments was that, by the late 1970s and early 1980s, sociological attention in Wales had begun to focus more closely on analyses of the relationship between the class structure in Wales and the rise of nationalism (Williams, 1981; Adamson, 1984; Day, 1984; Day and Suggett, 1985).

In part these studies were informed by a critique of the interventions by Hechter and Nairn. Hechter's volume, *Internal Colonialism: The Celtic Fringe in British National Development* (1975), advances the argument that the rise of nationalism in Wales was a response to its peripheral economic relationship to the dominant English 'core'.

Drawing on Marxist theories of underdevelopment, in Hechter's model Wales assumes the status of an 'internal colony'. Capitalist development is driven by the requirements of the core economy, surplus capital is directed back towards the metropolitan centre, and, as a result, the periphery is held in a state of dependency. This analysis of the exploitative economic relationship between core and periphery is, in turn, supplemented by a neo-Weberian account of social closure. Within the economy of the internal colony, positions of power are occupied by representatives of the metropolitan centre, while the indigenous population are largely denied the material benefits of modernization. In common with Gellner's account of the role of processes of social closure in sponsoring the development of nationalism, for Hechter the consequence of this 'cultural division of labour' is that the inhabitants of the periphery come to identify with the cultural identity which is the cause of their exclusion.

Subsequent research (Lovering, 1978; Day, 1980; Adamson, 1991a) has pointed to considerable flaws in Hechter's understanding of the development of industrialization in Wales in the nineteenth and early twentieth centuries. In addition, a major source of criticism of Hechter's theory lies in his problematic treatment of the cultural homogeneity of the indigenous population of the peripheral region; put simply, Hechter's thesis centres on the cultural domination of 'the Welsh' by 'the English'. Such an account does not fit with the economic and political realities of Wales during the latter half of the nineteenth and early twentieth centuries, when Welsh Liberal Nonconformists occupied many of the élite positions within Welsh society. Aligned to this critique is the failure to provide a satisfactory account of the significance of class divisions within Wales and with it an analysis of the complexity of the relationship between structural change and the growth of nationalist sentiment. For Hechter the situation is explained in terms of a straightforward clash of interests between dominant and subordinate ethnic groups; there is, as a consequence of this line of enquiry, scant recognition in this account of internal social differentiation within Welsh society.

Similar criticisms may also be levelled at Nairn's thesis (1977), which views the growth of a bourgeois cultural and linguistic nationalism in Wales as a response to the decline of the British state and in reaction to the consequences of uneven economic development. Nairn approaches the issue of the rise of neo-nationalism from a perspective which, despite his own criticisms of

Hechter's analysis (Nairn, 1986), echoes a number of the central tenets of the 'internal colonialism' thesis (Day, 1980). Nairn's study, however, places a more explicit emphasis on a Marxist account of nationalism than is evident within Hechter's work, arguing that the rise of nationalism should be seen as the attempt by peripheral élites to counteract the impact of uneven development. As with the critique of Hechter's study, it has been argued that Nairn presents an overly general account of social relations within Welsh society. Day (1979: 250), for example, maintains that Nairn's tendency to treat the population of Wales as one culturally unified group 'conceals . . . issues of spatial and social differentiation within Wales'. Furthermore, Adamson (1991a) argues that Nairn's conception of nationalism as a bourgeois ideology fails to explain the 'class-neutrality' (Adamson, 1991a: 177) of nationalist ideology in Wales during both the nineteenth and twentieth centuries.

Both Hechter and Nairn develop approaches which, in spite of the import of Marxist theory, closely resemble the 'diffusionist' model employed by Gellner (1964, 1983). While a more recent study (Rawkins, 1983), examining the relationship between uneven development and the rise of nationalism, attempts to counteract the weaknesses of Gellner's thesis by acknowledging that the form of, and adherence to, cultural/ethnic identity will vary within peripheral regions, it is apparent that, for many of the approaches discussed above, 'culture' and 'ethnicity' are examined as distinct from the structural relations within which they are, in reality, located. In this sense therefore it may be argued that these approaches are limited in terms of their potential to provide an understanding of the reasons for the emergence of differing, and competing, constructions of Welsh national identity.

On the other hand, it may be that the most serious flaws in the arguments of Hechter and Nairn lie not in their neglect of the variety of national identities but in their apparent belief that it is the job of the social theorist to try to distinguish *right* from *wrong* identities amongst those which might naturally occur. Both arguments also seem to depend on the assumption that the proper concern of social science is to advance sound reasons as to why the former should replace the latter and the popularity of these fundamental assumptions amongst other authors testifies to the influence Hechter and Nairn had on social thought at this time. For them identity can only be considered a problem worth studying in the British context because the wrong (British) identity has long been imposed on people for whom it is not appropriate and there are now compelling reasons why this mistaken identity will be cast off in favour of the proper ones: the alternative national identities of the 'Celtic Fringe'.

In Nairn's terms identity is problematic because the idea of a British identity has operated only as a smokescreen to obscure the self-interested operation of capital which is now, at the end of empire, more easily unmasked to be the ideological device it has always been, even when none but the very wise could see it. Hechter argues that some of the operations of capital that had been obscured in this way are internal matters concerning the exploitation of the Celtic Fringe – instances of 'internal colonialism'. The Marxist influence was never plainer than in the way that what real people said about their identities was treated in these accounts. Where such evidence might have contradicted the fundamental assumptions made about 'right' and 'wrong' identities it is dismissed as the product of ideology and the fruit of false consciousness, especially that sort of false consciousness that flourishes under colonialism. On the other hand, any evidence of enthusiasm for the alternative identities of the Celtic Fringe, even a minority vote for nationalist parties in Scotland and Wales, is considered to be proof both of the rightness of that identity and of the inevitable progress it will make in displacing that false consciousness. It must be admitted, however, that evidence on the views that the residents of Scotland or Wales (for example) took about their identities at the time was not central to the work of Hechter and Nairn.

Direct discussion of popular views on national identities was more prominent in studies which were concerned wholly or mainly with questions of national identity considered in a Welsh context, nevertheless these studies were still able to hold to the fundamental assumptions made by the prevailing orthodoxy about the distinction between 'right' and 'wrong' identities and the necessity to support the promotion of the former over the latter. Thus the careful sociological work of Bud Khleif – like Hechter, an American sociologist – included a detailed investigation of questions of national identity in Wales at the time of the first devolution debate in 1979, but for Khleif the whole point of the investigation is to allow him to describe the 'right' national identity for Wales and to estimate the chances of this identity being more commonly adopted in future.

Khleif (1978, 1980) makes explicit his intellectual debt to Hechter and the Marxist legacy is clear in the way Khleif distinguishes between the various sorts of Welsh identities he encountered in his fieldwork. The right identity is defined as that which puts the Welsh language at the centre of the national question. For Khleif those who hold to this view are grasping the truth that remains hidden from those who own allegiance to other versions of Welsh national identity, namely that Wales has long suffered from exploitation and disenfranchisement at the hands of the world's most successful colonial power. What Khleif calls 'the pro-Welsh' identity (meaning pro Welsh language in the first instance, but then by implication pro the Welsh nation) has a direct counterpart in orthodox Marxist theory in the stirrings of class consciousness: in the way the scales fall from the eyes of the leaders of a class-for-itself, whether in a colonial situation or in the more humdrum case of the proletariat facing a home-grown bourgeoisie. On the other side of the coin, Khleif's dismissal of what he calls 'the anti-Welsh' identity has a direct analogue in the Marxist theory of false consciousness and it is on exactly these grounds (but with the familiar internal-colonial twist) that Khleif dismisses – even condemns – those Welsh women and men who tell him that their versions of national identity do not centre on the Welsh language:

> In looking for an overall principle to interpret diverse phenomena, in seeing the whole of which a given phenomenon may only be a part, one has to go beyond persons to the objective or larger situation in which they are enmeshed. When one meets anti-Welsh Welshmen, especially those of an upper-middle socioeconomic standing, one perhaps cannot but think of what Macaulay had said about India: We will create a class of people as intermediaries between us and the natives we govern. When one meets pro-Welsh Welshmen, especially those of middle socioeconomic status, one cannot but think of rising élites in the Third World, of cultural nationalism in both the Third World proper and its equivalent regions in the First World. In terms of the sociological perspective [Hechter's] discussed earlier, both the anti-Welsh and the pro-Welsh Welsh are two sides of the same 'Internal Colonialism' coin. (Khleif, 1980: 54)

In large part the perspectives offered by Hechter and Nairn and represented in the work of Khleif and others on national identity have gradually been superseded by the work in the social theory of nationalism (in particular, that influenced by the work of Benedict Anderson and Ernest Gellner) which informs the papers collected in this volume and, as a direct result, those who write on these questions are now much more reluctant to make easy distinctions between right and wrong identities. There are, however, a very few social scientists – for example, one or two geographers – working in and on Wales who appear to have been untouched by recent developments in the social theory of nationalism and who still rely on unreformed, simplistic assumptions about right and wrong national identities. In addition other writers have tried to use alternative bodies of theory to allow them to retain some of what they see to be the advantages of the older approach.

Glyn Williams, for example, noting what he describes 'as an unfortunate tendency in much analysis of Welsh politics to treat nationalism as a residual unrelated to the "natural" class basis of politics in general' (1986: 189), attempts to analyse the particular discursive formations which give rise to concepts of 'class' and 'ethnicity'. Williams makes use of French discourse analysis and, to rather greater effect, the work of Ernesto Laclau, to argue for the retention of the old distinctions between appropriate and inappropriate identity on the basis of the sort of relativism which some might say denies the possibility of any sort of social theory. All the same, it was clear that by the early to mid-1980s social theory in and on Wales was much less dominated by the need to debate the problematic established by Hechter and Nairn.

Some writers (Rees and Lambert, 1981; C. A. Davies, 1983, 1989) sought to explain the growth of popular support for the nationalist movement in Wales within the broader framework of the changing dynamics of the British state. Davies (1983) argues that the development of a bureaucratic infrastructure has been central to the growth in popular support for the nationalist movement in Wales during the twentieth century, and particularly during the post-war period. Beginning with the establishment of Welsh departments as part of the welfare reforms and, in 1964, the creation of the Welsh Office, this infrastructure, Davies maintains, provides 'vital support for the movement, both by giving administrative reality to a separate Welsh identity and by helping to bring a degree of administrative, if not political, independence to Wales'; in addition, she adds, '[i]t also provides a much more accessible target for nationalist protest and pressure-group activities' (1983: 211–12).

Theories of uneven economic development featured prominently elsewhere within sociological discussions on Wales (Day, 1980; Rees and Lambert, 1981; G. Williams, 1981); however, within these studies the emphasis was on considering the effect of spatial variations in economic development, and the corresponding emergence of differing forms of division of labour, on the social structure in Wales and, in turn, on Welsh identity itself. In this way these later studies have sought to present an altogether more complex picture of Welsh society than those provided by either Nairn or Hechter. By now Anderson's representation of the nation as imagined community was gaining influence and researchers began to explore how people consciously experience a sense of national identity. More particularly, they were starting to think it was necessary to consider the *diversity* of Welsh experiences, the *differing* ways of 'imagining' Wales. From this time a central feature of the sociological work which has been carried out in Wales has been the desire to contribute to an understanding of the multiplicity of Welsh lived experiences. A crucial, although for some time not yet fully developed, element of this project has been the attempt to prise open a more inclusive debate on Welsh identities. As Day and Suggett (1985: 96) suggest:

> the question we ought to address is not that of the real 'nation' or national identity which lies behind concepts employed in political life, but that of the formation, articulation and propagation of the concepts themselves. Nationalist ideas, myths and definitions have to be deconstructed. This means that we need to treat 'Wales' as it has figured in successive, rival discourses, and consider the question 'How many Wales?' or 'How many ways of being Welsh?'

In the older discourses of nation and national identity – including, in some instances, academic interventions – conformity and uniformity were (too often) prioritized above difference and diversity. The consequence of this position was that many questions and alternative experiences – of the sort to which Day and Suggett draw our attention – were effectively factored out of the equation.

The first book-length exploration of the new possibilities was completed by Dave Adamson (1991a). While concentrating on the effect of economic restructuring on the social structure in Wales, Adamson also viewed the growth in support for Plaid Cymru, particularly among the 'new working class', as the result of the success of nationalist ideology in relation to other competing political ideologies. Shortly afterwards, a stimulus to the new social theory of Wales was drawn from an unexpected source: the apparently moribund (but once central) sociological concept of *community* (Cloke and Milbourne, 1992; Roberts, in Chapter 4 below; Borland *et al.*, 1992) and 'locality' (Day and Murdoch, 1993). The guiding theme for much of this work has been an assessment of the impact of social and economic change on rural and working-class 'communities' in Wales. More fundamentally, these differing contributions have, in a variety of ways, sought to open the debate on the meaning of 'community' and, in turn, its larger inflection in the form of the 'national community'. Drawing on Anderson's notion of 'imagined communities', Borland *et al.* examine the ways in which the idea of 'community' is implicated in processes of political mobilization. Within the work of both Roberts and Day and Murdoch (1993) the emphasis is on considering how social and economic restructuring has given rise to reformulations of social and national identities. This recent reappraisal of the concept of community and the move towards discussions of locality has served to provide a sharp contrast to the early Welsh 'community studies' of the 1950s and 1960s. In drawing our attention to the debates on the meaning of 'place', and in highlighting the tensions which stand at the centre of these changes, this work has underlined the importance of exploring the diversity of contemporary Welsh lived experiences. It is to this end that the chapters collected in this volume are dedicated and it is to the description of these chapters and the relationships between them that we now turn.

The Structure of the Volume

Each of the contributions to this volume is, in varying ways, concerned with addressing the kinds of social, political and cultural practices through which notions of the Welsh nation and Welsh identity are produced and sustained. There is, of course, as with any venture such as this, a considerable diversity of opinions and approaches among the different contributions. There are, for example, differences between those discussions which are concerned with a broader examination of social and political relations in Wales (as in Davies's, Gruffudd's and Williams's separate considerations of the interlocutions of discourses of feminism, rurality, racism and Welshness, respectively), and those which have, without losing sight of the links to wider forms of identity politics, elected to direct the spotlight on to more localized sites of identity-formation (as is the case for many of the other chapters in this volume). There are, in addition, differences in disciplinary backgrounds: from geographers to anthropologists, and from urban planners to sociologists. Increasingly in recent years, however, these kinds of disciplinary boundaries have themselves become rather more flexible to the import of ideas from other fields, although most notably to the probing of identities, borders and questions of difference which have been so characteristic of debates on postmodernity and postmodernism.

The arguments in each of the following chapters are, in large part, a consequence of this changing intellectual environment and, in particular, of the cross-fertilization of ideas across disciplinary boundaries. The ideas of writers like Benedict Anderson (1991), cited by virtually all of the authors in this volume, Homi Bhabha (1994) and, more recently, Michael Billig (1995) have been tremendously influential in prompting the questioning of collective identity-formations across a range of academic disciplines. The impact of these debates is evident in the work undertaken by each of the authors in this volume: in the way in which the authors here seek to unpack larger narratives of nationhood and through the manner in which they direct attention to localized sites of identity-formation, as well as in their concern to direct attention towards the kinds of identity politics which are so central to any definitional struggles over 'nation' and 'national identity'. A broad spectrum of views is represented in this volume but the objective of examining the kinds of social, cultural and political practices through which the categories of nation and national identity are materialized is a guiding theme of all of the contributions.

This volume also continues a process which was initiated by the BSA Sociology of Wales group in the mid-1970s (indeed Day's contribution makes the link to this earlier sociological 'community' more real than 'imagined'). The focus of this volume is, of course, narrower than the earlier sociological work in that the contributors here are concerned with a rather more specific conceptual agenda. The concern in this volume with nation and national identity in Wales has not, however, prevented the contributors from addressing a wide range of social, political and economic questions. As with some of the previous sociological volumes on Wales, in which the contributors were responding to particular kinds of theoretical and social issues, the contributors here use the category of 'nation' as a lens through which to examine the diversity of social and cultural experiences in Wales. Moreover, in directing our gaze towards issues of racism, rurality, feminism, heritage and migration, among other matters, these writers highlight the differing representations of Welshness as they have featured in various definitional processes. In following these lines of enquiry each of the following chapters point, in different ways, to some of the kinds of political issues which are central to these processes of organizing and representing Welshness. Some of the chapters (notably those by Adamson, Davies, Fevre *et al.*, Thomas and Williams) are directly engaged in discussions of the politics of Welshness, present and past. Williams, for example, considers the way in which the experiences of black people in Wales have been marginalized with regard to discussions of Welshness. Elsewhere Marks, and Dicks and Van Loon, point to the way in which a distinctive emphasis on Welshness has been downplayed in key sectors of the heritage industry in Wales. To take one example, in his analysis of the narrow-gauge heritage railways in north Wales Marks makes the argument that the public representation of this industry and the history associated with it has been repackaged in such a way that it is now almost devoid of any specific Welsh dimension. In other chapters (as in those by Day and Thompson, and Roberts) the discussion centres on more localized forms of contestation over differing forms of Welshness.

The organization of the volume into three parts – Nation, Place and Heritage – is a reflection of our intention to concentrate attention on the different sets of themes which are central to the contributors' analyses and to address some of the principal areas of work on nations and national identities in social theory. In the opening section, Nation, each of the authors are specifically engaged in considerations of questions of Welshness. The following section, Place, examines questions of space, territory and, of course, place with regard to how they are implicated in wider discourses of the nation as well as the way in which they feature as sites of identity and conflict. The final section on Heritage settles on issues which are indispensable to any discussion of the nation and national identity. Here the authors examine, in different ways, how the past is organized in such a manner as to present it as an ostensibly obvious feature of our identities. By way of an editorial commentary on each of these contributions, we begin with the section on Nation.

The first chapter in this section, by Day and Thompson, draws on recent discussions of nationalism and national identity to focus on what the authors term the 'local production of national identity'. This discussion argues that one of the most salient developments in this field in recent years has been the emergence of a critical theoretical stance towards questions of nation and national identity, particularly in engaging with naturalizing discourses of nationalism and ethnicity. Part of the significance of this line of enquiry is that it has begun to focus attention on how ideas of nationhood are embedded within everyday social experiences. Rather than taking as their starting-point generic assumptions about the relevance of certain factors, such as language or religion, for national identities, the authors maintain that it is instead necessary to consider the ways in which individuals imagine themselves as belonging to a larger national community. In general terms, as the final section of the chapter highlights, the underlying rationale for paying attention to the 'local' is that it encourages us to examine how national identities are embedded in routine social practices.

In the next chapter Adamson gives his account of the role of intellectuals and historiography in the development of Welsh national identity. In a similar vein to a later chapter by Gruffudd, Adamson examines the ways in which intellectuals in Wales have been recurrently implicated in the idealization of certain preferred readings of Wales and Welshness. Like Davies (Chapter 5), Adamson writes with considerable knowledge of political nationalism in Wales. Here he considers the role of intellectuals in the development of Welsh nationalism during the late nineteenth and early twentieth centuries. As he explains, intellectuals wield a remarkable influence by virtue of their position as producers of 'knowledge' across a wide array of fields of endeavour. In their writing on literature and music and the production of art, as well as their engagement with educational, political and philosophical questions, intellectuals have contributed much to the creation of the nation as an 'imagined community'. In his analysis Adamson elects to consider the influence of the intellectual in one key domain: the product of a national memory. Beginning with a critique of some of the sociological accounts of intellectual practice, he draws on the work of Gramsci to point to the hegemonic role of intellectuals in forging a 'national popular collective will' in Wales towards the end of the last century.

Day and Thompson's focus on the kinds of 'common sense' modes of talking about national identity, in general, and Welsh identity in particular, is brought back to mind in Williams's discussion of 'race' and racism in Wales. For Williams, multiculturalism can pose difficulties for many constructions of nation and national identity and nationalism cannot always be easily disconnected from racism. She suggests that, in the past, there has been a tendency to marginalize any discussion of race and racism in the construction of Welsh identity and so an ideology of a tolerant identity is maintained – in some cases in academic discourse – which has little to do with real race relations in Wales. In fact there are many obstacles to black people being allowed to claim Welsh identity, especially in those parts of Wales which loom large in the imaginings of nationhood. As she puts it, living in Wales is not enough to guarantee black people a passport to the 'substantive citizenship of Welsh life'. Multiculturalism and the dominant version of Welsh identity (supported by nationalists) do not happily coexist.

In exploring the relationship between nationalism and feminism in Wales, the following chapter by Davies brings attention to another area which has, until recent years, been a relatively marginal feature of academic debates in Wales. Discussions of feminism as situated within the context of social life in Wales have gained increasing public prominence with the publication of a number of pioneering volumes (Aaron *et al.*, 1994; Betts, 1995). Writing with detailed knowledge of mainstream Welsh nationalism and particularly of Plaid Cymru, Davies builds on both some of the recent discussions of feminism and nationalism in Wales and the developments in the more general theoretical work in this area. Nationalism and feminism are both universalizing discourses and must both cope with 'the epistemological problem of analysing the conditions of their oppression using the theoretical categories of their oppressor', but they can also come into conflict with each other. The discussion is based on the premise that the political movements of feminism and nationalism both depend upon and strive to produce particular forms of identity and belonging. Davies argues that one consequence of this shared project is that both 'intersections' and conflicts between feminism and nationalism find expression in the lives of individual women as well as at the discursive level. This is particularly obvious amongst those women with commitments to both movements. Davies asks how such women – activists in both the nationalist and feminist movements – seek to resolve these conflicts and to cope with what can amount to warring, dual identities.

The following section on Place begins with a chapter[2] which takes place of residence as its focus. In it Roberts reminds us how contrasts between the south and the north and west of Wales have always been at the heart of any discussion of either nationalism or national identity in Wales. South Wales experienced mass (historic) immigration, full-blown industrial development, urbanization, and (until comparatively recently) an accelerating decline in the number of Welsh-speakers living in the region. The north and west experienced these changes much more gradually and, in consequence, did not experience the same decline in the Welsh language or the same rise of labourism, but did provide a much more fertile ground for the growth of nationalism. Roberts looks at what happened in the south when those old differences with the north and west mutated with rapid de-industrialization. He finds evidence of changing views on identity and, especially, changing views on the Welsh language which offer at least the possibility that the old division in identities between north/west and the south might no longer be as strong as it once was. The empirical data on which Roberts draws in the course of his discussion do, however, point to a continued sense of a separate form of Welshness as perceived by residents in these south Wales Valleys towns.

Roberts's discussion of Welshness in the south Wales Valleys is informed by the desire to consider the impact of social and economic change on forms of social identities and to highlight residents' awareness of those changes unfolding around them. In the next chapter Fevre, Borland and Denney are also concerned with the relationship between such changes and identities but their chapter also shares some of the concerns of Williams with language and migration and with theorizing the relationship between race and nation. Fevre, Borland and Denney are necessarily embroiled in issues of difference and division within Wales since the changes which interest them include English immigration to those parts of Wales which are Welsh-speaking and which have frequently been perceived to be an external threat to nation and national identity. The authors argue that it is not possible to understand this reaction to English immigration (including, for example, suggestions for innovations in housing policy) simply in terms of a perceived threat to a community or way of life. Instead, they suggest that the conflict which coincided with immigration from England to Wales can only be understood as an expression of a perceived dispute over the national identity of the places in question. In this case Welsh national identity is defined primarily in terms of the first language of the population. According to Fevre, Borland and Denney, nationalism is required to give a place this national identity and nationalism should be seen as one of the necessary preconditions for conflict over immigration rather than as the necessary consequence of the immigration itself. As in the case of migration from the New Commonwealth and Pakistan to England in the 1960s, immigration acts as a 'disclosing agent' which allows us to see the fundamental character of national feeling and the notions of identity which underpin it.

The contrast between urban and rural Wales which informs the chapters by Roberts and by Fevre, Borland and Denney is even more prominent in the remaining two chapters in this section but here the focus switches from the place in which we live to place as symbol. The contrast between the urban and the rural is brought sharply into focus in the next chapter of the section on Place by Gruffudd. There are interesting comparisons to be made between Gruffudd's discussion and Dick and Van Loon's chapter, notably between the former's argument about how Wales as *rural* Wales is represented as a place apart from the rest of Britain and the latter's comments on how the particular representation of the history of the south Wales Valleys embodied in the Rhondda Heritage Park locates this region as central to the history of the British Empire and thus denies a distinctively Welsh identity for it. Gruffudd's analysis examines the processes in which the rural has acted as a metaphor for the regeneration of national identity in Wales. In common with this volume's concern with highlighting the diversity of ways of talking about Wales and Welshness, Gruffudd's chapter draws out the differing modes of representing the relationship between the land and the meaning of 'Wales'. Gruffudd, then, argues that the landscapes of Wales have frequently been contested and their inhabitants drawn into a variety of moral, aesthetic and political discourses as these contests take place. In support of this argument he looks at representations of rural Wales as they have been implicated in the process of imagining the Welsh nation (and treats at much greater length some of the topics raised by Williams, including the significance of the *gwerin*). The imaginings Gruffudd considers are those which have been expressed and elaborated in the work of those political and intellectual figures – including some of the intellectuals who featured in the earlier chapter by Adamson – who have made the rural act as a metaphor for the nation. Whereas Gruffudd's chapter offers a broad exploration of images of rurality in the imagining of the Welsh nation, Thomas's chapter is directed towards a specific consideration of the making of Cardiff as a national capital. With the exception of Williams, none of the other chapters in this volume have very much to say in a specific way about the largest city in Wales. In his chapter on Cardiff, Thomas searches for the different and contested meanings in and of the capital. To this end, he examines the two most important passages of spatial restructuring undertaken in Cardiff in the post-war period. In considering the urban regeneration programmes in different areas of the city, Thomas's discussion of Cardiff Bay has parallels with Williams's argument, especially in the former's comments that the treatment of this area as exotic (or as something to be hidden from outside view) is rooted in the disputed place of these populations within representations of the Welsh nation. His discussions of the regeneration of the city centre and the redevelopment of Cardiff Bay are presented with an eye to the significance of these projects in relation to the political enterprise of establishing and exploiting Cardiff's status as a capital city. The issues raised by Thomas take on added importance given the programme of imminent restructuring of the Cardiff Bay area, notably in the building of the home of the National Assembly. The decision to locate the Assembly in Cardiff was, of course, preceded by widespread public debate about what the location for the Assembly should mean in symbolic terms. As the work of the Assembly gets under way 'Cardiff' as both a place and as a site symbolizing the embodiment of the new political arrangements in Wales will undoubtedly continue to feature prominently in future political discourse. As Thomas suggests, the status of Cardiff as a capital city will undergo transformation in accordance with its increased public profile in the political arena.

Like the chapters by Adamson and Gruffudd, the two chapters in the Heritage section are orientated to analyses of the organization of memories of the past, although in focusing on two particular sectors of the burgeoning heritage industry in Wales they are more explicitly orientated towards examining the embodiment of these memories. In some senses these chapters may be read as examining the materialization of the post-industrial present which is so central to the processes of social and economic change as experienced by the participants in Roberts's chapter. Indeed, the second of these finds its empirical material – in the shape of a mining heritage theme park – in the Valleys of south Wales where Roberts undertook his research but the first, by Marks, draws its material from north Wales and the heritage industry built on the relics of the slate industry there.

In his discussion of that part of the heritage industry based on the narrow-gauge railways in north Wales, Marks turns our attention towards a crucial dimension of the history of Wales which is often obscured given the enormity of industrialization in the south of the country in the late nineteenth and early twentieth centuries. Moreover, Marks's discussion also interestingly points to how the depictions of this region as an almost timeless rural idyll (a phenomenon which is resonant of the representations of rurality considered in the chapter by Gruffudd) within certain publications of the tourism industry, and the reorganization of memories of the slate industry, have served to displace a vital element of the region's past. Indeed, it is this process of restructuring the past, specifically with regard to the heritage railways, which provides the central theme of Marks's chapter. Pivotal to his argument is the contention that the practice of moving from 'history to heritage' has served to amputate the heritage railways from their Welsh, working-class context. Marks finds that the history and identity of the north Wales working-class Welsh-speakers has been displaced by anglophone history or no history at all. Marks suggests that the representations promoted by the heritage industry based on the narrow-gauge railways of north Wales are unusual amongst those more frequently encountered in the rest of the British heritage industry, including the rest of the Welsh heritage industry, but his work finds unexpected echoes in the final chapter on the heritage industry in the south Wales Valleys.

Whereas Marks describes the narrow-gauge railways as constituting ribbons of an English identity in Welsh-speaking Wales, Dicks and Van Loon's chapter highlights the way in which representations of the south Wales Valleys in the Rhondda Heritage Park claim this region as a well of (one sort of) British identity in a south Wales Valley. There is no question of open conflict with (or ignorance of) any Welsh identity here but rather of the construction of a Britishness which seeks to incorporate a Welsh identity within it. Van Loon and Dicks argue that the heritage industry should be seen as giving both the locality and its history a British identity. This is attempted with representations which aim to integrate the region in two separate ways – one found through the history of the British Empire, the other in the history of the British welfare state – of constructing the British identity of place. This is to be done whilst preserving a distinct regionality, although not a Welsh identity.

The articles collected here describe several different versions of Welsh identity and a variety of different contests over such identities. They demonstrate not just the existence of variety and difference but the very process of identity construction in which identities are not simply being made and remade all the time but argued and even fought over. Although they are obviously influenced by socio-economic and political change, the outcomes of such processes are never predetermined. Sometimes identities seem to be imposed to the exclusion of others, sometimes identities merge, often people find ways to permit different identities to coexist, frequently individual people own to more than one identity. While all of this cannot help but improve our understanding of contemporary Wales, it is just as important to grasp how much the research and scholarship reported here can contribute to social theory. Just how vital it can be is explained by Thompson in the final, concluding chapter where he shows how the switch to the study of *multifarious* identity which our collection represents lights the way for social theory and the study of nations and nationalism. Thompson draws together all of the useful insights of existing theory and shows how the perspectives adopted here (in different ways by all the contributors) present our best hope of progress. Thompson's survey of the development of theoretical approaches to nationalism and national identity throughout the course of the twentieth century highlights some of the limitations of current academic discourses on these questions. The most important consequence of accepting Thompson's critique becomes clear when – after explaining the paramount importance of accounts of differing, and competing, constructions of nation and varieties of nationalisms – he delineates the most promising lines of development for future research. These are, unmistakably, to be found in the further investigation of national identity along the lines that have been attempted by all of the contributors to this volume.

After reading those contributions and the concluding chapter by Thompson we hope you will agree with us that this recent work in and on Wales has much to contribute to our understanding of important (and often disturbing) developments at the very end of the twentieth century. The increase in the salience of national identity is not what we might have once expected to be witnessing at this time. Of course the last ten years of world history have already disabused us of this expectation: renascent nationalisms can be found in many corners of the world and national identity is a very important component of social behaviour, and locus of social conflict, in many other places than Wales. We cannot expect that the perspectives that have emerged in the study of nation and national identity in Wales will tell us very much about the precipitate causes of such global phenomena (for example, reactions to globalization within the context of collapsing empires). Rather, the significance of work in Wales lies in its contribution to our understanding of the real processes by which national identity looms large as a determinant of human behaviour at such an apparently late stage in the game.

For all the 'creative tensions' between the contributions in this volume, they are united by more than their common interests in national identity, Wales and the social meaning of place. We are all agreed that it does not make sense to talk about national identity in a monolithic way. We are all agreed that identities have to be constructed and not simply uncovered. We are all concerned to show how this can be done in different and often conflicting ways (leading to contested identities). We may look for the proof of this construction (and contest) in different places, but all of the contributors whose work is represented here share one important opinion which gives them a common advantage over most of their predecessors. While older texts may discuss the construction of identity, and even conflict over identity, they do so on the assumption that there are, nevertheless, right (and so worth supporting) and wrong (being imposed, usually from 'outside' and thus worth fighting against) identities. The contributions in this volume strive to avoid this pitfall. Their authors do not assume that they know which identity is right for Wales because they all know that there is not one Welsh identity but many. It is this simple reminder of the absence of a right answer to the most fundamental of national questions that is the most promising potential contribution of these perspectives from Wales to social theory.

Perhaps this lesson applies to all the questions of social identity which interest social theory. When trying to explain the construction of all sorts of identities (contested and otherwise), social theory makes most progress when it tries to avoid slipping into the dangerous error of seeming to offer pseudo-scientific support to the idea that either the name or content of the national identity of a place and a people can ultimately be decided one way or the other. This volume contains a great deal of discussion of personal identity but, as far as conflict and the allocation of resources is concerned, the more important factor can often be what identity places are given. In such cases, personal identity is only relevant so far as the identities of the people play a part in the construction of, and contests over, the identity of place. This much is as true in Palestine and the Balkans as it is in Wales, and it is to the uncovering of the processes by which such identities are given that social theory should be dedicated, rather than to the unattainable goal of judging who has the right to give identities to places and who does not.

Notes

1. Three major volumes emerged from the work of the BSA Study Group: G. Williams (ed.) (1978); G. Rees and T. Rees (eds.) (1980); and G. Williams (ed.) (1983).
2. Reprinted by kind permission of the University of Wales Press having first been published in the journal *Contemporary Wales*.

PART I NATION

2 Situating Welshness: 'Local' Experience and National Identity

Andrew Thompson and Graham Day

> A man [sic] must have a nationality as he must have a nose and two ears; a deficiency in any of these particulars is not inconceivable and does from time to time occur, but only as a result of some disaster, and it is itself a disaster of a kind. All this seems obvious, though, alas, it is not true. But that it should have come to seem so very obviously true is indeed an aspect, or perhaps the very core, of the problem of nationalism. Having a nation is not an inherent attribute of humanity, but it has now come to appear as such. (Gellner, 1983: 6)

Introduction

These words, which open Gellner's *Nations and Nationalism* (1983), lay open a premise which stands at the core of much thinking on nationalism and national identity: the perception that the existence of nations and our possession of a national identity is natural and unavoidable. Discussions of national identity – whether in academic studies, political speeches, newspaper articles or in other social settings – often proceed from the unproblematic assumption that nations and national identities, as well as a nation's heritage and traditions are givens. In a recent special supplement of the *Western Mail* devoted to this issue – *Where Wales? The Nationhood Debate* – statements such as a 'nation that is sure of itself will want to be informed and entertained' (D. Smith, 1996: 4), and allusions to the need to 'forge a true identity for ourselves in Wales' (E. Morgan, 1996: 5), illustrate that beliefs about the 'reality' of the nation continue to exert a considerable appeal. Undoubtedly, the creation of elected assemblies in Wales and Scotland has raised the public profile of issues to do with national identity, although the debate can hardly be said to have caught fire. At times such as these, one would expect such questions to be more prominent in public life, but what about those periods when these issues are not high on the political agenda? Tim Williams (1996) argues that speculation about Wales and Welsh identity is largely confined to, and inflated by, those who have a professional interest in such questions, specifically the bilingual middle class. According to Williams (1996: 18), 'most of the Welsh never talk about Wales . . . For most of us, Wales is a team and a nice place from which to get a letter. It exists for the purposes of sport and sentiment.' There is, however, a difference between people's interest in, and readiness to talk about Wales, as a national entity and point of reference, and the frequency with which they find themselves addressing the question of Welshness, or of being Welsh. Wales, in some sense, always will remain a relatively remote abstraction, whereas a person's national identity is part of them, and can be exposed for consideration at any time. There are, undoubtedly, those – journalists, broadcasters, politicians and academics – for whom such matters are the subject of more sustained introspection, yet even if one accepts that most people in Wales (and elsewhere) do not explicitly discuss the form and significance of their national identity on a regular, or even irregular, basis it is unlikely to be something they have completely put aside or forgotten.

In this chapter, drawing on interviews conducted by one of the authors on the issue of Welshness as it is understood and described by people in one part of north Wales, we intend to consider the significance of what elsewhere we have termed the 'local production of national identity' (Thompson *et al.*, 1999). The use of the term 'local' in this discussion is intended to address two principal concerns. First, the notion of the 'local' refers to the ways in which individuals themselves talk about, and experience, their national identity. Here our aim is to draw attention to the categories and often matter-of-fact assumptions which individuals employ when talking about their Welshness. Our discussion utilizes the notion of the 'local' to examine how national identities are reproduced as a result of quite 'ordinary' social relations and experiences. In exploring this issue we suggest that while individuals may not necessarily conceptualize their experiences overtly in terms of questions of 'national identity', many of the events and encounters that occur locally are nevertheless significant reminders of difference and are therefore crucial for the ongoing reproduction of their sense of national identity. Rather than taking as our starting-point generic assumptions about the significance of factors such as language or religion for the national identity of a particular group, it is necessary instead to consider the ways in which individuals imagine themselves as belonging to a larger national community, often from a base of what they experience locally. The underlying rationale for paying such attention to the 'local' is that it encourages us to examine how national identities are embedded in routine social practices of everyday life.

National Identities as Natural Identities?

As we have suggested in our opening comments, discussions of national identity in the United Kingdom, particularly in Wales and Scotland, have currently moved more squarely into the public sphere by virtue of the debate attendant on devolution. In the week which saw the publication of the government White Papers on Welsh and Scottish devolution, the *Observer* (20 July 1997) dedicated three pages to consideration of questions of devolution and national identity, including one article which asked 'Where would you put your national identity in a list of defining features?' Outside these periods of public reflection, however, explicit deliberation about whether or not we are 'British', 'Welsh', 'Scottish' or 'Irish', and what these labels mean to us, may be rare.

Such labels or categories are nevertheless used prolifically to account for and describe the actions of those perceived to be members of other nations as well as to comprehend the differences between nations. Sports commentators, for example, may refer to the 'English game' to describe the problems which 'English' football players experience when playing 'abroad' or, alternatively, when 'foreign' players or managers come to 'English' clubs. In other instances, a whole range of practices – such as advertising, comedy, literature and cookery – regularly involve direct or implied references to different national 'ways of life' as well as stereotypes of 'national character'. In explaining the actions of particular individuals or even the 'actions' of a nation as a whole, references are often made to particular so-called 'national' traits: thus 'the English' may be described by some as 'cold' and 'detached', 'the

Germans' as 'serious' and 'methodical', while 'the Italians' are 'hot-blooded' and 'temperamental'. In each case, these categories are treated as 'common sense' or 'taken-for-granted'; it is presumed that when these categories are invoked no further explanation is required, as others already understand what we are talking about. In this way, then, national differences may be perceived as 'ordered' or 'organised'. According to Billig (1995), to explore the appeal of 'national identity' it is necessary to interrogate how such ideas of nation and nationhood are imbricated in 'common-sense' perceptions of the world; as he writes, 'nationalist thinking . . . takes for granted ideas about nationhood and the link between peoples and homelands; and about the naturalness of the world of nations, divided into separate homelands' (1995: 61). It is in this way that the existence of nations and the divisions between nations may be reproduced as real and objective. At the same time, however, it is within nationalist discourse that we would expect to find the precise content and meaning of national identity subjected to the most intense scrutiny, in an effort to raise it to consciousness.

Recent studies of nationalism have variously highlighted how ideas of nationhood permeate our thinking about politics and how discourses of nations and national identity are constant features of our everyday social environment. Calhoun (1995) explains that since the late eighteenth century nationalist discourse has provided the ideological framework within which notions of democracy and political legitimacy have evolved. At the root of the problem, as Calhoun identifies it, is that democratic theory has routinely taken for granted the 'natural' divisions between nations; as he writes,

> democratic theory includes few coherent answers to the question of why a political community has these members, with these boundaries, that do not depend on a heritage of nationalist discourse . . . Our whole approach to issues of large-scale identity and difference has been informed by naturalist presumptions usually left tacit. (1995: 273)

In a similar vein, Canovan (1996) argues that within political theory discussions of rights, democracy, social justice and 'the people' are all underpinned by certain implicit assumptions about the 'reality' of nations. Thus, for Canovan 'questions of nationhood are not an optional extra for political theory, but should actually be at the heart of the discipline. The reason for this is that nationhood is actually a tacit premise in almost all contemporary political thinking' (1996: 1). Billig (1995), in his study of what he terms 'banal nationalism', extends this line of enquiry beyond the realm of political theory by exploring the ways in which the language of nationhood and representations of the nation are embedded in routine social practices. The significance of pursuing such a strategy, he argues, is that it allows us to see how 'the routinely familiar habits of language will be continually acting as reminders of nationhood. In this way, the world of nations will be reproduced as the world, the natural environment of today' (1995: 93). These contributions clearly put the emphasis on the routine production, and reproduction, of nationality and the awareness of national identities.

Furthermore, thinking on the nation and national identity is often informed by assumptions about the collective bonds which hold the national group together and which underpin its members' sense of identity. 'Religion', 'language', 'culture', 'territory', 'history' and 'tradition' are variously employed to account for the behaviour of both groups and individuals. Discourses of the nation and national identity routinely invoke notions of homogeneity and cultural sameness. Indeed, the very idea of a national identity, as a collective identity, presupposes common understandings and agreement as to the form of 'our' identity. Such a conception of national identity itself is grounded in wider discursive practices in which the nation is constructed as an objective entity, one which is represented as existing above and beyond the social relations which constitute it. The conceptualization of the nation as a unitary body represents one of the central tenets of nationalist ideology, principally through the idea that the nation is the collective embodiment of the individual wills of its constituent members. In this way nations are accorded the ability to 'act', have 'duties' and 'desires' and, even, to 'speak' to other nations on behalf of their members (see Billig, 1995). Within such discourses it is taken for granted that members' outlooks, perceptions and beliefs are as one; questions of difference and the particular experiences of members are obscured from view.

There is little doubt that these assumptions are replicated in 'ordinary' people's views of national identity, and the ways in which they express them. To investigate how intimately the sense of national identity is bound up with a person's 'local' experiences, we make two main observations with regard to how individuals account for their national identity. First, we wish to develop further this question of the ways in which the possession of a national identity is held to be ostensibly 'obvious'. Secondly, we note how on the basis of treating particular factors as objective criteria of nationality, individuals categorize themselves and others. Our starting-point, then, is with the issue of the 'factuality' of national identity. Here we highlight how, in describing their national identity, individuals make references to various supposed 'facts' about it. The following remarks, taken from interviews with respondents in the north Wales town of Bangor, all presume that a certain inevitability and taken for granted quality attaches to the possession of a national identity.

(1) Everybody's born with a certain kind of nationalism in them. They're brought up to feel that way. So I think that people really stand their ground, that they want to be a part of their own nation, say England and Wales . . . They find it hard to integrate with each other, and they don't, to some extent, want to.

(2) Everybody's aware when they get to a certain age, that they're aware of their nationality. I think possibly more so in Wales because there is a great division between the Welsh and the English, isn't there? People in England don't say 'Am I English?' or 'Am I Welsh?' or 'Am I Scottish?' they are English and they don't even consider it.

(3) You know everybody wants a feeling of belonging to something and a feeling of identity, and for Welsh-speaking people the obvious identity is being Welsh, which is different to English. Everybody wants a sense of identity – and you get identity from the country you come from, the town you come from, and the village you come from, maybe . . . It's all to do with identity.

What is of particular interest in these extracts are the assumptions they contain about the universality of national identity, revealed in statements that 'everybody' possesses a sense of belonging to a national group. This assumption is rooted in the belief that a national identity is something which none of us can avoid. Each of the respondents, in stating that people are 'born' with, become 'aware' of, or 'want' to have a national identity, imply, indeed take for granted, that possession of a national identity is something which 'everyone' encounters. The statements begin from a variety of presuppositions: 'people want to be a part of their own nation'; that 'there is a great divide between the Welsh and the English'; identity is something which we 'get' from the 'country' (as well as town and village) from which we come; and that for Welsh-speakers their sense of national identity is 'obvious'. Here, the properties of having a national identity are treated as independent of their description of them: there will be a 'divide' between 'the Welsh' and 'the English' irrespective of their own views of this matter. While each of these respondents can provide explanations as to how we come to possess a national identity, there is little recognition that, in the course of making these references, they themselves are implicated in producing 'national identity', as they engage in the practice of accounting for what this category means to them.

When the respondents talk about national identity – in these specific instances 'Welsh' and 'English' identities – they draw on a range of references to describe what it is to 'belong' to a particular nation. Returning to the above extracts, we can see that people want to be a 'part of their own nation', that people belonging to different nations 'find it hard to integrate with each other and they don't, to some extent, want to'; that people want a 'feeling of belonging'. In explaining what it means to be Welsh, other respondents made similar statements. Responses included references to 'the bind of brotherhood. You're part of the same . . . you share the same values, not necessarily extremist values'; 'it's a special group, you know? We're small, we're a small people, we're strong, we're good together. We've got our own language within the UK. It makes you feel different.' In drawing attention to these statements we are highlighting what Tomlinson (1991) has referred to as the 'phenomenology' of national identity. Individuals do not regard their nations as something which they alone produce or are aware of; rather they proceed from the position that others too know that nations are 'real' and that there are therefore others with whom they can, and will, identify. For instance, for much of the time most individuals would not regard the existence of an entity called 'Wales' as something which is problematic, with the possible exception of when they encounter people from other countries; when they describe themselves as 'Welsh' they expect others to understand what this means. In each of the statements which we have highlighted the respondents, by making references to 'they', 'everybody', 'the bind of brotherhood', 'a special group', 'Welsh-speaking people', denote the collective and shared nature of 'belonging' to a nation. Thus, while respondents may describe something which makes them 'feel' Welsh, in perhaps quite a particular way, they do not perceive their understanding as unique. On the contrary, even the references to the emotional or 'subjective' dimensions of being Welsh, such as 'brotherhood', 'special group' and 'being a part', suggest that these are sentiments which are shared by all those who 'belong'.

As we have already intimated, if a crucial part of thinking about national identity is the notion of the universality of the world of nations – that 'everybody' has a national identity and that 'everybody' belongs to a nation – then an equally significant element is the idea of the particularity of 'our' nation. Billig (1995) illuminates this point when he observes that 'nationalism inevitably involves a mixture of the particular and the universal: if "our" nation is to be imagined in all its particularity, it must be imagined as a nation amongst other nations' (1995: 83). The interview extracts cited show some recognition of this among the respondents: that while we all have national identities, there are nevertheless clear distinctions between different nations and the identities that correspond to them – here, specifically between the identities of 'the Welsh' and 'the English'. The use of these collective labels to categorize 'us' and 'them' raises for us two points of interest. First, to employ these categories in talking of groups of individuals highlights a concern which Anderson (1991) explores in his use of the term 'imagined communities': namely, that people hold that there are others who, for whatever reason, are like them, but that this group has definite limits beyond which lie other imagined national communities, which are different. At this point, particular criteria must be introduced to determine the nation to which an individual belongs. The second point is that to grasp the full meaning and use of these criteria, it is necessary to examine the ways in which an individual's own experience – or local knowledge – is utilized in the production of these categories. The following examples show respondents bringing in these criteria as they set about explaining what it is to be Welsh, while at the same time utilizing what is clearly localized knowledge and awareness of particular situations and contexts.

(4) There are people who have firstly moved in from England to live here and they're English, and there's people who are born and bred here who can speak Welsh and they're definitely Welsh. There's definitely a middle group, where I come in, of either being born here or being bred here and considering yourself to be Welsh without being able to speak the language. I'd say if you're born here almost everybody thinks they're Welsh, even if they don't speak the language.

(5) A: It's just in me, it's where I was born, it's where I was brought up and I am Welsh. B: It's got 'Born in Wales' on my passport. A: That's what it is, aye. B: That's the only thing you need to be Welsh. If you're born in Wales you are Welsh.

(6) Someone who's Welsh would have to be Welsh-speaking 'cos you know you can be called English as well if you speak English. It's the language that makes me feel Welsh because I could leave Wales itself but I think the language – you'd have to speak Welsh to be classified as Welsh. You [a non-Welsh-speaker] can be a member of the nation but, you know, I'd call him a non-Welsh-speaking person who lives in Wales not a non-Welsh-speaking Welshman, you know what I mean? He's not Welsh, he's just a non-Welsh-speaking person who lives in Wales or who was born in Wales. If they really want to be a part then I suggest they learn to speak Welsh.

(7) More and more of my friends don't want anything to do with England, so they're becoming more Welsh now. They have more of an identity now. A Welsh person is somebody who can speak Welsh. The Welsh person who can't speak Welsh is no different to the English basically – they should've had an opportunity to learn the language. If they want to be Welsh they should learn the language. If they feel Welsh they should've been fluent by now, or tried to speak it, if not they shouldn't see themselves as different from the English.

At this stage of the discussion it is sufficient to point to how the respondents account for their particular categorizations of 'Welshness'. Local references are signified in these comments by things which are said to occur 'here' (birth, or living), by knowledge of how you might be 'called' or classified in social encounters, and by the immediacy with which respondents equate Welshness to the ability to speak the Welsh language. In each instance these categories are treated as pre-given, that is, as independent of individuals and their response to these particular criteria. For example, for certain respondents, the ability to speak Welsh is the defining characteristic of a Welsh identity regardless of the view one holds on the Welsh language ('You'd have to speak Welsh to be classified as Welsh'). In contrast, for others, being Welsh is something one acquires by virtue of being born in Wales, again a factor which exists whether one recognizes it or not ('If you're born in Wales you are Welsh'). The significance of the activity of categorizing is twofold. First, individuals hold certain criteria to be determining factors, in the sense that they are perceived as existing independently of their own personal views. Secondly, on the basis of assumptions about the 'objectivity' of these facts, individuals categorize others as to whether or not they are 'Welsh'. Thus, where speaking Welsh is treated as a fact of Welshness, in the instance of a person who cannot speak Welsh there is no alternative but to state that they are not Welsh ('If they feel Welsh they should've been fluent by now or tried to speak it. If not they shouldn't see themselves as any different from the English'). In each instance, the various ways in which individuals categorize what it is to be Welsh (and, obversely, what it is to be English) should be seen as 'rules' or resources which the respondents invoke in order to account for the national identity of others. More particularly, it is on the basis of these 'rules' that individuals are able to view the differences between 'Welsh' and 'English' as ordered and 'common-sensical'.

So far, our analysis has been concerned with pointing to ways in which individuals treat certain properties as facts of Welshness and to demonstrating how individuals, in turn, direct themselves towards others on this basis. Central to these considerations has been the contention that assumptions about the saliency of certain criteria (such as speaking Welsh) are viewed by respondents as 'common knowledge'. Thus the above statement that if non-Welsh-speakers 'feel Welsh they should've been fluent by now' contains an implicit assumption that such an understanding, that 'feeling' Welsh is inextricably connected with speaking Welsh, is one which is shared by both Welsh-speakers and non-Welsh-speakers alike. The denial of a Welsh identity to those who do not speak Welsh is, therefore, justified on the basis that they already know the 'rules' of belonging. Individuals, then, do not perceive the categories 'Welsh' and 'English' to be the product of their own 'subjective' accounts, but rather see them as part of a shared understanding of 'how things are' that is common to all those who have a certain identity. The relationship between the assumptions and their application thus serves to highlight the importance of what individuals take to be common understandings of national identity in the actual construction of such identities.

To confirm this, respondents provide practical examples of situations which lead them to believe that these assumptions are shared, and where the seemingly natural and evident possession of an identity inspires an automatic response. Thus a local Bangor man comments that:

(8) We never go out of Bangor without being involved in trouble. It's always Bangor, because it's predominantly English. Everywhere around Bangor's Welsh. So if we went up to Bethesda, Caernarfon, anywhere in Anglesey, it's always '*Sais* Bangor, English Bangor', and straight away there's conflict there. You can feel it as soon as you walk into the pubs . . . If me and my friends walk into a pub in Caernarfon we're strangers moving into their pub. You can feel the animosity as soon as you walk through the door. It's the same if they came into Bangor.

This extract highlights the use of proclaimed facts about the division between Welsh and English as situated 'rules'. In referring to Bangor as 'predominantly English', while stating that 'everywhere around Bangor's Welsh', this respondent illustrates how the categories of 'English' and 'Welsh' operate as a popular code for describing divisions between Welsh-speakers and non-Welsh-speakers. Although stated in a quite unproblematic manner, the categorization of Bangor as 'predominantly English', in contrast to the surrounding 'Welsh' towns, is controversial, not only because the city of Bangor is quite firmly located, geographically and historically, within Wales, and more than half of its residents have Welsh as their first language, but also because it implies that non-Welsh-speakers accept that speaking Welsh constitutes a clear marker of what it means to be Welsh. The respondent's remarks also draw attention to an understanding of how this shared knowledge is used to account for particular situations ('You can feel it as soon as you walk into the pubs'). The categorization of places as Welsh and English, respectively, proceeds from the assumption that the features which are the subject of this categorization are taken for granted. That people from Bangor and Caernarfon, for example, may refer to each other as 'Welsh' and 'English' is not, as a consequence, open to scrutiny: thus, 'we' in Bangor get 'in trouble' because Bangor is 'English'.

National Identity as Constructed Identity

So far, we have drawn attention to ways in which respondents appear to view nations as objective entities, from which they gain a definite sense of identity and belonging. Such ways of describing 'national identity' are also evident in the academic literature, since scholarly accounts tend to prioritize the collective dimension to nations and national identity to the detriment of individual experiences. For example, exploring the relationship between culture and national identity, Guibernau (1996: 75) writes that:

> Values, beliefs, customs, conventions, habits and practices are transmitted to the new members who receive the culture of a particular society. The process of identification with the elements of a specific culture implies a strong emotional investment. All cultures single out certain parts of neutral reality and charge them with meaning. Individuals are born within cultures that determine the way in which they view and organize themselves in relation to others and to nature.

At one level Guibernau is correct to suggest that individuals learn certain values and beliefs and that they participate in particular customs and practices; yet it is more problematic to state that 'cultures' 'determine' and 'organize' how individuals relate to others. In this one-sided account, which casts people as 'cultural dopes', there is little recognition of how individuals come to understand what 'their' culture means to them rather than having it simply 'transmitted' to them or how individuals negotiate the complex process of recognizing some others as like themselves while perceiving yet others to be different. In short, within such an account individuals play little part in producing their culture or national identity; rather, they merely reproduce what they are taught. The end result, then, is that 'culture' becomes a Durkheimian social fact: external to individuals and constraining upon them.

As they begin to develop more fully their understanding of Welshness, however, in several respects the reasoning displayed by our respondents leads us to conclude that, contrary to these naturalistic and essentialist assumptions, the realities of national identity, and hence of nations themselves, are both contestable and often contested. It is important to note here that the fact that in this instance we are addressing Welshness as an example is not intended to mean that other national identities – such as 'English', for example – are immune in any sense from the same processes and pressures; we do not seek to problematize Welsh identity as opposed to some other 'less negotiable' national identity. Although the level of contestation and negotiation occurring at any given time depends upon circumstances, all identities are problematic, at particular times and under particular pressures. A vivid example of this was provided following the death of Diana, Princess of Wales in August 1997, when the extraordinary popular reaction gave rise to a very considerable re-examination of the characteristics associated with the 'British', and/or of the nature of the 'English' and their 'Englishness' (e.g. *Guardian*, 4 September 1997). At the same time, it has been noted, by Bowie (1993) among others, that Welsh national identity may be especially pressurized or vulnerable at the present time, as is suggested by the very titles of some of the most significant recent published discussions of the topic: *When Was Wales?* (G. A. Williams, 1985); *Wales: The Imagined Nation* (Curtis, 1986); *Wales! Wales?* (D. Smith, 1984). The uncertainty conveyed by these phrases strongly suggests that there is no single way of talking about, or being, Welsh that has achieved total acceptance.

There is an alternative view, that, like social identity in general, national identity is not something fixed and given as an external, natural, fact but has to be made. This social constructionist position is now widely adhered to among social anthropologists, political scientists and sociologists. Thus R. Cohen (1994: 1), for example, notes how British national and social identity is 'continuously constructed and reshaped in its (often antipathetic) interaction with outsiders, strangers, foreigners, and aliens – the "others". You know who you are, only by knowing who you are not.' Cohen stresses that there is considerable ambiguity about both the 'inner' limits to this identity (where the line is drawn between 'Britishness' and its component of English, Welsh, Scottish, etc.)

and the outer limits (where larger identities such as being European come into play). This indeterminacy, he suggests, can be thought of as a series of blurred, opaque or 'fuzzy' frontiers surrounding the core identity. To complicate matters further, in a way which goes beyond the scope of this discussion, there is also a crucial interplay with other dimensions of identity (such as class, gender, religious affiliation), so that 'rather as one can twist the lens of a manual camera to secure greater or lesser definition, the degree of focus along different frontiers of identity can be varied situationally and temporally' (1994: 7). Similarly, R. Jenkins regards social identity as a practical accomplishment, a process, whereby 'selfhood is thoroughly socially constructed: in the process of primary and subsequent secondary socialisation and in the ongoing process of social interaction through which individuals define and redefine themselves and others throughout their lives' (1996: 20).

This stress on the provisional and malleable quality of our social identifications leads inescapably to an interest in how the boundaries of identity are managed and policed, which – entirely appropriately given his central preoccupation with questions of immigration control and maintenance of the outer boundaries of the nation-state – brings Cohen to employ the language of a surveillance system: gates, turnstiles, frontier guards, etc. Yet internal borders also have to be maintained and patrolled if the 'integrity' of a national identity is to be preserved, and it is here especially that we would see the significance of what goes on at a more local level.

Scattered throughout the comments of the people interviewed in Bangor are remarks showing how, beneath the apparent certainty, there lies a more problematic vision of Welsh national identity. From the extracts already cited, we learn that there are things about being Welsh which lead people to 'consider it' in a way to which those in England do not seem driven (extract 2). There are references to the existence of a 'middle group' who are neither fully Welsh nor fully outside it (extract 4) . People are capable of becoming 'more Welsh' and of achieving thereby 'more of an identity' (extract 7) . As a mark of their ambiguous position, Bangor people can be labelled as '*Sais* Bangor' by those who are (putatively) more Welsh (extract 8). Alternatively, as another respondent has it, they are 'Bangor-Welsh', 'half-and-half', with a very particular identity of their own:

(9) If someone asks you: 'are you Welsh?' . . . 'Yes, Bangor' . . . 'Oh, Bangor-Welsh, sort of half-and-half. You can't speak proper Welsh.' Once they know you're from Bangor they'll speak English to you, people from Bethesda or Caernarfon, or from the island, you know?

Elsewhere there are references to people who are 'proper' Welsh and 'sort of Welsh'. These phrases, and many others, conform well to Cohen's model of the fuzzy boundaries surrounding national identity, and bring the nature of Welshness much more into question than some of the earlier citations would suggest.

In elaborating upon this more open-ended, flexible, conception of identity, those interviewed adduce their own experiences in the course of their lifetime to show how identity is either cemented, or capable of adjustment, over time. It is even possible, they indicate, to switch between identities, according to the social relationships that surround the individual at the time:

(10) There are influences upon me. For instance, my girlfriend now is Welsh. So, at the moment, when I bother to think about it, I see myself as Welsh . . . When I was younger, a lot of my friends were English, so I perceived myself to be English. In the interim I perceived myself to be neither. I perceive myself to be Welsh insofar as I've lived here all that time, and there was that influence making me Welsh, and there was the influence of being English, of being born in England, and being English-speaking.

Such a view can be contrasted with those which present a picture of consistency of self-image, accounted for in the light of a set of supportive social conditions which underpin it. This could be said to characterize the position of the 'truly Welsh', those whose view of their Welshness appears entirely unqualified:

(11) I speak Welsh and I feel myself as being . . . tied to the history and culture . . . all my family are Welsh, a lot of them have married English people but they're basically Welsh, all of them . . . and my friends are Welsh, my boyfriend's Welsh, my parents . . . the community is mostly Welsh.
(12) I've always spoken Welsh, with my family, with all my friends, everybody. I suppose our parish is the highest Welsh-speaking parish in the whole of Wales . . . as I grew up all my friends were

Welsh and there was never any reason to think of myself as being anything else . . . I've never had any identity crisis (*laughs*).

Even here a change of circumstances will suffice to make someone different, in the sense of being more conscious of the way in which they regard themselves:

> (13) I've been made more aware of being Welsh now than I was before coming here from a totally Welsh place, basically absolutely Welsh. I've come here . . . there has got to be said ignorance on the English behalf here. It has increased my awareness being put in . . . even though it's Bangor, in the university it's basically England.

As in this example, in the course of formulating such a sense of their national belonging, individuals can reflect back on earlier times, reinterpreting and revising the meanings that they hold for them:

> (14) When I was growing up my parents never used to make me feel conscious of being Welsh at all, you know? They were never nationalistic, they were never anti-English, and they didn't have any attitude whatsoever. I just regard my family as a normal family which happens to speak Welsh, you know? We were not a family which was very conscious of being Welsh.

Thus people do engage actively in thinking about the various categorizations of national identity that are available to them, rather than simply reading them off some 'obvious' indicator. They formulate answers to questions about their own identity in the light of what they take to be common conceptions and solutions employed by others, so that in defining Welshness in particular ways, respondents are – for present purposes at least – including themselves within, or setting themselves apart from, membership of the category as they understand others to use it; as Cohen says, you know who you are by knowing who you are not. It is as if the responses we are given already form part of an ongoing internal dialogue, which briefly we are privileged to overhear.

> (15) Listening to Welsh songs and poems and watching so-called Druids does not make one any more Welsh.

(16) Why I don't claim to be Welsh is that when you talk to the so-called 'The Welsh' a lot of them don't know their Welsh history. Mention the Mabinogion and they think you're talking about a breakfast cereal, they really do. Unfortunately, while I am Welsh by birth and heritage, my first language is English. I'm classed not as a second class citizen but as a third class citizen. If I was black and wore a big bone through my nose I'd be better treated because at least I'd have a racial discrimination board to go to. I am quite often ostracised in my job because I am not fluent in the Welsh-speaking.

(17) Although I am not fluent in Welsh, I was born here, been bred here, and am proud of that. I always say I am Welsh, and not British, if asked.

In taking up positions of this sort, respondents are able to go further, and provide accounts which situate alternative conceptions socially, and show an awareness that these various versions of Welshness may be ultimately incompatible, that 'choices' may have to be made, and that there are limits to the degree to which melding and blurring can deal with discrepancies. This is particularly so, as the extracts confirm, with regard to the Welsh language, which for many in north Wales is the decisive signifier of Welshness. In *When Was Wales?*, the historian Gwyn Williams pointed to the

> denial of Welshness to the English-speaking Welsh, an exclusion which is becoming rapidly and increasingly and inevitably a bitter self-exclusion of the English speaking Welsh from the Welsh people and nation. The adjective 'Welsh' is increasingly applied, outside and inside Wales, only to the Welsh speaking component of the people. (1985: 93)

This is a view which finds its echoes among our informants:

(18) They're just digging up the past and it's all language. I tell you what, everybody in Bangor they are Welsh. Everybody in Bangor counts themselves as Welsh, and they are proud to be Welsh, but they are not fanatical about the language. The language to them is irrelevant really.

(19) Cymdeithas Yr Iaith gets its support from middle-class, Welsh-speaking families which are very conscious of being Welsh and who . . . maybe they've got a bit of an attitude towards the English. I've got no interest . . . I tend to associate it with farmers'

daughters, you know? Old-fashioned, boring Welsh people, and that's something I don't want to be associated with really.

(20) The people who are cultivating the Welsh language to make it sort of more academic are those who are privileged enough to go into higher education and the only work around this area for people with degrees is the public sector, so you get élitism. Unless you speak proper Welsh you just don't get in brother. It's as simple as that. I left north Wales when I was sixteen, yeah, because I was sick to death . . . my father's from south Wales and he couldn't speak Welsh – his mother was a Welsh-speaker – and as a boy I was sick to death of 'them' and 'us' situations. 'Them', the Welsh-speaking people, and the rest, the non-Welsh-speaking people . . . and it hasn't changed in twenty odd years, it's still there. In fact, it's getting worse because of so-called academic gobbledy-gook. I believe in the language but it seems to divide. We're classifying our own people through this which is our birthright . . . we're classifying our own people.

The other side of the coin is the stance taken by a Welsh-speaker who expressed his scepticism that people in south Wales could ever truly conform to his definition of Welshness:

(21) Even if you built hundreds of Welsh-speaking schools in industrial areas, I don't think you'll ever turn them to be Welsh-speakers, but you can keep the rural population . . . and I think that to get an understanding that if it is possible to isolate some areas without looking as if it is something racial or whatever.

In these responses, individuals can be seen to be actively producing Welshness as a category as they go about dealing with instances and possibilities that will not fit neatly into the simple and strict classification of 'us' and 'them'. In the words of respondent 20, 'we are classifying our own people' when 'we' resort to criteria of Welshness which intersect and collide with one another. Throughout, we see how 'the "people" themselves play the part of theoreticians in this field' (Ardener, 1989, cited MacDonald, 1993). Engaging in this activity leads some to conclude that the task is futile:

(22) You cannot define yourself as Welsh because 'Welshman' to one man is the ability to speak Welsh whilst to another man it is to help

your heritage and culture. If I was asked: 'am I Welsh?' I can claim to be Welsh by heritage and birth, having got family steeped in Wales and a lot of my mother's family were in the chapels . . . and had farms over on Anglesey. That way you can claim to be Welsh. But if you say to be Welsh is to go around bombing, destroying homes, tearing down signposts on walls, then I'm not Welsh and if you mean to be Welsh is to ostracise the English or any incomers . . . ask them have they ever been up Cader Idris? Have they ever walked around lake Ogwen? 'Aye we know where it is', and that's their limit . . . So if that's being Welsh, then I don't want to know.

Conclusion

The responses elicited from this group of respondents demonstrate that, despite initial appearances, Welsh national identity is not pre-given, but is very largely constructed and produced by people as they develop and express their understanding of situations, events, and other people as they arise. This impression of contingency deviates from the opposed tendency which treats national identity as a homogeneous, determined phenomenon. It also challenges some aspects of the nationalist 'project', in the sense that this frequently seeks to deny such contingency, by naturalizing identity and making it appear to coincide, inevitably, with predetermined boundaries (typically those of territory and birth). Differentiation and ambiguity is denied within the boundaries, while distinctions across boundaries are magnified. The result is what Balibar and Wallerstein refers to as 'fictive ethnicity'; that is, the population subsumed within the limits of the nation is represented as forming a natural community, whose members share common origins, culture and interests (1991: 96). Each individual is held to possess one unambiguous ethnic identity, and the whole of humanity is then divided up into mutually exclusive ethno-national groupings. Paradoxically, this makes the 'problem' of national identity, with which nationalist movements grapple, seem to disappear; and yet, as Balibar insists, such national groupings, or 'peoples', do not exist naturally and for all time. Indeed, from the viewpoint of the modern nation-state, the problem instead is to 'make the people produce itself continually as a national community' (1991: 93).

Balibar regards ambiguity as a key feature of identity, and we would contend that it is ambiguity and lack of clear definition – Cohen's 'fuzziness' – that lends national identity its extraordinary flexibility and survival power. From his analysis of Britishness, Cohen concludes that the constructionist approach offers four key insights: that identities are fragmented; that individuals possess multiple social identities, which can give rise to competing claims on their allegiance; that an important subset of identity constructs take a territorial (or spatial) focus; and that identities work situationally, that is, they represent a set of choices that are brought into focus 'as the context deems a particular choice desirable or appropriate' (1994: 205).

In an analysis of Welsh identity which prefigured these insights, Isabel Emmett (1982: 168) noted that:

> For some purposes, to be Welsh means to have been born in the Principality of Wales; for others, born and brought up there; for others, living in Wales and behaving in ways seen as typically Welsh and in particular not typically English; for others, living in Wales and speaking Welsh; and for most occasions, some mix of these things – and the list is not exhaustive . . . Such ways of attributing Welsh or any other group identity according to occasion to different categories of people are alternatives with a long history of use, and cause very little confusion.

We find plenty to support this position in the comments of our Bangor informants, among whom the way in which Welshness is comprehended and discussed involves a blend of many strands of thought, and many conceptions, which jostle with each other, interact, sometimes conflict and contradict, in people's minds and speech. Consequently identity, and that aspect of identity which is regarded as specifically 'Welsh', is hard to pin down, continually shifting, developing and adjusting according to context. We would suggest furthermore that the internal and external dialogues which result are rooted very largely in local social relations and experiences. While people may draw upon other sources, such as discussions in the media and their knowledge of the history, literature, etc. of Wales, it is in their encounters with others at everyday level, and in their awareness of events in the local context, that their sense of belonging to a given national community is lent shape. Our only disagreement with Emmett's interpretation is that this can generate a great deal of confusion, and sometimes conflict, particularly through those processes in which people's provisional and revisable constructions of national identity are systematized and formalized into features of nationalism.

Note

Our understanding of 'the local' draws, in part, on ethnomethodological notions of the 'local production of order' (Garfinkel, 1984) and 'mundane reason' (Pollner, 1987; Hester, 1991). The authors are grateful to Richard Fitzgerald for his various insights on these issues.

3 The Intellectual and the National Movement in Wales

David Adamson

Introduction

Attempts to theorize and explain the development of the political doctrine of nationalism have consistently identified a key role for the intellectual in the process of defining the nation. Intellectuals pursuing artistic, literary, academic, philosophical and political careers contribute significantly to the forging of national culture and the creation of national identity. In the process of 'imagining' of community (Anderson, 1983) it is the intelligentsia which provides much of the raw material of the national imagination as well as the leadership of national movements. This active intervention and participation has ensured that the role of intellectuals in nationalist movements provides a fundamental challenge to any conception of the intellectual as a detached, neutral observer of history, occasionally moved to intervene in the affairs of society. Instead we see passionate involvement in the creation and maintenance of national identity and associated programmes of political activism. It is no coincidence that for Benda (1959) the 'trahison de clercs' is most often committed in the pursuit of national identity (Gellner, 1994), or that for Said (1994) it is impossible to understand the nature of the intellectual without first considering the relationship between the individual and his/her and national identity.

This chapter explores the role of intellectuals in the creation and historical development of Welsh national identity. This is a complex task. Intellectual activity spans the full range of human endeavour and the burgeoning self-identity of Wales in the last century was evident in almost every sphere of Welsh society. To fully understand how an intelligentsia can contribute to the development of national identity we have to examine carefully its interventions in fields as diverse as literature, art, music, education, philosophy, politics, historiography and language. The unravelling of such a complex entity as the intellectual life of a society presents irresolvable difficulties. However, we can focus on specific aspects of this totality to begin to illustrate processes which may have a general significance for the development of national identities. By mapping one aspect of the role of the Welsh intelligentsia we can illustrate key features of the part it played in the creation of national identity. It is this more limited task which this chapter seeks to achieve by considering the role of intellectuals in describing and representing the history of the Welsh nation.

A key aspect of the definition of nationhood is some sense of shared history. For a people to identify themselves as one, there is an implicit assumption of shared experiences and cultural commonality. The building blocks of a shared identity will be drawn from a range of social and cultural characteristics which will include language, heritage, history of persecution, religious practice, folk traditions and ethnic lineage. The validity of such connections is defined by their longevity and the remembering of a shared history provides opportunity for defining the nation in the present. The role of the intellectual in this process is self-evident, whether as the formal academic historian, the author of revived or 'imagined' folk practices or the politician who weaves national heritage into contemporary political realities. Woolf (1996: 2) writes:

> From the earliest expressions of modern nationalism, historians, antiquarians and savants played a significant role in articulating a sense of national identity . . . History, language, folklore, territory, culture or religion could all be used to demonstrate the past traditions of a nation, symbolic evidence of its historic continuity and hence its authenticity.

Additionally, as social formations develop and become more institutionally differentiated, the process of remembering becomes formalized and professionalized in institutions which are defined as official and authentic representations of the history of the society. Museums become a significant bearer of national identity (Zolberg, 1996) and the work of several sections of the intelligentsia become channelled and focused to the public through the museum. Consequently, intellectuals engaged with conveying the past are uniquely placed to influence contemporary national identity. It is this process, in the Welsh context, which will be considered in this chapter.

The Intellectual in Theories of Nationalism

Whilst theorists of the national question have approached the subject from a diverse range of intellectual and political perspectives, there is a consensus that the intellectual plays a key role in the development of national identity and the organization of nationalism as a political programme. Indeed for the majority of commentators intellectuals are the leaders of the nationalist movements of the last century (Hooge, 1992). In Miroslav Hroch's much quoted study (Hroch, 1985) the intelligentsia are the 'strongest component' in all but one of the twelve nationalist groups he studied (cited in Schwarzmantel, 1992).

There is some dissent from this view which suggests that 'there are a large number of nationalist movements in which the intellectual leadership is not particularly marked' (Breuilly, 1993). The overwhelming opinion, however, is that the intelligentsia plays a key role in the emergence and development of both nineteenth-century, first wave national movements and contemporary movements in Europe and the developing world. It is not possible here to achieve any more than a brief review of this orthodoxy by identifying the central place of the intellectual in three seminal bodies of work on nationalism: by Elie Kedourie, Ernest Gellner and Anthony D. Smith.[1] Whilst these works have been subject to criticism - not least by each other – they represent between them modes of explanation which are now well established in the literature on nationalism.

For Kedourie (1960) the intelligentsia are found at the centre of three causal processes in the emergence of nationalism in the nineteenth century. They carry the responsibility for the 'invention' of the doctrine, to satisfy their 'need to belong' in a rootless world in transition from traditional social formations to the condition of modernity. Equally, they seek to establish the nation-state to create a place where their full worth is recognized and their status is in accord with their self-perceptions. Finally, it is they who break with the traditions of the past as encroaching modernity prevents the transmission of conventional political values. Instead they form movements of national identity to bring into existence the state of nationhood which they desire. In summary, for Kedourie, it is the intellectual who bears the 'spirit of an age' which nationalism becomes in the nineteenth century. Kedourie's theory is entirely idealistic and lacks any grounding in analysis of the cultural, political and economic context of nineteenth-century Europe (Adamson, 1991a). For Gellner (1983: 126) Kedourie presents us with a 'bizarre' suggestion that such a powerful, global ideology could emanate from the 'obtrusive lucubrations of philosophers'.

In his own writings, however, Gellner (1964, 1983, 1987) pays equal attention to the role of the intellectual in establishing nationalism as the most influential ideology of modernity. In contrast to Kedourie's idealism, Gellner presents an understanding of the emergence of nationalism in the nineteenth century which is rooted in the material conditions of societies engaged with the transformation to modern industrial communities. Indeed, for Gellner it is this process of transition which creates the conditions which give rise to the ideology of nationhood. Drawing from both Durkheimian and Weberian perspectives (James, 1996), Gellner (1964) sees the production of 'effective citizens' as the primary function of the modern state, achieved by the creation of an official language and an education system to promote literacy and adaptation to an ever-changing division of labour. The constant need for 'generic training' (Gellner, 1983: 27) requires a national education system which can only be maintained by the nation-state. In this way the state becomes inextricably linked with a particular linguistic and cultural configuration and the first wave of nationalism in Europe is created.

Additionally, by combining concepts of modernization with patterns of uneven development, Gellner creates an explanation in which practices of social closure by dominant modern élites prompt a reaction in intellectuals in communities where the benefits of modernity have been denied. For Gellner (1964) the wave of modernity progresses with an uneven front and those who gain advantage first exclude others by mobilizing factors of ethnicity, religion and language as mechanisms of social closure. In response, intellectuals in the excluded cultures are educationally equipped to reject the dominant culture and assert their own culture in its place. In this they attempt to create their own modern nation in which they will achieve full status, in much the same search for recognition identified by Kedourie. In their battle for control they also enlist the working class, calling to their aid the very criteria of ethnicity, religion and language by which they are excluded from modernity. Gellner (1964: 172) claims that in the short term the working class identify a common interest with the intellectuals, willing to exchange 'hardship-with-snubs for possibly greater hardship with national identification'. In Gellner's thesis the intellectual has progressed from the bearer of a 'spirit of an age' (Kedourie, 1960) to become the leading force in the nationalist movement for secession.

Similar functions are ascribed to the intellectual by Anthony Smith (1971, 1979, 1981). In his model of nationalism, modernity is established in the form of the 'scientific state' which bureaucratizes and homogenizes in pursuit of efficiency. As for Gellner, a key component is the need for an official language of state, the emergence of which creates 'sociological minorities' (Smith, 1971: 235) discriminated against because of their language and culture. The modernizing process both attracts and repels the intelligentsia of the minorities creating a crisis of 'dual legitimation' in which they are presented with two sources of authority; the state and their religion. This crisis is resolved by one of three possible responses: 'traditionalism', 'assimilation' and 'reformism'. Smith sees nationalism emerging from a complex fusion between the reformist and the assimilationist position in which the former seeks historical validation of religion in an ethnic past and the latter seeks to redress the inequalities of the 'scientific state' by adopting the ethnicity of the reformers. In combination, nationalism is created and again intellectuals are central to the process.

In these three seminal works we find that intellectuals are ascribed the key role in creating nationalism. However, there is little explanation of why this is the case. Kedourie, Gellner and Smith fail to reveal why the social conditions they describe determine these specific behavioural outcomes in the intelligentsia. More fundamentally, none of them consider that alternative choices were available to the intellectuals. Specifically, no explanation is given in Kedourie as to why intellectuals experienced a crisis of status, a 'need to belong' or why they failed to inherit the political traditions of their society. Gellner gives us no reasons why minority intellectuals reject the dominant culture, preferring a form of resistance through celebration of their own culture. Smith gives us no explanation for the attraction and revulsion for the 'scientific state' experienced by his intellectuals. All three fail to consider the possibility that their agitated intellectuals could have chosen alternative paths to the quest for nationhood.

One clear alternative was a ready acceptance of the benefits of modernity brought by the dominant culture and a consequent sacrifice of their local tradition, language and religion for the alternatives of affluence, progress, science, secularism, even if experienced from a slightly marginal position in relation to the dominant cultural group. It is this choice which prevailed as the norm in modern Europe until the resurgence of ethnicity in the mid-1960s. Additionally, there is no consideration of the development of socialist or collectivist ideologies by intellectuals in both dominant and subordinate national cultures (Schwarzmantel, 1987, 1992), which was evident as a frequent response to changing socio-economic conditions in all European countries during the nineteenth century.

To address these and other failings in these dominant paradigms of nationalism, in *Ideology and the Nation* (Adamson, 1991a) I turned to the Marxist tradition to excavate a theory of nationalism which offered more sophisticated analysis of the economic, cultural, political and ideological climate which gave birth to the nationalist doctrine in nineteenth-century Europe. Of crucial importance in that theory was the writing of Antonio Gramsci (1971) which fused the analysis of the role of the intellectual with the national question. For Gramsci these two fundamental issues were inextricably linked and part of the same social and political process; the struggle for ascendancy in society by distinct social groups. Identifying a paradigm in Marxism which reached from Marx through Lenin and Gramsci, I developed a theory of nationalism which employed the Gramscian concept of the 'national popular collective will' to describe a process whereby nationalism exists as a 'free floating' ideology which cannot in essence be ascribed to a particular class, as is often the case in Marxist discussions of the national question.

For Gramsci, the national question is a central aspect of his discussion of 'hegemony'. In theorizing the concept, Gramsci developed the view that the power of the bourgeoisie did not rest simply on economic domination but was also dependent on relations in the political and ideological spheres. Distinguishing between 'coercion' and 'consent' (Femia, 1981), Gramsci drew attention to the realms of culture, morality and beliefs in maintaining the social order. Gramsci grounded much of his analysis in 'civil society' (Gramsci, 1971: 12) in which non-state institutions play a major role in reproducing a consent for the dominance of the ruling block. It is this consent which forms the basis of hegemony, legitimizing the ruling class, normalizing class relations and obscuring exploitation. It establishes a belief system in which the class system and its protection of class interests is presented as a general will operating in the interests of the whole society.

Central to this process is the creation of a 'national popular collective will' (Gramsci, 1971: 131) exemplified by the French Jacobin movement which successfully synthesized class interests, creating an historical block from a diverse set of classes. Gramsci argued that no such hegemony had been created in Italy. This had led to a political vacuum into which the proletariat could step by itself, bringing together the specific national characteristics of Italian society to create a 'national popular collective will', dominated and shaped by the proletariat. This struggle would take place primarily in civil society and Gramsci saw a central role in this process for the intellectuals of the workers' movement. In contrast to Marxist orthodoxy in which intellectuals were always the 'hired prize-fighters' of capitalism, Gramsci saw a unique role for intellectuals in classes which were emerging and establishing for themselves a conscious and active identity (Thompson, 1994). In struggling against domination they were engaged in an act of creating a counter-hegemony in opposition to the beliefs and values of the current hegemonic block. Gramsci termed these leaders, organizers and thinkers of the class, 'organic' intellectuals.

Gramsci (1971: 240) saw the organic intellectual weaving together the 'original and unique' internal relations of a culture to create the national popular collective will. National characteristics form an important component of hegemonic and counter-hegemonic appeals in support of attempts to create a fusion of class interests and the formation of political alliances. In this sense nationalism can be employed by a dominant class in society to justify and legitimate its position or it can be mobilized by classes and alliances of classes seeking to challenge their domination.

Nationalism is ascribed its character by its insertion into this 'war of position' and its actual form will be determined by the alliance of class interests which employs it.

The remainder of this chapter examines how this process occurred in the formation of Welsh nationalism in the late nineteenth century as an emerging indigenous bourgeoisie attempted to weave a national popular collective will grounded in Welsh linguistic identity, religious Nonconformism and political liberalism.

Representing the Past: Nationalism, Ideology and the *Gwerin*

The emergence of a clear sense of national identity in Wales is the result of a process which unfolded throughout the nineteenth century and is fully described in Adamson (1991a). Conditions in both the rural and emerging industrial sectors led to the development of a strong, self-conscious national élite by the end of the century. Its development was the consequence of a coincidence of interests and cultural characteristics between a largely impoverished rural tenantry and a developing indigenous bourgeoisie.

The Welsh-speaking, Nonconformist tenantry were in conflict with a primarily Anglicized and Anglican landlord class. Insecurity of tenure, price inflation, tithe conflicts and politically motivated evictions served to politicize this tenantry by the 1860s and the inherent economic conflicts were overlaid with cultural differences of language and religion. At the same time, in the industrial communities of south Wales an indigenous bourgeoisie was emerging and the opening of the Welsh coalfields triggered a huge expansion of economic activity and wealth creation in which local entrepreneurs came to the fore. Initially, in close alliance with the nascent working class around issues of electoral reform and religious dissent, by the 1890s the relationship was becoming increasingly conflictual. This Nonconformist, Welsh-speaking bourgeoisie resisted the Anglicization and secularization of the working class by an emphasis on language and religion as the basis for national identity and shared interests. This was articulated largely through the Liberal Party in Wales attracting the support of the rural tenantry which required an organized means of expressing its interests and overcoming its traditional dependency on the landlord class. The result was the fusing of these interests within a hegemonic block characterized by Welsh Nonconformist radicalism, a political movement which was able to draw together a rural tenantry, an indigenous bourgeoisie and a nascent working class until late into the nineteenth century. This configuration gave rise to a celebration of Welshness. The hegemony of the Welsh Nonconformist élite was founded on issues of language, religious dissent and Liberalism welded together in Welsh radicalism to become a political and cultural force which swept Wales into the twentieth century, forging a literary, political and cultural base for nationhood.

Its most visible expression was in the realm of politics where it gave rise to an articulate and organized expression of Welsh national identity. Welsh politicians occupied pivotal places in the British polity and English Liberalism was dependent on its Welsh support for electoral success (K. O. Morgan, 1963). Welsh Liberals actively pursued policies of Home Rule, Disestablishment of the Church and generally sought to reflect the unique characteristics of their 'imagined community' in legislation affecting Wales. Cymru Fydd, the London-based Welsh society which came into existence in April 1887, became the voice of Welsh Liberalism. Publishing in January 1888 the first edition of its journal of the same name, the society began to form branches in the Welsh towns in the opening years of the 1890s. The group was dominated by a collection of Welsh London intellectuals in exile and the flowering of a Welsh intelligentsia was a crucial process in the establishment of such a vociferous national identity (K. O. Morgan, 1981). The key figures in the Cymru Fydd movement were T. E. Ellis, D. A.Thomas and Lloyd George (K. O. Morgan, 1963), supported by a core of Welsh Liberal MPs who together forced the attention of the British Parliament onto Welsh issues.

The period of influence of Cymru Fydd, however, was short. By the dawn of the new century it was a spent force, although the nationalism it had so clearly articulated remained an embedded facet of Welsh political and social life. Successful merger in 1894 of Cymru Fydd and the North Wales Liberal Federation was not replicated in the south where, for Morgan (1963), there was an inherent distrust of the rural emphasis of the movement on the part of the more commercially orientated southern Liberals. Morgan also attaches significance to personality clashes between members of the leadership. A more likely explanation for the demise of Cymru Fydd is the resolution of conflicts between landlords and the tenantry in the rural sector coupled with an increasing emphasis on the politics of industrial conflict in the south (Adamson, 1991a). These factors shifted the ground of Welsh political debate at the same time as key members of the organization moved centre stage in British politics.

The influence of Cymru Fydd nevertheless continued far beyond its limited lifespan. It had raised a debate on Home Rule and had successfully campaigned for legislation specific to Wales. In this it raised aspirations and demonstrated the potential for the creation of national institutions and a Welsh political and cultural life separate from England. The movement had given structure and form to the expression of Welsh national sentiment. Alongside the political debates of the movement there had been parallel developments in the cultural sphere. In keeping with the flourishing of national cultures throughout Europe at this time there was a 'renaissance' of Welsh literature and a flourishing Welsh-language press (Butt Philip, 1975). Butt Philip (1975) paints a picture of Welsh intellectual life at the turn of the century dominated by a concern with issues of national identity. Intellectuals, influenced by the European debates about nationality, discussed and wrote about the ideas of Mazzini, Garibaldi and other nationalist figures.

The creation in 1893 of the University of Wales had opened a period of nation-building expressed in the desire for national institutions that reinforced the cultural and artistic life of the emerging nation. For Morgan, the campaign for the 'People's University, Prifysgol y werin' (1995: 26) was deeply symbolic of the burgeoning national culture. Education was to be a pivotal point in this movement and the addition of national institutions such as the National Library in 1907 was seen as consolidating the intellectual development of the Welsh nation. The process also contributed significantly to the development of a specifically Welsh intelligentsia rooted in the Welsh-language, Nonconformist traditions. Its intellectual heart could be found in rural Wales, its language was Welsh and it celebrated Cymric culture and heritage. It developed and embellished a sense of continuity and antiquity, an unbroken lineage reaching back to the Welsh princes. By the time of the formation of Plaid Cymru, the nationalist party, in 1925 the process of 'imagining' Wales was complete and the character of the national movement was centred on the hearth of a rural, pre-industrial golden age.

The emergence at this time of a Welsh intelligentsia is crucial to the development of Welsh nationhood. Almost every aspect of Welsh social, cultural and political life was imbued with the sentiment of a clamouring nationhood. The political intellectuals of Cymru Fydd were joined by poets, writers, journalists and Nonconformist clerics all advancing a sense of Welsh nationhood and themselves drawing inspiration from the intellectual climate they were themselves contributing to. In literature and academia figures such as O. M. Edwards, John Morris-Jones, John Edward Lloyd and Crwys Williams celebrated the Welsh past and the common bonds between its people, establishing a shared sense of people and place which became embodied in the concept of the *gwerin* (P. Morgan 1986b; K. O. Morgan, 1995).

The concept of the *gwerin* is central to the development of this sense of nationhood. Lacking a clear English translation, the term came to signify a particular conception of the Welsh people and its significance lies in the 'symbolic usage' (P. Morgan, 1986b) it acquired as an expression of Welsh identity. Prys Morgan (1986b: 134) traces the growing currency of the term *gwerin* as a form of 'propaganda from the 1890s onwards'. The term signified a heroic Welsh people rising from their subjection to claim nationhood. The idealistic imagery of contemporary art and literature portrayed the *gwerin* as the ancient Welsh, successful in their resistance to invasion, steadfast in their language and culture and pure in their Christian faith. The *gwerin* were perceived as a rural people; industrial workers were inserted into a largely rural imagery and assumed to be bound to the countryside by ties of language, blood and faith. The 'imagined community' (Anderson, 1983) was classless and free of the conflicts associated with industrialization. Early nationalists saw manifestations of proletarian organization such as the Scotch Cattle and Owenite trade unions as the work of 'English agitation' (Adamson, 1991a: 118). Prys Morgan summarizes this conception of 'the people' which stood at the heart of Welsh national identity:

> By 1900 the common folk of Wales had become a remarkable phenomenon: according to this ideal, a classless society, progressing rapidly yet retaining a closeness to the soil, educated, religious, cultured, keen to own its own land and property, hard-working and methodical, law-abiding. Temperate in drink, respecting the Sabbath, and an example to the world. (1986b: 139)

This idealized interpretation of past and present permeated Welsh politics, culture, art and literature. Its action as an ideological device was to obscure the internal class tensions between the working class and the Nonconformist élite and to establish a world-view which emphasized the common language, culture and religiosity of the Welsh people. The industrial revolution in Wales was creating an urban proletariat with an increasingly complex division of labour. Political and social conflicts characterized by a class component were manifest from the late seventeenth century onwards. For Gwyn A. Williams (1980: 24), there was the emergence of a 'visible and audible' working class by the early nineteenth century and organizations such as the Scotch Cattle and Chartism demonstrated the increasingly conflictual relationships between workers and their employers. In particular, south Wales saw an increasingly secularized and radicalized working class by the beginning of the twentieth century. However, the 'myth of the *gwerin*' (P. Morgan, 1986b) evoked an image of a common people, in harmony and at prayer until the 1930s.

This could only sustain a hegemonic structure of Welsh radicalism while the working class were still drawn primarily from the rural hinterland of the industrial areas (G. A. Williams, 1980) and shared the need for electoral reform and religious freedom with the indigenous bourgeoisie. As the century progressed increased external immigration created an Anglicized working class less attached to Nonconformism. The basis of the hegemony broke down (Adamson, 1991a) and the industrial working class turned increasingly to radical, secular beliefs which, by the end of the first decade of the twentieth century, were characterized by Marxist, socialist and syndicalist ideas (K. O. Morgan, 1995).

Despite this loss of political grip on significant elements of Welsh society and the early failure of the political project of Welsh nationalism with the collapse of Cymru Fydd, the sense of Welsh nationhood had become an embedded element of Welsh culture. The sense of *gwerin* and a shared past continued to bear influence long after the specific social conditions which brought it into existence were eroded. This vision of Wales has remained a central tenet in the political nationalist movement in Wales. By the 1930s the perception of the Welsh nation as a rural idyll characterized by a classless *gwerin* had become enshrined in the political programme of Plaid Cymru. In the inter-war years policies were primarily cultural, seeking advancement of the language and culture of Wales (D. H. Davies, 1983) rather than any expression of political independence. Economic policy was based on a vision of pre-industrial Wales and the 1934 economic policy statement *Ten Points of Policy*, penned by Saunders Lewis, saw deindustrialization as the key solution to the crisis of the Welsh economy (Adamson, 1991a). However, Plaid Cymru is not the sole surviving site of this ideology which continues to exert influence in key cultural institutions from the Eisteddfodau (Urdd and National) to the branch museums of the National Museums of Wales. As a final illustration of the way intellectual activity contributes to the establishment of national identity, it is useful to examine one of the paths by which a concept born of the cultural configuration of the turn of the century continues to bear influence today.

Museum Representations and National Continuity

Representations of the past are a crucial component of any attempt to build a unifying ideology. The centrality of the 'national popular collective will' in Gramsci's analysis suggests that issues of national heritage, national identity and components of these are essential to the creation of the social cement which binds together potentially antagonistic groups within the hegemonic structure. Icons as varied as flags, buildings, literature, folk customs, artworks, musical forms and language are interwoven in the process of 'imagining' the community of the nation. This unifying national identity serves to obscure difference of wealth, privilege, status and power. It establishes a sense of commonality of aspirations and beliefs which naturalizes the social hierarchy and depoliticizes subordinate groups. Contestation of the meaning of the past and of heritage artefacts, however, also provides a fertile ground for 'counter-hegemonic' representations to the extent that the meaning of the past is constantly reinterpreted according to the exigencies of life in the present (Urry, 1996).

The 'organic intellectuals' of the late nineteenth and early twentieth century in Wales erected a complex national culture, part excavation of the past and part invention, to establish a firm sense of nationhood traceable to the Welsh princes and beyond into

Celtic and Druidic culture. Wales was not alone in this process of 'inventing tradition' (Hobsbawm and Ranger, 1983) as it became a key component of nation-building throughout Europe. This process of 'invention' was not exclusive to enthusiastic amateurs such as Iolo Morganwg (K. O. Morgan, 1983) but is evident in the work of leading historians of the time. The historical analysis produced in this period was subject to the same ideological milieu and reflected this powerful sense of a nation and its people. The burgeoning colleges of the federal Welsh University produced scholars steeped in the sense of *gwerin* and nationhood.

Gwynfor Evans paints a picture of a Welsh intellectual élite engaged in the propagation of a sense of national identity, reawakening the spirit of the common people. For Evans, O. M. Edwards was 'the brightest star in this scintillating company' (1988: 276). Edwards himself had felt that the failure of the Cymru Fydd movement[2] had been the result of a lack of historical understanding on the part of its leadership (Rees, 1963) and he felt the need to 'give the nation her memory back' (Evans, 1988: 278). The result in his book *Wales* (1901) was a text which foregrounded Welsh history prior to the Tudors and had little to say about the industrial revolution (Rees, 1963). In describing Edwards's work, Evans (1988: 279) states that 'in writing of his country's history, as in everything he did and wrote his eyes were on the *gwerin*. The glory of the *gwerin* was at the heart of his vision.'

Edwards's work was typical of a historiography that was bound up within the fervour of nation-building which characterized Welsh intellectual life in the first decades of the twentieth century in Wales. More importantly, such a view dominated Welsh intellectual life and informed the view of the literati and educated élite.[3] It was this view of the past, authenticated by scholarship and reproduced in all cultural endeavour, which formed the backdrop to the formalization of national memory with the establishment of the National Museum of Wales.

The creation of a museum movement in Wales took place within this ideological context of nation-building. The National Museum of Wales, founded in 1907, was one element of a ready recognition of Welsh identity by the Liberal government of the period and continued the practice of institution-building initiated by the creation of the University of Wales.[4] The formation of a national museum was perceived as reflecting the continued cultural development of Wales and educated nature of Welsh society. In keeping with the times, the Cardiff museum celebrated high culture in the European tradition with a strong fine art collection. More significant for the investigation in this chapter is the establishment of the National Folk Museum in 1947. There had been discussions from early in the century about the desirability of establishing a museum of folk life in Wales but the gift of a site by Lord Plymouth provided the first such opportunity to bring the ideal to realization. Set in the grounds of St Fagans Castle, an Elizabethan manor on the outskirts of Cardiff, the museum adopted the model of the open-air Scandinavian folk museums (National Museum, 1974). The strategy was to create a collection of reassembled buildings representative of Welsh folk architecture.

Ehrentraut (1991) identifies a European-wide trend for the establishment of museums of 'vernacular architecture' from the end of the nineteenth century onwards. Embedded in nationalist discourses, the establishment of such museums was an integral element of the nation-building activities of national bourgeoisies. Ehrentraut raises a number of issues in his analysis of Austrian *Freilichtmuseen* which are of direct relevance to this analysis of the relationship between the myth of the *gwerin*, the hegemony of Welsh nationalism and the modes of museum representation.

First, he identifies a use of contrived landscape to create impressions of timeless rurality either by shielding or incorporating external views, depending on whether the wider horizons reinforce or challenge the sense of rurality. At St Fagans the visitor, having passed through a modern entrance and exhibition area, is transported thereafter to a pre-modern world. A network of narrow paths meanders through a widely dispersed series of restored buildings which, to the uninformed, seem to display a contemporary relationship to each other. The layout suggests a village as it might have existed prior to the industrial revolution. Careful use of rare-breed livestock confirms the pastoral scenery and woodland and hedgerow screening prevent any visual intrusion by the twentieth century. Until the mid-1980s every display at the museum was of rural origin. Craft demonstrations similarly were of rural crafts. Growing criticism of the museum's failure to represent industrial Wales eventually resulted in the rebuilding of a row of early industrial workers' cottages[5] and more recently the inclusion of the Oakwood Miners' Institute. However, the inclusion of these buildings does nothing to challenge the illusion of ruralia. The cottages are presented with no sense of context and are in juxtaposition to a general stores rescued from a mining community but which in this wider context takes on the appearance of a village store.

Secondly, Ehrentraut identifies an absence of social history from his Austrian examples. No information is offered about 'the course of geopolitical events, the relationship of farmers to their secular and ecclesiastical overlords, and the internal differentiation of rural society itself' (1991: 54). Similarly, at St Fagans there is no information about social hierarchies or the position of the occupants of the exhibits in the social structure. The impression of a timeless, village existence is reinforced by an absence of reference to external, political and social events. The focus of the display of workers' housing is the furniture of successive decades. No information about social and work conditions or the workers political responses to them are given. These houses span the years of Chartism, the Merthyr Rising of 1832, two World Wars and the economic devastation of the Great Depression. The occupants endured cholera epidemics and yearlong lockouts from work. They participated in religious revivals and the formation of the modern socialist movement. The museum demonstrates instead the minutiae of daily life.

For Ehrentraut (1991: 50) these features of folk museums can be explained in functionalist terms as 'institutional mechanisms of pattern maintenance' or in radical terms as 'cultural production of the ideological state apparatuses'. The latter perspective supports the view of the myth of the *gwerin* as an ideological strategy brought to bear by a Nonconformist élite in Welsh society. Ehrentraut suggests that heritage architecture is a 'visual ideology' of the dominant class which reinforces the pattern of class relations. Whilst we might accept a more sophisticated understanding of the ways in which museum representations are read as 'subtexts' (Vergo, 1989: 3) by the general public, the St Fagans mode of representation has clearly been the product of an intellectual milieu which defined Wales as rural and pre-industrial. It draws on and sustains the world-view which was hegemonic at the turn of the century but which since has withdrawn from mainstream culture and politics to the realms of Welsh institutions and cultural organizations populated largely by the graduates of the University of Wales. The survival of that intelligentsia in command positions within Welsh cultural institutions demonstrates its ability to recreate itself through the mechanisms of internal recruitment and effective education and socialization within the colleges of the University of Wales. In this sense the ideological construct of Welsh nationhood and the role of the *gwerin* has survived considerably beyond the social conditions which brought it into existence.

Much of this extended influence of the conception of Welshness embodied in the *gwerin* is due to the failure of any alternative to emerge within the nationalist movement itself. Despite the central arena of Welsh politics having moved from the rural to the industrial community by the turn of the century, the predominance of romantic cultural nationalism ensured that the nationalist movement did not engage with the political implications of industrialization until the 1960s. The fact that the majority of the population lived in industrial south-east Wales, and had, at best, an ambivalent attitude to issues of Welsh language and culture, was not a concern for the party until the resurgence of nationalism post-1963 brought an increasing membership drawn from that population.

Rawkins (1979) provides a useful framework for the analysis of this period. He sees the initial concern for the perceived crisis of Welsh in the 1960s culture being expressed by the traditional membership of the Welsh intelligentsia and literati. Characterized by their attachment to the Welsh language, Nonconformism and a rural lifestyle these 'fortress nationalists' are seen by him as a rural middle class concerned with threats to the stability of the social order which they inhabited. Additionally, Rawkins suggests that the failure of these traditional members of the nationalist movement to stem the tide of change promoted the adoption of more radical action by Welsh youth and the emergence of what he terms 'militant cultural nationalism'. Often connected by family ties and common cultural and educational backgrounds, Rawkins stresses the common grounding of these two nationalist strategies in a Welsh middle class separated only by generation.

More importantly, Rawkins identifies a growing interest in nationalist politics from the urban areas of Wales, particularly in the south-east. He identifies from 1966 onwards an emergence of 'modernists' who were to take the party away from its traditional concerns with a Welsh way of life into a 'radical political commitment to economic and social justice' (1979: 453). Characteristically English-speaking and English-university-educated 'modernists' developed the movement in the industrial valleys of south Wales and penetrated the party apparatus at senior level. D. H. Davies (1983) sees the party moving increasingly towards a socialist policy base and distancing itself from the politics of cultural nationalism. By the 1970s Plaid Cymru was posing a serious threat to the Labour Party in its heartland, the mining valleys of south Wales.

In terms of nationalist ideology this radicalization of Welsh nationalism also entailed a redefinition of Welshness. No longer could use of the Welsh language be the primary criterion for Welsh identity. Similarly, traditional cultural institutions such as Eisteddfodau were not seen as the sole expression of Welsh culture. There emerged a new sense of identity best described as Anglo-Welsh and distinct from the rural Nonconformist identity, which had been embodied in the prevailing concept of the *gwerin*, examined earlier. Authors writing about Wales, but in the medium of English, came to the fore and the imagery of Wales became more identifiable with the culture of the mining communities and its associated choral and sporting traditions.

This ideological transformation of Welsh identity also had complex associations with work emerging from the academic community. By the 1970s the major focus of Welsh historiography was the Welsh working class and the industrial legacy. Pioneering work by scholars such as Glanmor Williams, David Williams and Gwyn A. Williams[6] had demonstrated a far more complex and conflictual model of Welsh history than their earlier counterparts. These historians were to place Wales at the centre of the examination of the development of the working class in Britain. Central to this emerging school of analysis was the department of History at the University College of Cardiff where the enthusiasm of Gwyn A. Williams and the nature of his key texts generated an army of historians excavating the industrial communities of south Wales. A key role in the dissemination of this work was played by the journal *Llafur: The Journal of Welsh Labour Historians*, which contributed significantly to the genesis of interest in Welsh industrial history. Gradually, a comprehensive picture of the importance of Welsh industrial communities emerged and demonstrated the complex link between the rural and industrial sectors in the formation of modern Wales. The key role played by Welsh organizations and individuals in the emergence of the British labour movement demonstrated the enormous significance of the Welsh coalfields in wealth generation and the political development of British society. A view of the Welsh people as rural, Welsh-speaking and Nonconformist was difficult to sustain in the face of this new imagery of Wales. The conception of the *gwerin* adhered to for so long by the Welsh intelligentsia bore little examination as reality. Implicit in this reconstruction of Welsh identity is that the self-perception of the Welsh people itself has changed. Insufficient space here prevents an analysis of the impact of Welsh industrial history on the new generation of museums and heritage sites which have mushroomed in industrial south Wales, often in attempts by local authorities to replace some of the post-war job losses by leisure and tourism. Sadly, many such attempts have achieved little more than a 'commodification' (Urry, 1996) of the past. Conforming to all the worst stereotypes of singing miners, the experience offered to the consumer of contemporary heritage obscures the heterogeneity of working-class life, both past and present (Adamson, 1991b). Plaid Cymru has made concerted attempts to establish an electoral base in south Wales with some success in local politics and the demand for Welsh-medium education demonstrates that a major re-evaluation of Anglo-Welsh identity has arrived at a new 'social image' of Welshness (B. Roberts, 1994). In reality in the late twentieth century a plurality of Welsh identities coexist, determined by local factors as much as by more generalized features of nationhood (Thompson *et al.*, 1999). The *gwerin*, created as myth by the Nonconformist intelligentsia as the century opened, has not survived its end.

Conclusion

The chapter has argued that the role of the intellectual is central to the creation of national identity. Identified as such in all major theories of nationalism, the weight of historical evidence paints a picture of intellectuals actively engaged in the creation of the material of nationhood. Following earlier work (Adamson, 1991a) in which it was argued that nationalism is a free-floating ideology which is mobilized by classes and social groups in pursuit of hegemony in society, this chapter has attempted to illustrate the contribution of the intellectual to the creation of a 'national popular collective will'. In the Welsh context this role was largely enacted through the creation of a Welsh past which became embodied in the concept of the *gwerin* as an expression of almost timeless unity of the Welsh people. The *gwerin* operated as a means of inclusion that enabled definition of who the Welsh people were. In reality it excluded significant proportions of the working class, but at the ideological level it wove them into the definition by denying the existence of the culture in which they existed. The *gwerin* was an intellectual construct evident in all spheres of intellectual activity in Wales, reproduced as the image of the nation and itself reproducing that image. It was created by the 'organic intellectuals' of an emerging indigenous bourgeoisie and reached its zenith just as that class began to lose its hegemony over the increasingly radical working class. These intellectuals were not the detached observers praised by Benda (1959). Their 'treason' was absolute as they campaigned with vigour and conviction for the creation of a Welsh nationhood. These intellectuals were not on the sidelines but at the front of the national movement, creating and articulating the sense of nationhood for a popular audience. In this they behaved as 'organic' intellectuals in the Gramscian sense, giving voice to the aspirations and world-view of an emerging class.

Central in this process is the specific sphere of intellectual activity associated with representing the past. In academic historiography and in the formalization, institutionalization and professionalization of collective memory, specific images of Welshness have prevailed. Most evident in the museum function these images have been slow to erode and difficult to challenge. In complex relationship with national identity itself, it required a body of historiography grounded in the industrial culture of the south to challenge the hegemony founded in the rural conditions of late nineteenth-century Wales. Post-war educational reforms and popular entry to higher education were the vehicles for the creation of the 'modernists' (Rawkins, 1979) who provided this challenge and dismissed thoroughly the conception of the *gwerin* which has prevailed in the cultural institutions of Wales.

Notes

1. I have elsewhere given a fuller treatment of these three writers (Adamson, 1991a), in which the full weaknesses of all three theoretical models are tested.
2. Edwards had been joint editor of *Cymru Fydd*, the journal of the Cymru Fydd political movement.
3. A similar perception of Welsh society dominated sociological and anthropological analysis of the 1950s. Community studies carried out within the framework of the Aberystwyth school of anthropology have been criticized for their projection of a timeless, conflict-free rural communities. See Owen (1986) for a discussion of the Welsh community studies of the post-war period.
4. The same term of the Liberal government saw the establishment of the National Library, the National Council for Agriculture, a Welsh Department of the Board of Education and a Welsh Insurance Commission as well as a recognition of Welsh interests in legislation of the period.
5. The cottages were rescued from the demolition of The Triangle at Merthyr Tydfil, a unique setting of early industrial housing which was destroyed to make way for industrial redevelopment. This act of official vandalism did much to force a public recognition of the importance of industrial heritage and the threat which existed to many important sites in south Wales.
6. These and other historians had begun an evaluation of political and social upheaval in the nineteenth century which challenged the perceptions of a classless *gwerin*. For Gwyn A. Williams (1980: 24), there was the emergence of a 'visible and audible' working class by the early nineteenth century and organizations such as the Scotch Cattle and Chartism demonstrated the increasingly conflictual relationships between workers and their employers. David Williams (1955) had demonstrated that even the rural idyll was in reality shattered consistently by corn, toll and tithe riots. Perhaps most fundamental was the evidence that the Welsh working class had been at the forefront of the development of British radicalism, held under the sway of their Nonconformist masters for only the briefest periods of the mid-nineteenth century (Williams, 1966).

4 Passports to Wales? Race, Nation and Identity

Charlotte Williams

Interest in the development of nationalism and its relationship to the contemporary manifestation of racisms in European countries has continued to grow as multiculturality becomes a more conspicuous feature of modern societies (*Race and Class*, 1991; Delanty, 1996; Rex, 1996). The history and articulation of racism within British nationalist ideologies is well documented (Gilroy, 1987; Miles, 1993). However, British nationalism is by no means a homogeneous ideology or indeed evenly developed across differences of class, gender, place, ethnicity and other social and spatial divisions. These factors operate to shape significantly the way in which nationalism is expressed and produce specific ideological constructions with their own boundaries of inclusion and exclusion. In this way regional and highly localized subjectivities have emerged, reflecting particular relationships between ideas of nation and 'race'.

One of the continuing issues in the construction of the British national collectivity has been struggles which exist over its internal borders. 'Welsh' as a deviant status within a wider British ideal has always challenged any unified concept of the boundaries of a British national collectivity. The strength of this challenge has varied at different historical moments and along different axes whether overtly political or by appeal to a specificity in terms of language, culture and identity. Nairn (1977) long envisaged the break-up of Britain as a result of such struggles. At times these struggles have been racialized as peoples from the Celtic countries, in particular the Irish, have been regarded as inferior or a dangerous 'other' in British history.

In contemporary Britain elements of this racialization persist. Note, for example, the recent controversy over the reference in a national newspaper to Welsh people as 'dark ugly trolls' (cf.

Western Mail, 2 January 1998) and the collective criminalization of the Irish as dangerous terrorists (Yuval-Davis, 1993: 44). This racialization of the Welsh is, however, a contradictory construction as by turns the Welsh have joined the hegemonic colonial ethnicity – white British and, to a certain extent more latterly, white European. White Welsh have in this way both challenged the boundaries of the national collectivity but also claimed access to the power and privilege it confers. Beyond the level of jibes and stereotyping, it is fair to say that the Welsh diaspora have not incurred any significant ethnic discrimination. It should nevertheless be noted that Welshness and Britishness do not coalesce in quite the same way as Englishness and Britishness. There is a distinctiveness that does not easily converge under the umbrella term 'British' and a certain sense in which marginalized nations such as Wales are able to reject British national concerns.

By contrast with this somewhat ambivalent juxtaposition of Welshness and Britishness, the peoples of the New Commonwealth countries and their descendants have been systematically and unequivocally placed outside the boundaries of the British national collectivity and racialized as inferior through both political processes and civic culture. The nature of the interrelationship between the British nation-state and racism is debated but its potential not disputed within nationalist writings. However, the extent to which the so-called 'Celtic' nations are yoked to this hegemonic ideology is less well explored. In their discussion of Scotland, Miles and Dunlop (1986) illustrate the potential within these nations to resist the hegemonic codes of exclusion by design or distraction, as well as simultaneously allowing for identification with the dominant British nationalism. Any consideration of the link between racism and nationalism within these nations must therefore proceed from an acknowledgement of the potential for a particularistic constellation of national ideology with race whilst also recognizing the influence of the wider British nationalist ideology.

The task of theoretically conceptualizing the relationship between nationalism and racism has been afforded little discussion by writers on Welsh nationalism (Adamson, 1991a; C. A. Davies, 1989; G. Williams, 1985). Anderson (1983) and Nairn (1977), although not addressing the issue within the Celtic nations specifically, do offer a theoretical starting-point. For Nairn (1977) racism is a derivative of nationalism and its post-war resurgence can be attributed to the lack of any major mobilizing myth of nationalism. His thesis on the break-up of Britain cites the political decline of empire and economic collapse as the spur. Anderson (1983), by contrast, is interesting because he frees up the notion of a fundamental interrelationship between nationalism and racism, arguing that the two are distinct ideologies that travel autonomously. For Anderson, racism is essentially antithetical to nationalism because nations became possible through printed languages which popularized culture and not through biological and kinship references which are seen to be the stuff of race. Anderson suggests both race and nation as imagined communities, although nationalism is not of necessity negative in the way that racism is; he sees them as very different sentiments:

> The fact of the matter is that nationalism thinks in terms of historical destinies, while racism dreams of external contaminations transmitted from the origins of time through an endless sequence of loathsome copulations . . . On the whole racism and anti-Semitism manifest themselves, not across national boundaries but within them. (1983: 136)

Gilroy (1987), Rex (1996) and Anthias and Yuval-Davis (1993) roundly reject this dichotomy. Gilroy's thesis on British nationalism illustrates the potential for a blurring of conceptions of 'race' and nation in which biological and cultural references overlap and in which the discourses on 'race' serve to reinforce national boundaries proscribing inclusions (who may legitimately belong) and exclusions (those whose origin, sentiment or citizenship assign them elsewhere). For Gilroy 'race is bounded on all sides by the sea', suggesting 'race' is coterminous with the boundaries of nation in the British context (1987: 45). He argues that nationhood may well be malleable but the links with discourses of class and 'race' and the organizational realities of these groups are such that it is by no means arbitrary. Rex adopts a historical analysis and points not only to the common historical origin of ideologies of racism and nationalism but shows, contrary to Anderson, that 'race' can be deployed with positive evaluation to demarcate a supraclass population; an example of this could be whites in South Africa. His conclusion is that 'the dialectic of inclusion and exclusion that is integral to the formation of imagined communities around the ideas of "nation" and "race" produces more complex patterns of identification and organisation than Anderson recognises' (1996: 78). Anthias and Yuval-Davis take this a step further, suggesting that, whenever a delineation of boundaries takes place, processes of inclusion and exclusion are operating and most ethnicities of hegemonic national collectivities contain elements of racist exclusion within their symbolic orders. Racism cannot, therefore, simply be set free from nationalism in the way Anderson suggests. Indeed there are particular paradoxes and dilemmas that contemporary multiculturality poses for specific constructions of nationalism and historical analyses of nationalist ideologies reveal clear examples of racist articulation.

There have been very few attempts to examine Welsh nationalism and 'race' and the inclusionary or exclusionary assumptions of Welsh national identity. One of the earliest forays is that provided by Denney, Borland and Fevre (1991). Their starting-point is that ideas that constitute nationalism within Wales are highly differentiated in nature such that it is impossible to speak of a Welsh nationalism but more appropriately Welsh nationalisms. These positionings will in turn embody different conceptualizations of 'race' and racism. Whilst they acknowledge both 'race' and 'nation' as constructs, they argue that it is possible to delineate loosely structured positionings around 'nation' from which some analysis of the relationship to racism can proceed. Denney et al. draw up three ideal typifications which they refer to as the *racial separatists*, the *socio-linguists* and the *cultural pluralists*. By selecting fragments of text (journalistic, literary and academic), they build an argument to illustrate the potential for racist discourse within the frame of the grouping they call the racial separatists. This grouping is themed by notions such as soil, blood, roots and ancestry as the core markers of Welsh nation and identity and in this sense, given its genetic overtones, the discourse is racially bound. The two other constructions examined have overtly cultural themes which, it is argued, are independent of 'race'. The socio-linguists' grouping, largely based on their understanding of the nationalist activities of Cymdeithas yr Iaith Gymraeg, emphasize the Welsh language as central to nation and national identity. The others, the cultural pluralists, referenced by the work of Plaid Cymru, focus on issues of Welsh territoriality, distinctiveness and the need for self-government. Denney et al.'s analysis concludes with only a tenuous link being found between nationalism and 'race' in one of their three groupings.

The proposition of these writers is tentative and probably rather cautious in that it fails to acknowledge the extent to which 'cultural ideologies' are overlaid with 'biological connotation' and become exclusively drawn. They state, for example, that the 'importance of Welsh national cultural distinctiveness is stressed above other factors such as 'race' (1991: 156–7). This ready distinction has not, of course, stood the test of time as more rigorous examination of the *new* racism shows it to be precisely culturally rather than biologically based or indeed a complex interplay of the two. A simple example of this overlaying might be seen in the popular use of the phrase '*native-born* Welsh-speaker' when used as a form of social closure, with its inherent evocation of genetics within the frame of culturalist arguments. What is needed is an analysis which begins with a definition of racism as it is popularly formulated and an exploration of nationalist ideologies that accommodates the ways in which exclusions claimed on the basis of culture are indeed racialised.

The Denney *et al.* piece has been pilloried not least for being developed on rather thin evidence and loose sociological concepts (G. Williams, 1994). Williams finds it methodologically indefensible, pointing specifically to the many limitations of typologies and taxonomies in the creation of a dynamic theory of nationalism. He argues that what is offered are essentially static pictures based on a haphazard selection of miscellaneous evidence for which there is no sound sociological justification. Further, he suggests, the selection of the evidence is based on the wholly negative presumption that a link between racism and nationalism can be 'proved', in effect ignoring the Andersonian proposition that the two do not necessarily coalesce. Williams's attack is directed against a search for universal 'truths' that somehow are understood to stand free from the interpretations of the writers as subjects themselves in the construction of this theory. He posits that this should be replaced by an understanding of 'meanings' we attribute to 'nation' which will be continually contested and in the construction of such meanings we as contributors to the discursive frame are all implicated: 'What is at stake in nationalism is the competition over the meaning of nation' (1994: 99). This point is well made. However, within Williams's own astructuralist positioning, based on

Foucault's discourse analysis, further difficulties lie. In the rather relativistic mêlée offered, 'Wales', 'nation', 'race' and racism are constructs and sites of permanent struggle and contestation. In this formulation there is only text, narratives and discourses which are each apparently afforded equal validity such that the logical conclusion might be that the narration racism is as valid as the narration equality. He argues: 'the relationship between power and knowledge is treated in terms of how relations of power define the fields of knowledge and produce objects of knowledge be they "race", "racism", "nation" or some other object' (1994: 101).

In the process of constructing racism in this way we are obliged to accept that discriminations, abuse, oppressions and other forms of social closure towards those with particular ascribed characteristics which are systematized within certain societies have no objective reality and no historical reference and are really only subjects for interpretation. This might be a happy and convenient conclusion for those whom it does not particularly affect and it effectively dispenses with the presumption that any link can be made between nationalist ideas and racist ideology, for there is no such thing in such a framework as ideology.

Williams's critique also raises the issue of the identity of the speaker and gives significance to the question 'Who has the right to speak?' which is common to so many debates in Wales and in which Williams himself colludes. Whilst bound by his own methodological assumptions, he cannot overtly question the right of Denney *et al.* to contribute to the discursive formation; he nevertheless implicates them, if only by inference, in neo-colonialism. Although heavily qualified and disguised, the import of phrases such as 'transient voyeurs casting a fleeting eye over the natives' (1994: 87), 'aggrieved ethnocentrists' (1994: 95) and 'Welsh, a language with which none of the authors is familiar' (1994: 93) is not missed.

The implicit claim within this type of critique is to ethnic absolutism. The tendency here is to reify fixed and rigid categorical groups and to confer on these groups specific attributes that become privileged and exclusive. This operates to narrow the field in terms of who is regarded as a legitimate commentator and who is not, effectively determining who is insider and who is outsider. This represents a potentially powerful strategy of silencing alternative versions of Welsh national identity that confront the hegemonic images, denying the legitimacy of these counter-formations often before they are even formulated. This is achieved by denying the authors of these alternative versions the right to speak.

The silencing of 'race' within the Welsh context is a phenomenon I have addressed in a previous article (C. Williams, 1995). In raising issues of 'race' and racism as they are associated with Welsh national identity-formation I breached certain unspoken codes, namely many of the assumptions of white Welsh tolerance and simultaneously the role of black people in Wales as essentially silent and passive, geographically contained and making no public demands on Welsh national identity. Again the policing of this publication indicated the difficulty of mounting any open and free debate about national identity in our country. The response to this article, like the Denney *et al.* piece, evoked the 'who has a right to speak' strategy most especially because it encroached on highly guarded territory around issues of Welsh language and Welsh national identity. It could be suggested that the article became controversial precisely because it shifted a focus from a consideration of racism concentrated in the south of Wales, in particular Cardiff, which might be considered 'non-authentic Wales' or 'English Wales' to a discussion that confronted a Welsh-speaking Wales and indeed came from within the heartland of Welsh-speaking Wales (see *Golwg*, 1 February 1996). In doing so it challenged both the physical territory of white Wales and powerful constructions of Welsh national identity. The response was also characterized by the citing of individual examples of instances of harmonious relations between white Welsh and individual black people with little acknowledgement of the processes of cultural and institutional reproduction of racisms (*Golwg*, 7 February 1996).

These academic exchanges highlight several significant factors. Two things emerge starkly from the Denney *et al.*–Williams debate and in particular from the G. Williams (1994) response. The first is that it is essentially a white English–white Welsh debate, a tussle on the borders of an England and a Wales in which the treatment of racist discourse relates to insider/outsider ideology along this axis. The 'us' and 'them' has yet to include some analysis of the position of New Commonwealth peoples and black settlers within Wales which can indicate much about conceptions of 'Welshness'. What my own contribution illustrated was a tendency to contain any debates on 'race' and racism to areas not considered 'proper' Wales or certainly areas more under English influence. In this way prevailing versions of Welsh national identity that privilege ideas of white tolerance (as opposed to multiculturalism) are protected. The second and related issue the debate highlights is the construction of Welsh identity and nation that protects a certain silence around 'race' or promulgates the idea of 'race' as a *non-Welsh issue*. Not only are we to accept racism as an autonomous movement in Andersonian style but we should understand it is a feature of the British hegemonic nationalist ideology in which Wales appears not to be implicated. The proposition becomes: why go searching for it if it is not there? The defence of any suggestion of a link between racism and particular Welsh nationalist ideologies or projects is rebuffed by referring to the construction of racist discourse. That is, we as speakers become implicated in constructing racism (G. Williams, 1994). Ironically perhaps G. Williams himself argues:

> There are also silences in the sense that certain things cannot be said within a given discursive formation. It is here that we locate the concept of power, in the manner in which discourse determines what can and indeed, must be said, within any given place. (1994: 100)

It is not that Wales is any more or less racist than anywhere else that is at issue here (this point has been discussed elsewhere: S. Evans, 1995; C. Williams, 1995). What the foregoing discussion illustrates is the way in which the academic debate in Wales is affected by the politics of national identity and the processes of marginalizing and discrediting those whose contribution challenges strongly held beliefs.

Another perspective on the issue of 'race' and nation comes from an examination of social and political life. The lack of a bureaucratic structure or any clearly unified political voice to orchestrate a homogeneous or specific form of political nationalism within Wales must be noted as limiting any concerted effort to resist dominant British codes of exclusion. However, what is now recognized is that a distinction can be made between the civic nationalism to which, for example, Plaid Cymru currently makes appeal and ethno-cultural nationalism. Delanty suggests the former refers to membership of a political community and is primarily defined by reference to the State and the latter refers to membership of a cultural historical community. It is apparent that the great modernising expressions of civic nationalism are today being overshadowed by ethno-cultural nationalism . . . Nationalism no longer appeals to ideology but to identity. (1996: 3)

It is often argued that there is more to Britishness than a passport and similarly therefore there is more to 'Welshness' than legal residence. Access to membership of a national collectivity is mediated by the more substantive citizenship of belonging, attachment, recognition and identity — within the realm of the cultural. One of the most pervasive forms of this type of nationalism is what Billig (1995) has referred to as 'banal nationalism'. This is the nationalism of everyday life in which political conflict is articulated more in terms of cultural contestation than in ideological terms. This milder banal nationalism serves to legitimize and sustain the more extreme expressions of nationalism through the more diffuse 'ways of life'. Thus the newer forms of nationalism have a distinct culturalist terminology. It is in this realm of expressions of Welsh identity that hints of the treatment of 'race' become manifest.

What characterizes the cultural scripts of Wales? Borrowing Anderson's idea of the 'imagined community', the narratives of Welsh nation are inscribed with notions of egalitarianism, solidarity, hospitality and tolerance. Frequent references, both literary and populist, parade these characteristics of Welshness. Tennyson portrayed Wales as tolerant and welcoming (N. Evans, 1991). As a value base of nation this proposition is both safe and unsafe, as it can be read as both a firm moral foundation or as an unreliable assumption serving to mask a different reality. There can be no single explanation for this widespread and culturally sustained myth. It most likely relates to a constellation of factors, the oldest of which is probably the *gwerin*. The *gwerin* refers to a distinctly Welsh form of community: 'a cultivated, educated, often self-educated, responsible, self-disciplined, respectable but on the whole genially poor and perhaps small propertied people straddling groups perceived as classes' (G. A. Williams, 1985: 237). The '*gwerin*' is a concept that epitomizes the tendency towards national myth-making (Hosking and Schopflin, 1997). It is an idea that evokes a supportive, cosy and genial commonality unique to Welsh people, unhampered by much of the competitiveness and snobbishness that characterizes the English way of life. It can be said that the *gwerin* transcends other social divisions such as class and promulgates a nationalist ideology that is not class but culture based. It is in essence a most principled community and in certain connotations an internationalist one appealing across national boundaries to wider struggles for equality and rights.

The foregoing represent deeply held ideas about the nature of Welsh community. The idyll of the rural Welsh community, in particular, is referenced as evidence of such reciprocity, mutuality, integration and harmony. This sense of community becomes a powerful metaphor in the construction of the Welsh national identity. Yet the *gwerin* is essentially an appeal to a notion of cultural homogeneity and embodies a vision of culture and identity which is essentialist, static and based on ethnic absolutism. It promulgates the imagining of a Welsh character and a national consciousness that is fixed and to an extent exclusive and leads to rigid constructions of 'Welshness' associated with community in which individuals are seen to share or not share highly specified attributes. Day's (1998) exploration of the notion of the rural community suggests a much more diverse reality than is often recognized.

'Race' as an intersection with *gwerin* has a troubled history. Evans's (1991) examination of the treatment of immigrants in Wales over a period of 150 years finds two parallel accounts. One appealing to the harmony of the *gwerin* in its imagining and another hard document of intolerance, animosity and overt racial violence in the face of multiculturalism. In the more rural areas of Wales, it must be noted that the *gwerin* has not been significantly challenged by the immigration of peoples of a different colour and culture to the majority community. What is clear, however, is that tolerance is not a static and inherent quality of Welshness and can be granted and suspended as significant threats are perceived, whether based on miscegenation, economic and resource scarcity or on ideas of cultural invasion. In Welsh history and indeed in contemporary Wales, racialized boundaries have been raised and lowered around all areas of social life. The factors of racial discrimination and disadvantage as well as open hostilities are not arbitrary but institutionalized inequalities in Welsh life.

An image associated with these ideas of tolerance is the depiction of the Welsh as an oppressed people empathetic to the oppression of others. In this vein the concept of 'internal colonialism' remains a central and continuing theme of Welsh nationalism. First put forward by Hechter (1975) the idea was uncritically accepted and embraced by the nationalist movement. This thesis expresses a predominant view of Wales as the object of English oppression. Borrowing the core–periphery distinction from Marxist theories of underdevelopment and Weber's (1968) notion of social closure, Hechter has posited the Celtic Fringe nations as subject to a process of annexation and imperialism in which the different cultural and ethnic groups were deliberately held in a state of backwardness whilst élites belonging to the core culture held control over these internal colonies. This state of affairs was manipulated by a form of cultural stratification within the labour market with key posts in social, commercial and state institutions held by the dominant class. Hechter's work has been subject to extensive criticism for, amongst other things, its conception of class and its assumption of a one-way exploitative relationship between the English core and the Welsh periphery (G. Williams, 1985; Adamson, 1991a). What has held more currency is the proposition of 'cultural imperialism' and oppression which has been widely adopted and also specifically and powerfully applied to the Welsh language speakers within Wales (Bobi Jones, 1974). It is clear that something of Welsh national identity is born within this idea of resistance to external domination and external contamination. As Hechter himself suggested: 'there is always the possibility that the disadvantaged group in time will reactively assert its own culture as equal or superior to that of the advantaged group' (1975: 257). Although the idea of a culturally homogeneous Celtic people held in oppression by an English élite may be disputed empirically, the ways in which these ideas are reproduced in 'banal nationalism' cannot be dismissed and in turn these ideas have a bearing on the treatment of 'race' and racism. The language of 'race' is frequently deployed to depict parallels with the oppression of black peoples and the forces of imperial colonialism. For example, Meibion Glyndŵr's popularized expression 'white settlers' in reference to immigrants and pop songs that have used phases such as 'John Boy, nigger boy, John'. In common with Ireland there exists a powerful anti-imperialist, Nonconformist and radical sentiment within Wales. It is not uncommon to hear the expression 'I'm not white, I'm Welsh', which reflects both a distancing from the forces of English imperialism and an articulation of the solidarity this sense of oppression produces. From this springs a sense of alignment with other oppressed peoples. Cymdeithas yr Iaith Gymraeg, for example, in this vein often cite their links with the anti-apartheid movement.

Yet another dimension of this alignment with oppressed peoples relates to the proletarian solidarity of the mining communities of Wales perhaps most popularly expressed in the film *The Proud Valley*. This class oppression and the sense of adversity won through industrial strife again opens up the potential for empathy. Whilst these parallels might be empirically unwarranted, they do hold important implications. One offshoot of this sense of identification with other oppressed groups is to regard racism as a problem of English nationalism and of 'Englishness'. This allows for a distancing and detachment from the issue of racism, with the Welsh claiming something of the moral high ground. The formula is: oppressed people cannot be oppressors. In its imagining Wales therefore does not carry the burden of an imperial and colonial past but embraces the egalitarianism of the underdog based on a type of common-enemy theory. Plaid Cymru's most recent manifesto explicitly raises this theme of detachment from the hegemonic imperialist agendas:

> Our principles do not arise from a history of imperialist exploitation of other nations, nor from any Welsh tradition of conquest and domination of other peoples . . . we gain our inspiration from the experiences of the communities of Wales which survived long years of oppression, neglect and scorn. (1998: 8)

There are several obvious problems with this position. The conflation of minority experiences obfuscates important differences in the nature, history and articulation of the oppressions (C. Williams, 1995). The view suggests some type of cultural homogeneity that would be difficult to sustain, but more to the point the notion of the Welsh as an empathetic and therefore tolerant peoples unsullied by imperialist contamination cannot be empirically substantiated. Evans's historical review suggests 'there is little evidence of inherent tolerance in the Welsh psyche' (1991: 21), nevertheless it is an important and continuing expression of some type of shared community sentiment that has come to form the basis of moral and political ideas; the style of imagining. The claims of tolerance and mutuality present a fundamental paradox in Welsh everyday life, countered as they are by overt hostilities to outsider status. Within both banal and more politicized nationalist reference in north-west Wales, immigration is viewed negatively as a threat to community and culture. Here 'race' necessarily becomes suspended or deflected by the concerns of the external threat of 'Englishness'. 'Race' in effect produces an awkward complexity on the rigid boundary of English/Welsh animosities in which the interaction with wider racist ideologies becomes apparent. On the one hand it is possible to argue that this boundary is not racialized but claimed in protection of cultural distinctiveness. Immigration of any type is viewed as a threat to particular conceptions of Welsh culture if not directly to the threat to the Welsh language. In this depiction, 'English' becomes necessarily homogenized in such a way as to make ambiguous the position of black non-Welsh-speaking settlers or black immigrants to Wales, a conventionally institutionalized 'other'. The pervading and spontaneous assumption that to be black is to be non-Welsh (with a few localized exceptions, notably Cardiff) reflects the racist logic not only of the wider dominant racist ideology of the British nation but highly specified notions of who is and who is not Welsh. There exists, therefore, an ambivalent boundary in relation to those English with black faces that is bound to imply that what needs to be done to maintain the image of tolerance is to 'keep the English out but not the black ones'!

Consider the ascription given to a group of black people speaking English in a 'Welsh' pub in Caernarfon, a heartland of Welsh-speaking Wales, by contrast with that given to a group of white people speaking English in the same pub. Consider these same groups of people seeking to purchase property in the area. It might be suggested that in the first instance a level of acceptance, albeit temporary, might be extended to the black pub-goers given the common-enemy theory, especially if they were sporting, say, Nigerian, as opposed to Liverpudlian, accents. In the second instance both groups seeking to purchase property might experience hostilities based on wider British racist ideologies, in the case of the former, and anti-English sentiment, in the case of the latter.

It is pertinent to explore therefore the ways in which the cue skin colour can operate to cut across boundaries raised by the cue 'English-speaker' to confer belonging, acceptance, welcome or otherwise, or collide with them to reflect wider racist ideology. The expression of nationalist sentiment based on the cultural divide English/Welsh is highly problematic, often ignoring the treatment of 'race' within it and precariously locating black Welsh identity. The only safe positioning for black people becomes therefore confessional cues of accent, the Welsh language or the expressed heritage claims of those of mixed descent. It is by evoking everyday 'banal nationalism' that symbolic border guards operate to identify people as members or as non members of this specified collectivity and to proscribe a cultural inventory that is shrinking rather than expanding. Credentials such as customs, literary and artistic codes, name, dress and, of course, accent and language are increasingly narrowly defined sites of Welshness. These border guards maintain the mythical unity of the Andersonian 'imagined community', demarcating points of inclusion and exclusion in what is an increasingly problematic hegemonic construction of the collectivity. In reality, it is more accurate to speak of 'Welsh cultures' than a Welsh culture, which acknowledges the fact that Welsh cultural identity is multi-dimensional, and the attempt to cling to notions of cultural purity and retreat into a Welshness that distrusts difference serves only to weaken the search for a national identity.

Black people in Wales are strangely placed in these constructions of nation. For example, in the localized culture of Cardiff the border disputes of 'race' may be diminished by claims of place, long settlement, accent and the fact that many Cardiffians, black and white, regard the 'real Wales' as somewhere beyond. To those in the north, south Wales from Newtown onward is identified as multi-racial. From the point of view of the Valleys, 'white' Wales includes Swansea and Bridgend and stops at the Cardiff city limits. For some in Taff-Ely, Cardiff is also seen as very white. Outside of the Cardiff area, in more sparsely populated areas of Wales, individual black people may at times be able to claim a sense of belonging through intermarriage or a long history of intermarriage, in ways in which newer settlers or those of more distinct cultural grouping cannot. In a recent study conducted in Torfaen it was observed that 'Valleys culture' was accepting of those black people of mixed Welsh origin in a way that was not extended to non-racially mixed Asian families (C. Williams, 1998). The facts of settlement claims, residence or legal citizenship do not necessarily confer a passport to the substantive citizenship of Welsh life.

In effect, the nature and spatial distribution of the black communities of Wales have served to pose no significant threat to Welsh national identity. The pattern of friction documented historically, for example the Cardiff riots of 1919, relates most significantly to economic threats rather than cultural ones. Indeed the spatial distribution of black and ethnic minority groups in Wales indicates that the Welsh heartland remains relatively undisturbed by incomers of this background. Of the 41,000 people who registered as black and ethnic minorities in the last census, over half live in the Cardiff area with the remainder scattered in small pockets right across Wales. Wales did not experience the migration waves that England did in the 1950s and 1960s. It is also home to one of the oldest black communities in Britain with all the consequent type of rooted identities this confers. These factors indicate that the relationship with the dominant community is of a different order. The long settlement and lack of spatial concentrations has served to defuse the black communities of Wales as any type of internal threat.

The other side of the coin is that, with the exception perhaps of the Cardiff caucus, the black and ethnic minority communities are so diverse and often so small that any sense of themselves as a collective and political power is weakened, ensuring that 'race' is not forced onto the political agenda from below. Political participation and democratic involvement of these groups in Welsh institutional life remains low and some may argue is kept low. It remains to be seen how effectively these minorities will be incorporated within the functioning of the new Assembly. It might well be that the national imagining which claims that it is peculiarly tolerant and indeed anti-racist demands that the black communities be acquiescent and do not take an active part in the creation of identity because what is being privileged is the tolerant and not the multicultural community.

Migrant communities are not homogeneous and within themselves they mobilize their ethnic identification in a complex patterning – by reference to a country of origin, by reference to a country of settlement within which they have to struggle for acknowledgement as well as cultural distinctiveness, and by reference to a potential land of onward settlement (Rex, 1996). These axes are not necessarily mutually exclusive nor the preserve of particular black communities. They do, however, point to different types of relationship to nationalist ideologies or national identity amongst these groups. The claims of black and ethnic minority peoples to 'Welshness' is consequently extremely diverse and has its own internal dynamic. There can be no Tebbit test. The assumption that all members of a specific cultural community are equally committed to that culture is misplaced and tends to treat the minority communities as if they speak with a unified voice. The boundaries of black collectivities are not necessarily coterminous with the geographical boundary 'Wales' or the boundary 'Welsh culture'. Migration, nomadism, diaspora and the facts of multiculturalism confront the arbitrary boundaries of nation and the assumptions of national belonging. Individuals of diaspora communities can evoke attachment to place, patriotism and national sentiment but at the same time hold allegiance beyond the boundary. It is more fitting therefore to speak of Welsh cultures in acknowledgement of the multiple identities that defy simple categorizations that many constructions of nation seek after. The whole notion of multiculturalism stands in opposition to essentialist units of culture with fixed boundaries. The Welsh response to hybridity has largely been assimilationist, holding on to a comforting 'they all blend in' and 'there is no problem here'. This approach resists the plurality of Welsh identities and defies the realities of the constantly changing parameters of the national imagined communities. In building nationalist discourse it fails to hear the counter narratives which arise at the nation's margins generated by its cultural hybrids of the diasporas. These hybrids fracture the totalizing narratives of nation by both evoking and erasing them (Bhabha, 1990a). The existence of minorities challenges the nation's cognitive map and the quest for homogeneity as the viable basis of nationhood. In these ways minorities form a complex intersection with nationalism that is at times complementary and at times conflictual.

There is no good reason for believing that Welsh political consciousness has been immune to the influences of wider British racist ideology. Historical involvement in the slave trade and missionary involvement has ensured Wales's co-option in it. The activities of the British National Party within Wales continue to make news, most recently in their recruitment amongst the Welsh farming communities (*Western Mail*, 7 May 1998). However, it must be acknowledged that 'race' is not raised as a political issue in Wales as it is in England for a number of reasons other than the Welsh general distaste of the issue.

In England post-war labour migration of peoples from the New Commonwealth countries produced a situation in which race relations was forged as an issue on the national agenda. The English national character distinguished by ideas of tolerance and fair play was keenly tested by the reaction to immigration from the New Commonwealth and Pakistan which showed just how much the dominant imagining had always been of a white nation. It was very much a white England that was tolerant and did so much for the peoples of the world (as Thatcher suggested) and it would not be England any more if it was not white. In response to this perceived threat from within, a plethora of immigration legislation, a Race Relations Act, and a number of nationalist statements riven with racist overtones have subsequently characterized English politics. The ability of Wales to distance itself from these hegemonic codes has been largely by appeal to the tolerance thesis, although without such significant immigration there was correspondingly less need for the invisible ink of national identity to become visible. Yet there are other reasons for this apparent depoliticization of 'race' in Wales.

Wales is internally divided – north/south, urban/rural, Welsh-speaking/non-Welsh-speaking, native born/incomer – to the extent that finding common concerns or any sense of common history and common destiny so central to nationalist projects may be problematic. This fragile and fragmented hold on Welsh identity means it is more difficult to see what it is that might be threatened by the presence of black incomers and settlers. These divisions are not entirely arbitrary in their constellations and it remains pertinent to ask on which side of these axes most nationalists in Wales can be found. The English, with all the advantages of a dominant people with a language, values and identity that are seldom questioned, may well have a more pronounced sense of national identity but boundary markers can readily become heated up or mobilized when actors develop identity investments as a result of economic, cultural or political investments. Black and ethnic minority people in Wales have not yet been perceived as a significant threat to political investments in the way that the more general marker 'English' has.

Miles and Dunlop (1986), reviewing the situation in Scotland, have argued that the focus of the national question there has acted partially to displace the influence of 'race' in setting the political agenda. In similar ways language politics neutralizes the racialization of politics in Wales. Language entered the political discourse of Wales in the early 1960s about the same time as 'race' entered the English political agenda. Many people in Wales feel that they have had to adopt 'race' concerns from England but that they have low salience for them. There is a sense that the 'race' debate is distant from Wales and this produces a widespread indifference to the issues. It is true to say that 'race' is not a boundary marker heated up to the degree it is in England. It might well be that other divisions within Wales are so many and deep-seated so as to militate against the formation of an established in-group that in so many countries has evoked a racialized boundary coterminous with nation. In essence, while the symbolic 'border guards' police the English/Welsh borders 'race' will be subsumed. The national question in Wales is more significantly influenced by the threat of an *external* concern, centralist rule, and the xenophobia is most acutely directed towards the English. This therefore has contributed to the depoliticizing of 'race' in Wales.

The issue of language deserves closer inspection given that it has been increasingly suggested in recent decades that the Welsh language has become a key boundary of Welsh nationhood and is associated with exclusive and authentic claims to Welsh identity (Bowie, 1993; B. Roberts, 1994). Although there is much ambiguity and some ambivalence about this position, this undoubtedly represents a key line of division (with the potential for social closure) in Wales. This is very pertinent to the black and ethnic-minority communities of Wales who may find a Welsh nationhood located in the Welsh language inaccessible and meaningless. Yet, in as much as the Welsh language is a boundary marker, it has been argued that this is not a racialized boundary since it is a permeable one. It is suggested that access across this boundary is open to all who would wish to learn to speak Welsh and therefore share in the benefits in-group membership confers (Morris and Williams, 1994). However, this is not as straightforward a proposition as might be suggested. First it oversimplifies the issues of language acquisition and identity in presenting the case as unproblematic irrespective of age, 'race', locality, ability and migration. Secondly it dismisses the apparent development of language hierarchies within Wales. For example, there are clear distinctions made between the status of 'Welsh-learner', 'mother-tongue speaker' and 'native-born Welsh-speaker'. The latter is a particularly interesting construction in its claims to place and ancestry as well as to ability. These boundaries therefore are variously raised and lowered with the potential for social closure and exclusion. It is difficult to conceive of a nation in which notions of who is 'proper Welsh' and who is not are so frequently bandied or in which the claims of the non-Welsh-speaking Welsh to Welsh status are disputed so vociferously (Bowie, 1993). If within the new linguistically conscious Wales, proficiency in the Welsh language now confers no small amount of social prestige and economic opportunity and indeed the potential for a form of cultural élitism, this has clear ramifications for the sense of belonging and attachment that more open and generic definitions of Welsh nationhood can confer. In Wales to be authentically Welsh is still largely to be white, and increasingly to be Welsh-speaking. A notion of multiculturality is not demonstrably present in Welsh cultural life or in popular conceptions of Welshness, so that the construction of a black Welsh identity is fraught with difficulty.

In the lead-up to the recent devolution vote, the BBC *Video Nation* series featured a black Welsh-speaking young woman arguing a case for Home Rule in Wales (BBC 2, *Video Nation*, March 1998). This powerful mixed metaphor for nation both rejected and claimed ideas of Welsh cultural roots and identity – claims made by the distinctiveness of language were countered by the black ancestry of this young woman. So the appeal was to a nationalism which transcends a racial boundary in the way that *gwerin* collapsed class into national identity. Increasingly such representations challenge more traditional and heavily guarded notions of Welsh national identity, yet at the same time there remain few artefacts, symbols or cultural markers that signify acknowledgement of black Welsh identity. Plaid Cymru's manifesto has made explicit its inclusive appeal based on a notion of civic nationalism with phrases such as: 'Our civic nationalism welcomes all those living in Wales', and 'Plaid Cymru stands and fights for every single person in Wales whatever their background, their birthplace, the colour of their skin, their religious belief or the language they speak – be it English or Welsh' (1998: 1). These are important and bold statements based on ideas of civic nationalism and appealing to radical and socialist traditions within Wales. More cynically, these proclamations may be the result of Plaid Cymru searching for new tactics to broaden its appeal given its motivation to make electoral headway. Passports to nation, however, remain meaningless where access is denied to national identity by 'ways of life' based on exclusive ethnicities. It remains questionable the extent to which Plaid Cymru will be able to continue with this broad sweep in order to attract new voters whilst remaining accountable to its natural constituency, once access to the levers of power via the new Assembly is established.

The success of the 'Yes' vote on devolution may well attest to the existence of something called a Welsh nation, however fragile, but, as Ned Thomas has argued (1998), devolution in itself solves nothing: it merely brings the responsibility of finding solutions closer to home. In 1989 Dafydd Elis Thomas suggested that, with devolution, 'there is an opportunity to pull Wales out of a British way of thinking'. Within Wales the slim success of the devolution vote has produced a new opportunity structure and a new cultural space for formulations of Welsh national identity that can operate to resist the racisms within British nationalism and build nationhood freed from this potential. Writing on feminism and nationalism, Davies has pointed out that nationalist ideologies parade the idea that other inequalities 'will be readily resolved within the context of native national institutions once national liberation is secured. Indeed inequalities within the nation are often attributed to the presence of an external oppressor in national life' (1996: 253). The widespread complacency around the issue of 'race' within Wales and the denial of responsibility for racial discrimination within the national agenda do not bode well for the development of a clear departure from wider British racist ideologies or for the incorporation of genuine multiculturalism into national identity.

Nation-states typically seek after common cultural codes and homogenizing markers to cement differences within them. The issue of multiculturalism and hybridity poses a continuing challenge to the 'imagined communities' of Wales in the construction of Welsh national identity, to notions of right and wrong identities and the privileges of passport these confer. At the same time within the black and ethnic minority populations there is also an internal modernizing dynamic in which attachment to place, belonging and identity claims are constantly shifting.

'Race' has not been politicized in Wales's public agenda in the ways in which it has formed part of the British hegemonic ideology of nation. Several reasons explain this distancing from the overarching British agenda, most specifically a formulation of Welsh national identity as tolerant and empathetic to the oppressions of others and the lack of any perceived threat to that imagining from the black communities of Wales. Whilst racism may not have been rehearsed overtly in political proclamations of nation, it may well be that hegemonic codes which embrace racist notions lie deep in the cultural assumptions of Welsh national identity – that is to say, within powerful constructions of who is considered Welsh and what the attributes of 'Welshness' are seen to be. It has been argued that these imaginings have barely been tested and where they have, for example within the realm of academic debate, particular strategies have been deployed to deny the legitimacy of alternative constructions and to locate the debate on 'race' in a way which ensures widespread national myth-making remains untouched.

5 Nationalism, Feminism and Welsh Women: Conflicts and Accommodations

Charlotte Aull Davies

This chapter is concerned with the relationship between nationalism and feminism, with particular reference to the significance for women in Wales of the contradictions between these two discourses and their associated social movements. I begin by considering various intersections of feminism and nationalism, both in their ideologies and political practice and in the social theories that seek to explain them. These intersections of nationalism and feminism encompass characteristics which they share as well as contradictions and dilemmas each creates for the other. Second, I look more specifically at how these various intersections are reflected in both nationalist and feminist movements in Wales. Finally, I turn to the question of the relationship between such social movements and personal identities, in particular the identity conflicts they may engender. I consider how Welsh women who belong in various ways to both feminist and nationalist movements address the issue of conflicting identities in their discourse and practice.

Intersections of Nationalism and Feminism in Political Practice and Social Theory

In spite of their differences and contradictions, nationalism and feminism have certain basic similarities. One is their tendency towards a universalizing discourse that gives primacy to a particular difference, whether national identity or gender. A second similarity is the epistemological dilemma that an oppressed category faces in attempting to analyse the circumstances of their oppression and how to overcome it without inadvertently employing the analytical categories of the oppressor.

Both nationalism and feminism base their political movements on analyses of society in which one characteristic is believed to assume primacy in establishing bonds within a particular collectivity based on shared experience. In the case of nationalism, that characteristic is shared national identity; in feminist ideology, it is gender. Thus each assumes an essential homogeneity, which takes precedence over other internal differences, uniting a collectivity and opposing it to others that do not share this primary characteristic. Clearly, then, any salient cross-cutting category, such as class, may be perceived as threatening by such universalizing ideologies and, furthermore, each of these ideologies can become a problem for the other. Nationalist discourse has dealt with the two major cross-cutting categories of class and gender very differently. An examination of the nature of this difference and the reasons for it will clarify further the relationship between feminism and nationalism.

Most theorists follow Weber (1946) in arguing that particular nationalist discourses first developed among intellectuals in eighteenth-century Europe and that the appeal of the nationalist project was initially greatest among the new urban middle classes, especially the professional classes. However, nationalist ideology maintained that rightful sovereignty inhered in a larger collectivity of individuals comprising the nation and that such sovereignty should be recognized and institutionalized by national political institutions. This national collectivity was usually identified on cultural grounds such as common history, language or religion. Such a basis of legitimacy expands the national collectivity beyond the middle classes that first propound national unity and hence creates the necessity to establish a sense of solidarity that can overcome class difference. Responses of the liberal democracies established by the historic 'nation-states' of the West, as well as the large variety of other subsequent nationalist movements, to the problems posed by class divisions have been varied. But it is probably correct to say that they have generally attempted to minimize class difference, sometimes by making significant concessions to working-class demands. In contrast, the response of national governments and nationalist movements to gender difference has more commonly been to emphasize it, through promoting essentialist interpretations of gender which legitimate and consolidate existing, and usually unequal, gender relationships. Such a treatment of gender divisions has penetrated very deeply into nationalist discourse, and is also to be found in most social theories about the origins of nationalism.

The androcentric perspective of most theories of nationalism may be seen at various levels, the most obvious being the lack of theoretical attention given to women's contributions to nationalist movements or to how they may have been affected by these movements. Gellner, in his hypothetical example of the growth of a self-conscious national élite, describes how 'some Ruritanian lads destined for the church, and educated in both the court and the liturgical languages, became influenced by the new liberal ideas . . . ending not as priests but as journalists, teachers and professors' (1983: 60). In a similar vein, Anderson's analysis of the creation of a self-conscious national élite in the Americas describes how the colonial power limited the careers of American-born creole functionaries and inadvertently encouraged them to imagine new national communities.

> [T]he 'Mexican' or 'Chilean' creole typically served only in the territories of colonial Mexico or Chile: his lateral movement was as cramped as his vertical ascent. In this way, the apex of his looping climb, the highest administrative centre to which he could be assigned, was the capital of the imperial administrative unit in which he found himself. (1991: 57)

Anderson further emphasizes the shared fraternity among these creole bureaucrats engendered by their experiences of colonial administrative practices – fraternity which was the basis of national consciousness.

The totally male composition of this emerging national élite goes unremarked and, in fact, is taken as unproblematic; hence any role women may have had, not to mention any significance associated with their absence, is unexamined or seriously underplayed. Yet, while not sharing the career experiences of these emerging nationalist male élites, women clearly were involved in and affected by them, if only as mothers, wives, sisters and daughters. The argument for analysing the significance of such familial ties is strengthened when we consider the importance assigned to certain family forms by nationalist ideology, and the way in which women are subsequently defined and controlled by the nationalist image of the family as the backbone of the nation. In one of the few theories of nationalism that does take gender differences and sexuality as central, Mosse (1985) analyses the links between the rise of middle-class respectability and nationalism in western Europe, paying particular attention to the embourgeoisement of the family in the development of German nationalism early in the nineteenth century. He demonstrates, for example, how representations of Queen Luise of Prussia de-emphasized her considerable political activity and depicted her as having 'found fulfilment in marriage and her domestic tasks . . . Nationalism and respectability were thus linked, and the restricted, passive role of women legitimized' (1985: 96). In an analysis of the growth of nationalism under very different circumstances, in colonial India, Chatterjee (1986, 1990) also describes a similar identification of a particular family form with the nationalist movement. In trying to apply Western nationalist ideology to their own society, Indian nationalists had to grapple with a contradiction in which their adoption of the progressive material attributes of European culture appeared to endanger the distinctive national character whose preservation was the *raison d'être* of their movement. They resolved this contradiction by locating the distinctiveness of Indian national culture, and its area of superiority over the West, in its spirituality, which was centred in the home and nurtured by women. The similarity of this resolution, insofar as its effects on the lives of Indian women was concerned, to that associated with Western nationalisms as described by Mosse is striking. In particular, Indian nationalists developed an ideal of the new nationalist middle-class woman, whose positive identification with the private domestic realm was encouraged by stressing her superiority both over Western women in her greater spirituality and over working-class Indian women in her educational achievements and enlightened running of the home.

Feminist theorizing about the origins of nationalism emphasizes very different aspects of the process. Nationalism from this perspective is seen as an attempt to build national unity, both ideological and social, upon a particular idealized family form. The effects of this family form were differentially experienced by men and women, with women's lives being restricted and controlled by men as a result. From a nationalist perspective, this ideology had the further advantage of helping to decrease class divisions among men at the same time as it increased them among women.

How did this come about? Both Gellner and Anderson emphasize the importance, in the formation of a national élite, of a particular kind of male career experience, which produced both a sense of fraternity based on common national culture and an awareness of common disadvantage *vis-à-vis* another national élite. Yet a feminist reading suggests that of equal importance may have been a common desire by this emerging nationalist élite to exert greater control over their women. Such an outcome became more practicable for middle-class men as their careers increasingly allowed them to do without women's economic input to the household. Women could thus be effectively restricted to concerns about home and family, while at the same time the reason for so doing was projected as of the utmost public importance, that is, the preservation of the nation's cultural identity. Such duality meant that women could be allowed into the public realm, as for example in the provision of education for middle-class women, without compromising their essential restriction to private domestic concerns (cf. Rowbotham, 1992). Working-class men could use this ideology of the family to secure their own dominant position within their family units, thus giving them a greater stake in the nationalist project. But working-class women often became domestic servants, working for middle-class women who could then pursue their education and professional careers while still maintaining traditional domestic arrangements. Such relationships could not help but exacerbate class differences among women.

As this suggests, feminism, too, as a universalizing discourse with historical origins among white Western middle-class women, may be criticized for disregarding the significance of cross-cutting categories, such as race, class, nationality and sexual orientation. The resulting conflicts between feminist and nationalist ideologies have been particularly apparent in national liberation movements in the Third World. The Bolivian activist, Barrios de Chungara, for example, has been scathing in her denunciation of feminism as a folly of wealthy women (1983: 41), and a more theoretically based analysis of the position of women in such movements concluded that 'it is impossible to liberate women in countries that are economically dependent on the West' (Gilliam, 1991: 231), in other words, accepting the frequent nationalist argument that national liberation must precede women's liberation. Feminist responses to such challenges from cross-cutting categories have paralleled those of many nationalist movements in, first, accepting the criticisms and attempting to broaden the concerns and perspective of the movement, while simultaneously trying to maintain some common core based on concern for women and women's issues to unite the movement.

Before looking at how this is attempted in the discourse and practice of Welsh feminist and nationalist movements, I consider briefly the second characteristic that nationalism and feminism have been said to share – their tendency to develop an understanding of their own situations of exploitation and oppression using the analytical categories and epistemological assumptions of their oppressors. This problem has been thoroughly explored by very many feminist theorists. For example, Rosaldo (1987) discusses the implications of studying women using theoretical dualisms, like public/private, that incorporate an essentially androcentric perspective; and D. E. Smith (1987) suggests that women's ways of knowing have been systematically excluded from sociological theorizing. Theorists of nationalism have not generally been as concerned with these epistemological issues. However, Chatterjee (1986) explores the Western bias of most theories of nationalism, arguing that they take for granted a liberal-rationalist political philosophy and epistemology which entirely overlooks the problems posed for dominated peoples who attempt to employ, for their own liberation, a discourse which originated in the very colonial power relations they seek to overthrow. Clearly women who are committed to both nationalist and feminist movements may find themselves reflecting, and having to untangle, biases from either source or both.

Types of Nationalism and their Significance for Women

Before turning, in the next section, to a consideration of some of the ways in which Welsh nationalists and feminists have addressed issues such as those discussed above, I want to correct an implicit assumption in the discussion so far that both nationalism and feminism may be treated as unitary phenomena. This is clearly incorrect as regards both their discourse and practice. Rather, the variability in their ideological formulations is manifest in the great internal differences within the political movements each may be seen to stimulate and support. Certainly, as has already been suggested, the nationalism associated with the first wave of 'nation-state' formation in western Europe is to be distinguished from both the nationalism that supported movements of liberation in colonized territories as well as from the minority nationalisms that have arisen within these historic 'nation-states'. In recognition of this variation, numerous typologies of nationalism have been advanced (for example, Kohn, 1944; A. D. Smith, 1971; Greenfeld, 1992). However, as already noted with more general theorizing about the origins of nationalism, little consideration has been given to the different gender relationships and feminist responses that are likely to be associated with different types of nationalism.

A distinction between forms of contemporary nationalism that has recently come to prominence is that between nationalisms based in ethnic versus civic definitions of belonging to a collectivity. This distinction has moral overtones suggesting that the ethnic type of nationalism is 'bad' (closed, intolerant, exclusive) and leads to conflict and even 'ethnic cleansing', while civic nationalism is 'good' (open, rational, inclusive) and can accommodate difference (Ignatieff, 1993). On such a dichotomous classification, Welsh nationalism, with its greater dependence on cultural bases, particularly language, is commonly characterized as an ethnic form of nationalism whereas the Scottish variety is definitely civic nationalism. However, since the sectarian conflict in Northern Ireland, with its ideological bases in religion, is likewise seen as a form of ethnic nationalism, and the recent history of the province contrasts with the strikingly pacific nature of the Welsh nationalist movement, the classification and its implications seem very unsatisfactory, particularly as regards Welsh nationalism. A more useful approach to this classification, suggested by Yuval-Davis (1997), does two things. First, she breaks down the ethnic category into two distinct bases for nationalism, that based in a myth of common origin and that based in shared cultural heritage. The cultural basis is less vulnerable to charges of exclusivity in that its criteria of belonging (language, religion, food, and other cultural markers) rely on features that can be acquired by incomers, although the ease with which this is done and the degree to which such acquisition does genuinely provide access to the collectivity will vary between movements. (It should also be recognized that even those movements based in a common origin myth will normally have a mechanism for incorporating outsiders through some form of adoption.) Second, Yuval-Davis argues that these so-called types are better regarded as dimensions, tendencies that are present to greater or lesser degrees in all forms of nationalism. The assignment of a particular nationalism to one of these types depends on which dimension it seems to emphasize and such emphasis can change over time as well as vary among the different organizational expressions of the movement. Furthermore Yuval-Davis points out that the construction of gender relationships and particularly the relationship of women to a specific nationalist movement will depend on the relative importance of these different dimensions. A nationalism for which the genealogical dimension, that is, the myth of common origin of a people, is central will be particularly concerned to control women's bodies as the material reproducers of the nation, both guarding their 'purity' and promoting fertility. The role of women in nationalisms that emphasize cultural factors is usually more closely related to their role in childrearing, particularly early socialization, rather than childbearing. This dimension is particularly likely to stress the importance of the family and domestic life in the reproduction of the nation and as such to emphasize as well the distinction between public and private, tending to restrict women to the latter. Civic nationalism is based in an ideal of equal access to civil and social, as well as political, rights and responsibilities (Marshall, 1950), and as such would appear to provide women with the best opportunity for full and equal participation in the national collectivity. However, in practice, access to such rights is commonly gendered, with women being a separate category for some laws and social regulations.

Thinking about the three principal minority nationalisms within the UK – in Wales, Scotland and Northern Ireland – in terms of these dimensions, it is clear that a simple categorization is misleading at best. For example, the conflict in Northern Ireland, while using the cultural criterion of religion as the principal boundary marker between the two 'communities', has had an explicit genealogical element expressed for example in concern about the relative birthrates of the two 'communities'. This dimension has not been much in evidence in Welsh nationalism, although one section of the language movement has argued that the future of the Welsh language is entirely dependent on the maintenance of a

Welsh-speaking heartland, with one of its advocates in the 1970s calling for 'a birthrate far in excess of that of English speakers' (Betts, 1976: 28). However, this dimension has been a minority element even within the language movement; and the broader language movement, while having important if complex links with Welsh nationalism, cannot be taken as the defining characteristic making it an ethnic as opposed to a civic form of nationalism. I have argued elsewhere (Davies, 1989) that the Welsh language has been at least as important for the nationalist movement in its contributions to the establishment of a Welsh organizational infrastructure, both governmental and non-governmental, as in its symbolic importance for Welsh cultural identity. This role for the language links it to the growth of a civic form of nationalism rather than tying it unproblematically to the ethnic/cultural dimension. Certainly considerations of language preservation are highly gendered insofar as they emphasize the continuance of the language through its acquisition as a first language ('mother tongue') and its transmission primarily in the home. On the other hand, when the language campaign moves into the public realm of state educational provisions and official status, the links between cultural preservation, the private sphere and women can sometimes be challenged, as is discussed more fully below. Furthermore, given that the Welsh language has been a minority language in parts of Wales for most of this century, Welsh nationalism, particularly in its party-political form, has faced a dilemma regarding the basis of its appeal and the nature of its constituency virtually from its inception. Nationalist political activists for the most part did not choose to address this dilemma by an insistence on the restoration of the language but rather by promoting a civic form of nationalism that recognized the existence of two language communities and defined Welshness in terms of citizenship. However, as already noted, an emphasis on the civic dimension of nationalism does not necessarily reduce gendered inequalities nor eliminate the inherent conflict between nationalism and feminism. In this context gender may still be used to determine the degree and way of belonging, and women may still find that they are denied full access to political and civil society and social equality. These issues have been pursued in terms of women's position in and contributions to the various organizational expressions of the Welsh nationalist movement, as discussed below. Certainly an important example of this process is to be found in the gender issues raised in the wake of the 1997 referendum that ensured the establishment of a National Assembly. This fundamentally important political development provides both a greater impetus for the development of the civic dimension of Welsh nationalism and another site for contesting gender inequality, as, for example, in the composition of its members and the degree of women-friendly procedures and practices to be incorporated into its working arrangements.

Intersections of Nationalism and Feminism in Wales

In this section I will consider ways in which nationalist and feminist movements in Wales have affected one another as well as how they have responded to the epistemological dilemma each may be said to confront. The main organizational expression of the Welsh political nationalist movement in the twentieth century has been Plaid Cymru (the Party of Wales, known as the Welsh Nationalist Party until 1945). Although women were active in the Welsh Nationalist Party from its inception in 1925, their contributions have not been fully explored nor acknowledged (cf. C. A. Davies, 1994). Nevertheless, it is clear that women activists in the party in that early period did not constitute a challenge to its male-dominated character and patriarchal assumptions. In the first place, the contributions of these women were highly individualistic; they were not involved in the party primarily as women, nor did they share a common outlook on important issues, whether the establishment of a socialist position for the party or the role of the Welsh language in the movement. Although a women's section was created as part of the party organization in its Inaugural Summer School in 1926, it 'never became a prominent feature of party organisation' (D. H. Davies, 1983: 70). It did not develop a coherent position on women's issues nor was it a focus for the activity of those women who played important roles in the party. These women were all middle-class, well-educated and, with few exceptions, Welsh-speaking, and in this they were collectively of similar composition to the men who made up the party in its early days. Additionally, they tended to be women who had a career or some independent means of support. Most were unmarried; those who married and remained active in the party did not have children.

Their family circumstances thus permitted, both practically and ideologically speaking, activities in this male-dominated sphere. Due to their particular circumstances, their success in a male domain did not challenge the patriarchal assumption that the participation of most nationalist women should be confined to a secondary supportive role which complemented their primary domesticity. And aside from this handful of activists, the majority of women in the party fulfilled these expectations – engaging almost exclusively in fund-raising projects like jumble sales and coffee mornings.

Through the decades of the 1950s and 1960s, even fewer individual women attained prominence in the party and the role of the women's section did not alter. The emergence of Merched y Wawr, a Welsh-language version of the Women's Institute, in the late 1960s may have been partially responsible for this, in that its linguistic nationalism doubtless attracted many women who might otherwise have been politically active. However, by the mid-1970s, while Plaid Cymru's women's section retained its traditional role, the broader women's movement had begun to affect the attitudes and expectations of individual women within the party. These individuals rejected the helpmate role that had characterized the women's section and began to press both for greater attention to issues of particular concern to women and for adjustments to the party's formal structure so as to include more women. These women mainly came from the urban industrial areas of south-east Wales where the women's movement was strongest, and in the early 1980s they secured control over the women's section and transformed it into a political unit through which women could work together to secure equal rights within Plaid Cymru. These activities are the main example of gender as a cross-cutting category directly impinging on Welsh political nationalism through feminists acting within Plaid Cymru. The party responded by giving some concessions to women but successfully resisted making the positive discrimination of the 1980s, in which the women's section was allocated additional representatives on the executive committee, a permanent feature.

One of the reasons for this was that only a very few of the women who had been instrumental in this transformation were primarily pursuing feminist goals within a nationalist context, and, of those who were, most subsequently left the party. The majority of women who remained active beyond this period of positive discrimination in favour of the women's section placed their nationalism on a par with, or ahead of, their feminism. Thus, they did not pursue the contradictions between feminism and nationalism but sought out accommodations in practice. Even so, as the prospect for a Welsh parliament re-emerged in the 1990s, women in Plaid Cymru, again working to some degree through the women's section, once more began to place the issue of women's participation more prominently on the party's agenda, arguing for measures to ensure gender balance in any elected body. In the event, they failed to obtain an agreement for twinning constituencies that would have meant 50 per cent of the party's candidates for the National Assembly were women. However, the party officially resolved to use the regional lists of Assembly candidates as a way of improving gender balance. Furthermore, the selection of a woman to head the party's slate of European candidates – where they appeared to have a reasonable chance of winning one seat – was doubtless partly in response to the debate about gender balance among Plaid representatives.

Although women have arguably been more visible in the broader nationalist movement, particularly in the language movement, than in Plaid Cymru, the effect of feminism on its organizational expressions is even less apparent. Young women played an important part in the campaigns of Cymdeithas yr Iaith Gymraeg (the Welsh Language Society) from the 1960s onwards. They represented a large proportion of activists and many went to prison in pursuit of their beliefs. At the same time, it was assumed that their careers as language activists would naturally culminate in a marriage that would produce several Welsh-speaking children. Thus it is not surprising that Cymdeithas yr Iaith did not have a woman as chair through the 1960s and 1970s, although several women were elected to the post in the 1980s. One of them has written that it is not meaningful even to ask about gender divisions in the organization. '[Women] don't stand out as a separate or a peripheral group in Cymdeithas. They are the group. Take the women from Cymdeithas, and it wouldn't be the same movement at all. That's why, . . . we've never had a "women's section" in Cymdeithas' (Tomos, 1994: 259). While this says a great deal about working relationships in a group that relies heavily on direct action, it leaves unanswered many questions about the relationship between gender and language production and reproduction which a feminist perspective can pose.

Another major arena of the Welsh-language movement, that of campaigns for Welsh-medium schools, has allowed for rather different experiences for some women who managed to invert the process whereby women were consigned to concentrate on childcare in order to ensure the survival of their national language. These women, non-Welsh-speaking themselves, wanted to ensure that their children acquired fluency in the language. Clearly they could not secure this end by confining their activities to childcare and the domestic sphere. Instead they had to become involved in the public realm in the campaign for Welsh-medium education, and many women, particularly from south-east Wales, managed to build an active public career on such campaigning.

Thus particular forms of campaigning in the support of nationalist goals may facilitate women's challenging unequal gender relations at the interpersonal level (as in Cymdeithas yr Iaith) or gendered expectations of appropriate spheres and kinds of activities (as in the campaigns for Welsh-medium education). Nevertheless these activities do not in themselves constitute feminist practice nor necessarily lead to a more feminist consciousness. This appears to be a common occurrence across nationalist movements. Thus, in her study of women and Irish nationalism, Ward recognizes that, in spite of their demonstrably critical role in the movement in all historical periods, 'at no stage were [women] accepted as equal members' (1983: 2), nor did nationalist women tend to develop a feminist consciousness as a result of their activities. In a similar vein, Latin American women who organized as mothers to protest the disappearance of their husbands and children transformed their political consciousness while still rejecting any feminist interpretations of their activities (Schirmer, 1989). The next section will consider further the effects of such activity on individual women and how they may deal with associated identity conflicts.

While nationalist organizations cannot be said to have been profoundly affected by feminism, neither have feminist organizations in Wales been overly responsive to the priorities and concerns of Welsh nationalism. Perhaps the best example of feminist organization on a Welsh dimension is Welsh Women's Aid, which assists women and children escaping domestic violence. The fact that this organization has a bilingual policy is one indication of its acceptance of cultural nationalist concerns, and its organization as a distinctive Welsh unit gives some credence, although not intentionally, to political nationalist claims for Welsh political distinctiveness. However, some of the activities of women's refuges in rehousing women from outside the local community in Welsh-speaking areas may be seen as conflicting with nationalist attempts to protect the language. This particularly poses a dilemma for individual women who work in these refuges and may reflect such conflicts in their personal identities, an issue that will be discussed further in the next section. Another organization which has perhaps most fully succeeded in combining nationalist and feminist practice in its activities and aims is Honno, the Welsh women's press founded in the 1980s.

Before turning to a consideration of the ways in which individual women may experience some of these conflicts between nationalism and feminism in their own identities and how they attempt to deal with them, I want to look briefly at the second way in which I have suggested nationalism and feminism are linked, that is, in a particular sort of epistemological dilemma. As already noted, it has been argued that Third World nationalist movements must cope with a fundamental contradiction in their attempts to frame a discourse of national liberation working with analytical categories and understandings taken directly from the oppressor. Minority nationalisms within the boundaries of the historic 'nation-states' of the First World face a similar dilemma. Saunders Lewis, one of the founders of Plaid Cymru and its president from 1926 to 1939, both recognized this problem and attempted to find a way out in his address, entitled 'Principles of Nationalism' given to the Welsh Nationalist Party's first summer school in 1926. He began with the assertion that 'the thing that destroyed the civilization of Wales and ruined Welsh culture, that brought about the dire plight of Wales today, was – nationalism' (Lewis, 1975: 5). He developed an analysis of this form of nationalism as essentially 'materialistic and cruel, leading to violence, [and] oppression' (1975: 9) and proposed an alternative based not on independence but responsibility within an international community. In a more recent response to the same epistemological dilemma, Lord Dafydd Elis Thomas (former Plaid Cymru president and member of Parliament for Meirionydd Nant Conwy) has argued that the party should drop its identification with nationalism, which he regards as a political position discredited by contemporary events, and instead concentrate on greater Welsh autonomy within an evolving European framework. If nationalists face difficulties in trying to separate their movement from the influence of the assumptions of those they regard as oppressors, Welsh women, in common with women of other minority ethnic groups, may be regarded as doubly oppressed both by the dominant ethnic group and by men of their own ethnic group. Nationalist movements have tended to deny responsibility for the oppression of women within the national group, arguing rather that it is a consequence of colonial status and will vanish with it. Ward notes, for example, that Irish Republican ideology has tended to assume that women's oppression is just another aspect of Ireland's oppression and hence requires no separate consideration within the national movement. 'In Republican mythology, Irish men used to be non-oppressive and this dubious proposition somehow becomes transmuted into an assurance that they will automatically become so again – as soon as the contaminating effects of "foreign influence" are removed' (1983: 255). One example will suffice to illustrate the interweavings of these two sources of oppression for Welsh women. Williams has shown that in the second half of the nineteenth century, Welsh women's periodicals developed and projected a view of the ideal Welsh woman that emphasized domesticity and religiosity and stressed women's responsibility for 'the preservation of the mother tongue and the upholding of the character of the nation' (S. R. Williams, 1991: 88). The fact that these periodicals were primarily under the editorial control of Welsh men could suggest that the main source of the oppression experienced by Welsh women came from them rather than from the English. On the other hand, one of the principal stimuli for the development of this idealized Welsh woman, with the concomitant pressures on women to emulate her, came from the 1847 *Report into the State of Education in Wales*. In this notorious report, a commission of three Englishmen portrayed the Welsh as immoral and uncouth, and much of the development of Welsh national sentiment over the subsequent half-century was in response to its accusations. So it could be argued that the actual source of the oppression to which Welsh women were subjected was English prejudice.

> The late-nineteenth-century Welsh woman seems, then, to have been presented with three possibilities in terms of choosing an identity. Either she abandoned her Welsh allegiances and adopted the English middle-class model of refined femininity . . . or she defensively asserted her Welshness in the face of insult, and, to prove its virtues, clad herself in an armour of strict propriety which would inevitably have entailed self-suppression . . . or she accepted the English definition of herself as the libidinous hoyden of primitive Wild Wales. None of these possible identities afforded her a voice of her own . . . (Aaron, 1994: 188)

As this suggests, the sources of oppression and hence the choices women must make in terms of the movements through which they resist such oppression are not clear-cut. Furthermore, the contradictions and conflicts between nationalism and feminism are not simply matters of organizational aims and priorities. They are also reflected in the identities and actions of individual women. The final section of this chapter looks at how some women, nationalists and feminists, have understood these contradictions and addressed these conflicts in their everyday practice.

Feminism and Nationalism: Conflicting Identities?

Women who are committed to both of these social movements, feminism and nationalism, face conflicts between the two. Such conflicts occur at an institutional or organizational level in that each movement makes universalizing claims which appear to devalue the aims and reverse the priorities of the other. However, because such social movements are also engaged in constructing a collective identity which forms a part of the personal identity of those who belong to them, the conflicts between movements may also become identity conflicts for individuals who have allegiances to more than one such movement. Generally speaking, many individuals organize their commitments so that their practice tends to give greater emphasis to one of the two aspects of their identities, but they do so without fully relinquishing the other, so that they deliberately maintain a tension in their discourse and practice between the two. For example, feminists in Plaid Cymru, while usually placing their nationalism ahead of their feminism and investing most of their political energies in nationalist campaigns, still work to ensure that feminist concerns remain on the party's agenda. Thus their practice clearly rejects the nationalist argument that promises an automatic end of gender-based oppression once national freedom is attained (cf. C. A. Davies, 1996).

Another study (Charles and Davies, 1997) looks at identity conflicts experienced by women working in a feminist organization, namely refuges established by Welsh Women's Aid in Welsh-speaking communities. Women given shelter in these refuges and often seeking to be rehoused in local Welsh-speaking communities not infrequently are non-Welsh-speakers who require, and are legally entitled to, housing away from their home communities for reasons of security. Welsh-speaking workers in these refuges, who may also be nationalists, can thus find themselves assisting in an activity that may be viewed as undermining the Welsh language and the integrity of Welsh communities in these areas. Thus they face in their everyday working lives a conflict between their feminist convictions as a part of Welsh Women's Aid and their cultural-nationalist loyalties. Again, these women have developed various ways of retaining a creative tension between the two aspects of their identity, rather than relinquishing either of them. Thus, although in their discourse they normally give priority to the needs of women, they also stress their belief that Welsh-speaking communities have a right to preserve their integrity, and their practice attempts to fulfil feminist priorities while limiting their impact on nationalist concerns.

Aaron (1994) maintains that in fact it is not really possible to choose between these two aspects of identity, feminist and nationalist, in that Welsh women in attempting to overcome one form of repression are inevitably forced to address the other. Two different women's descriptions, coming from different directions, of precisely that experience will conclude this section. Menna Elfyn, poet and activist with Cymdeithas yr Iaith, reports that she 'went to prison . . . as a language activist, but came out a feminist. Imprisonment brought home to me the existence of another silenced war, waged this time against women' (Aaron, 1994: 282). She says that she had to find her voice as a woman, apart from the Welsh male poets she had admired, through maintaining the kind of tension between feminism and nationalism suggested in women's practices discussed above. In contrast, Roni Crwydren, born in Wales but 'coming from a family of English-speaking outsiders' (Aaron, 1994: 94) came to nationalism via her convictions as a lesbian feminist.

> I felt it was easy for me, as a woman, to appreciate what it was to be the victim of patriarchal oppression, but not so easy to find out what part I was or could be playing as perpetrator of English colonial oppression in Wales . . . It felt crucial, therefore, for me to learn to speak and read Welsh, for both political and personal reasons. (Aaron, 1994: 295)

Conclusions

Nationalism and feminism may be said to share certain characteristics; specifically they are both universalizing discourses and each has to confront the epistemological problem of analysing the conditions of their oppression using the theoretical categories of their oppressor. Paradoxically their similarity means that their associated social movements tend to be in conflict, in that each calls forth a division in the collectivity the other portrays as homogeneous and seeks to unite in political action. Furthermore, at the epistemological level, each strives to develop ways of knowing that disentangle its perspective from that of the oppressor. But here the similarity breaks down – for women who are feminists, the source of their oppression is dual, based in gender as well as national difference; for male nationalists, gender difference is not experienced as a source of oppression. The social movements that nationalism and feminism each support have responded variously to these conflicts, sometimes by denying the importance of the other form of social division, sometimes by attempting to accommodate it. In general, nationalist movements, particularly national liberation movements in the Third World, have succeeded in asserting a prior claim to women's allegiances, and, for the most part, this has been the case in the Welsh nationalist movement as well. This is not surprising given the dual nature of oppression experienced by women in minority collectivities and the complexity of the interweaving of these two sources of oppression. Men who belong to ethnic national movements may see feminist demands as an undesirable complication in their movements for national autonomy, but women as a collectivity cannot be said to represent another source of oppression for them. What is of note is the way in which women who are both nationalists and feminists strive to keep feminism on the agenda of the nationalist movement, deliberately seeking out and promoting a creative tension between these two movements, which is reflected in their practice in nationalist and feminist organizations as well as in their personal identities.

PART II PLACE

6 Welsh Identity in a Former Mining Valley: Social Images and Imagined Communities

Brian Roberts

The Social Image

Even in recent research, studies of mining communities have tended to follow a conventional sociological wisdom, with the rather simple connection made between action and a traditional (usually class) consciousness (G. Rees, 1993: 311). Here I propose to move beyond this view by stressing the complexity and 'rootedness' of tradition as lived, transmitted and interpreted, and also by focusing on the missing dimension of 'ethnic identity'.[1]

Much attention has recently been given to questions of ethnic identity and social imagery in relation to place and nation (see, for example, Anderson, 1983; A. D. Smith, 1986, 1992).[2] The idea of the social image has been an attractive conception in understanding group outlook (for example, as put forward by Lockwood in his influential article on working-class imagery) but has suffered from theoretical imprecision (Lockwood, 1966; Willener, 1975). Here it will be used in two senses: as a 'project for action' (H. H. Davis, 1979) and as involved in the making and reinforcing of boundaries of local, ethnic and national 'communities' (Anderson, 1983). In this view, social image and 'community' (which also fell into disfavour, see Stacey, 1969) are retained as important terms in locality and other research (see Day and Murdoch, 1993) due to a recognition that individuals are part of a number of communities which provide the contours of identity.

Ethnic identity, following Smith, will be taken to be a collective, 'long term ethnic persistence', based on 'the social and cultural properties of ethnic communities, that is, collective cultural units claiming common ancestry, shared memories and symbols, whether they constitute majorities or minorities in a given state' (A. D. Smith, 1992: 437). An interesting feature of the Welsh context, in regard to ethnic identity, is that the history of the relations between Wales and England, and recent population shifts and economic restructuring, have produced a 'fractured and fragmented' Wales (Cloke and Milbourne, 1992: 367). There are difficulties in relation to the notion of a common and distinctive Welshness (Day and Suggett, 1985). Any sense of the Welsh nation as a whole has to take into account the variety of meanings it may encompass. As Balsom suggests, a 'three Wales model' can be identified. The 'Welsh Welsh' can be said to be in a specific but ambiguous position in terms of ethnic identity, since their Welshness is within a British setting. The 'Valley Welsh' of the industrial Valleys, containing strong Labour support and traditional radicalism, is caught between the more Welsh-speaking and nationalist heartland ('Y Fro Gymraeg') and 'British Wales' along the coastal belts and areas adjacent to England, where Welsh identity may be weaker and some strong support for the Conservatives can be found (Balsom, 1985; see also Borland et al., 1992; Cloke and Milbourne, 1992: 367). We can say, then, that a range of social images of 'Welshness' (and other identities, see Devine, 1992) can be held within a given area or even a group. These images are not isolated entities but, at least in part, defined in relation to one another.

Imagined Social Boundaries

The interrelation between local, ethnic and other experience and wider values and forms produces the context for the shaping of images or 'imagined communities' (Anderson, 1983). In our study, based on the Welsh valley communities of Blaina and Nantyglo, social images are examined as ways of mapping the changes in identity within local communities. We suggest that a re-creation or exploration of a local Welsh ethnic identity is apparent in the area, stemming from the interplay of internal and external cultural and social factors, for example in family, work and consumption patterns (see Adamson, 1988). To be fully understood, the re-working of 'Valley Welsh' ethnicity must be placed within the complex historical relation between Welsh and English culture and the subsidiary–core economic connection between Wales and south-east England:

> Ongoing industrialisation has not been associated with a shift from status group to class political cleavages throughout Great Britain as a whole. Instead, this process has been limited solely to those contexts which have been culturally dominant in the polity. Peripheral counties, that is those which are relatively poor and culturally subordinate, have continually manifested status group political organisations over time. The basis of these orientations appears to have been the sense of Celtic ethnic identity. (Hechter, 1975: 339)

For Hechter, in short, industrialization does not necessarily eradicate ethnic solidarity or status-group politics and, indeed, may sustain a 'segmented cultural division of labour' (Hechter, 1985). A further paradox, according to Rees and Lambert (1981), is that a form of nationalism, as a 'regional consensus', has been supported by the state, through special measures to maintain central hegemony at a time of increasing economic and social dislocation in Wales.

Here, we cannot lay out all the interconnections between a local community and wider socio-structural patterns. However, we can suggest that the analysis of sectional, class and other relations can be further enhanced by reference to the nature of social boundaries; one such application which can be explored is 'community closure' (derived from Weber) which can be reinterpreted to refer to how groups draw socio-spatial boundaries through the application of social images of inclusion and exclusion (Neuwirth, 1969; Eyles and Evans, 1987: 57–60; Parkin, 1979; Jackson, 1989; Rodger, 1992):

> Communities are defined in terms of the solidarity shared by their members, which forms the basis of their mutual orientation to social action. Solidarity is not seen as a function of ecological residence, but rather as a response to 'outside' pressures. It is manifested in those relationships and communal actions which are part of the members' positions within the larger society or relative to other communities. (Neuwirth, 1969: 149)

Communities are not necessarily homogeneous; they may contain various subgroups, may have an internal hierarchy, and communal norms may be enforced by coercion. 'Community closure' results from the attempt by a community to monopolize resources for social, economic or political advantage and is accomplished by excluding others along racial, ethnic, class, gender or other dimensions. In this account, an allowance can be made for differentiation between communities (for example, ethnic communities and status communities) and for the position of the underprivileged (those denied economic and political opportunities and, therefore, social esteem) who are unable to improve their position and enforce closure due to the dominance of other groups (Parkin, 1979). Thus, social imagery of in-group and out-group is used to maintain group solidarity within a community for social advantage (Neuwirth, 1969: 151–2; see also Rodger, 1992).

Social boundaries are not fixed. In the area examined, social contours are in flux because the foundation of cultural life is shifting due to rapid economic and social changes. The result is that Valley people are questioning the meaning of 'local' and 'Valley' identity and are re-examining 'Welshness'. In short, new identities are being *explored:* a sense of Welshness that is neither of the Welsh-speaking areas nor of British Wales, but may take cultural elements from both and incorporate them within the revival of its own traditions, may result.

The Boundaries of Welshness

The following discussion and material is based on research carried out in Blaina and Nantyglo during 1990–1. The study sought to investigate how a local community was responding to rapid social changes, with particular reference to identity, within the area.[3] The idea of social images was used to show how boundaries are formed and reformed which underpin a range of interrelated social identities, such as the 'valley', 'the Valleys' and 'nation'. According to this view, 'Welshness' can be seen as expressed through these (and other) simultaneously held, social identities.

We can say that a 're-formation' of identity is taking place in the valley. By the term 're-formation' I am recognizing that social identities are subject to change and that 'traditions' (as in the mining valleys) are not simply fixed at some point in the past. It is also a realization that traditions are experienced and lived and that any discussion of social identities must relate them to the sociohistorical context in which they arise. Sometimes shifts in social identities are relatively rapid, at other times their key elements (communal images) appear more permanent.

The strength of a 'feeling of Welshness' was a surprise in the research on the valley, given the traditional portrait of the south Wales Valleys as having dominant mining and class identities (Francis and Smith, 1980; Rees and Rees, 1983; Cooke, 1985). Francis has noted the 'lasting rebellious anti-establishment *class orientated* attitudes, over many generations' which remained as an oral tradition in the most solid coalfield in the 1984–5 Miners' Strike (Francis, 1985: 267). Interestingly, he quotes Phil Abrahams of Nantyglo, a Communist county councillor in the 1930s and a leader of the unemployed, who was jailed in a well-known means test protest, to confirm the historical sense of class and industrial identity in the area:

> Talking about tradition, my grandfather was born in 1825 . . . in Abergavenny, he was buried in 1920 . . . and he was in the Chartist Uprising (in 1839), . . . he had a blue scar, down here . . . I said 'Grandfer, what happened to your head, what give you that?' 'The Bloody militia . . . they came at us from all sides . . . and when they shot twelve . . . at Newport . . . we run over the mountains . . .' Now it's interesting you say about our people being left wing or revolutionary. Of course, it goes back to the Chartist Movement . . . We were the first to suffer the ignominy of the Industrial Revolution. (Francis, 1985: 267)

Writers have noted for some time that the social outlook of the Valleys has been shifting, even prior to the strike and recent economic restructuring. Adamson argues that a 'new working class' is emerging which expresses a new Welsh identity separate from traditional political practices (Adamson, 1988). Our research was conducted in 1990–1 and, therefore, cannot simply compare changes in social orientation after the national dispute and recent job losses in mining and other industries with a prior tradition.[4] However, two previous research studies were undertaken in the villages in 1937 by Massey and in 1942 by Tarrant which give some basis for a longer historical perspective and comparisons (Massey, 1937; Tarrant, 1942; Roberts, 1992). From the evidence of these studies, the area showed both a strong mining identity and a sense of long struggle against exploitation and disadvantage. They revealed a very strong local attachment to the area and a view that other parts of the country knew and cared little about mining communities. However, the 'class orientation' or level of class consciousness is more difficult to gauge from these accounts. By the late 1930s Labour had gained a political ascendancy and the Communist Party, while few in number, could count on several hundred votes in local ward elections. Massey's view was that there was discontent on issues such as levels of Public Assistance, but '[t]here is no general understanding of the meaning of socialism; the average man votes for a working-class candidate who will try to get something for the workers and against a ruling class candidate who won't' (Massey, 1937: 40). In our research, class was not used frequently as a reference point for identity. The 'full class conflict' view was usually expressed only by a number of retired miners who, typically, had been active in the union. Much more often people spoke in terms of the valley and the Valleys in relation to the south Wales coastal belt and, especially, south-east England. The following is the common view on regional disadvantage: 'I divide it by the M4 motorway. Below the M4 tends to be the main economic zone of Britain and a great deal of the wealth and power' (M/20s/white collar).[5]

However, sometimes the regional view was conceived in class terms: 'You have north and south. There is no doubt a class division because of geographical position within the country' (M/50s/unemployed). Class and industrial identity may have been in decline for some time due to economic restructuring; certainly a class-conflict view of society was not widely expressed. However, it is also the case that the way in which working-class consciousness has been perceived by writers in the past has insufficiently recognized the diversity of experience, the change in traditions and circumstance, and the variety of expression of class identity. There is a need for a more complex model for the interpenetration of social identities in the south Wales Valleys (and elsewhere) which takes more fully into account local situated experience and relationships with other sources of identity. Equally, other social identities or 'imagined communities' such as ethnic, regional and national identities have been undervalued when portraying the social outlook of the Welsh Valleys.

The general reason for a new phase of identity within the locality has to be found in recent socio-economic change: the loss of the mines, the return of high unemployment and new social divisions. The changes have a *symbolic* meaning, being interpreted according to experienced markers: for example, high unemployment brings local reference to the hardships of the 1930s, while the grassing over of the slag heaps and the pit head is a loss with a deep meaning for the local community. The 'greening' of the valley brings the uncertainties of renewal. Traditional cultural elements are being reasserted, renewed or re-created and placed within new elements and practices. Locally some groups may have additional reasons for affirming Welshness (alongside the sense of security a firm identity brings); for instance, a local élite with wider connections may see a reinvigorated Welshness not only as an indicator of status within the community but as an extra lever, especially at a time of diminished resources, to pressure the government to meet the special needs of a region and ethnic group. In the latter case, the stress on ethnic background and language are potential symbols of difference and may strengthen disaffection from the socio-political central core.

Ironically, by meeting claims for special economic measures for Wales and its regions, the British state may be also supporting a form of nationalism as a 'regional consensus' (Rees and Lambert, 1981) – as a means of managing the rebuilding of the economic and social structure. This support is double-edged as far as national identity is concerned; it may pacify some national sentiment by accommodating it, but at the same time it is a confirmation of difference. For example, for some, the tourist industry's promotion of Welshness may be dismissed as creating a vulgarized identity but, again, government and commercial support for a 'heritage Welshness' could stimulate and aid the creation of a sense of ethnic separateness or cultural nationalism. In all this we must keep in mind that a sense of Welshness or of Wales has been continuously made and remade historically across the generations (G. A. Williams, 1985).

Welsh Identity

The reshaping of a Welsh identity was examined through responses to questions on 'Welsh roots', 'Welshness' and 'Welsh character', the Welsh language and nationalism and independence. The responses to these questions can be considered as expressions of difference or similarity, of inclusion and exclusion; they are implicated in the construction of social boundaries. The 'imagined communities' of the valley, the Valleys, and nation depend on the drawing of boundaries which arise through the formation of 'images' of who 'belongs', and who does not, to the group or area (Borland *et al.*, 1992).

Welsh roots

For some, the question of the roots of Welshness, 'Do you consider yourself Welsh?', brought the following 'common-sense' response: 'Well, I don't know if you can describe it, its a feeling you've got, you're Welsh. I suppose like an Englishman, you're born in England. If you're born in Wales, you're Welsh' (M/60s/ex-miner). Giving Welsh identity, often first, according to a geographical definition – boundaries containing meanings about 'place' – gives an immediate reassurance of an identification with an area. But even this geographical definition has its ambiguity. Reference is made by older residents to the area being part of what was Monmouthshire, a cultural borderland between Wales and England, 'belonging' to neither. The expression of a 'national identity' still exhibits some of the splitting of the area caused by its Anglo-Welsh population being caught between a Welsh-speaking hinterland and the English Midlands. This discomfort was evident in the apparent defensiveness in many replies to the initial question 'Do you consider yourself Welsh?' The usual reply was a 'mundane' statement of Welsh national identity as located in rugby competition, communal singing and (rather less now) the chapels. This was never the complete picture or reality of identity in the Welsh Valleys. It was always a symbolic shorthand, prone to stereotyping from outside, but there is certainly now a searching for a new sense of identity composed of old and new elements.

One common reaction to questions concerning the basis of local identity revealed an important dimension. Respondents often immediately seek to establish a Welsh pedigree or 'roots' by mention of Welsh antecedents and, wherever possible, their forebears as Welsh-speaking: 'I like to think that I am Welsh. My father was Welsh-speaking. There was a group of Welsh-speakers that he went to school with, if he started to talk Welsh he was not allowed of course' (M/60s/ex-carpenter). The ambiguity of being non-Welsh-speaking, strangely, is often felt more keenly when outside Wales. Welshness as a boundary, as confirming 'belonging' to an 'imagined community', was placed in doubt due to people asking questions which (it seems) touch on the sensitive roots of their identity, for example someone met on holiday asking 'Where are you from?', 'Do you speak Welsh?' and being unable to answer, 'Yes, I speak Welsh'.

To be Welsh, for many, gave a sense of exclusivity; it is to be different from the majority. Perhaps, this is a common 'positive' interpretation of a boundary by a minority, dominated culture: 'I certainly am Welsh. It means something nice and slightly exotic, there are only 2–3 million of us – we are still a minority. I don't mind, I like being Welsh' (M/20s/professional). But, to be 'non-Welsh-speaking Welsh' creates a doubt around identity, since Welsh-speakers elsewhere (and those in the Valley learning the language) are often seen as making a claim of greater exclusivity and identity. Hence, people say 'Yes, I am Welsh', then apologetically, 'But, I can't speak Welsh', which is immediately and emphatically followed by – 'But, I am just as Welsh'.

Welshness

The older generations were more likely to mention the local traditions of communal singing or the town band when defining Welshness. Again, the Welsh language intrudes. For one elderly woman: 'Well, I love the Welsh singing, you only wish sometimes that you could understand what it is. It's too late for us to learn now' (F/70s/ex-shopworker). For a substantial majority, the sense of Welshness was more than a geographical connection or something that is routinely given expression in national sports or through an unfocused sense of pride on St David's Day. For them, the traditional Valley identity – which contributed to their idea of Welshness – was more than a cliché; it carried certain grounded meanings, although its basis was withering. Those in middle age tended to have a more 'reflective' and uncertain view of the question than older residents, searching for new definitions. In particular, the more politically active saw the question of Welshness and its expression as rather deeper and more fundamental than a limited nationalism that may find its outlet in support of the national rugby team or as an 'over-ritualized', once-a-year celebration on the National Day:

It gives you an identity. There's something that people tend to feel, it is private. Maybe because we've got an inferiority complex, I don't know. Being Welsh is something that you can boast about. It's not only about being Welsh on the National Day. It's not simply being anti-British – it's something more than that – people who are conscious of it. It's more to do with your culture and your history. (M/40s/white collar)

There is some evidence, as witnessed in the schools, of a revival in the significance of the National Day itself:

There is an increasing interest in St David's Day, especially within the junior schools. They do an Eisteddfod and it's good. There is an interest there. Because it died out over a few years – now the headmistresses are reviving it. People are probably finding pride in their nationality. (M/50s/unemployed ex-miner)

A new dimension is also becoming more noticeable which may take on some significance for the construction of local Welshness as the old industrial base is eroded and the 'greening' of the valley emerges: 'It's seeing all the green valleys – which makes you take pride in the valleys and the mountains. People have started to take more pride in their homes as well, in the Valleys' (F/40s/cleaner).

Welsh character

It is probably difficult for anyone to summarize the characteristics of their nation. There are, of course, stereotypes or common emblems or activities associated with a country (or part of it) which may have some basis and be a source of pride for its members. Again, south Wales is often portrayed in terms of the mines, rugby, singing and chapels. However, these activities are now indicators of a declining tradition – used as a simple view of Welshness from outside, while becoming 'endangered' inside. For those in the Valleys, these activities were merely part of a more general culture; they were among its outward features, growing from the rhythms of mining life and embodying a deeper Welsh character and communality associated with the area. It should be noted at this point that the decline in these 'traditions', especially the chapels, is not a recent phenomenon. There is even a strongly felt sense that Valley life is Welsh character, due to a sharp awareness that the hardships of the mining communities produced a distinctive and vibrant culture which aided physical survival and enriched a shared experience. The experience of shared exploitation, struggle and isolation produced an affirmation of cultural difference and a celebration of communality. Now it is perceived that a traditional social identity, in decline for so long, is at a final turning as its content and symbolic boundary markers are challenged.

This Welsh character, usually described by local residents in terms of communal values (for example, friendliness, sharing and helping), may now be fading due to the decline of the close knit between work and communal patterns. Its relative strength depends upon lines of inter-family connection and the fact that people tend to move away rather than enter the locality from far afield. Welsh Valleys' or local valley character, then, is usually seen by residents as the same 'communal life'; individual 'character' is interpreted through a communal 'meaning'. Few were able to point to 'Welsh character' in terms of personal differences from other ethnic groups. A widespread view was that Welsh character could be different across Wales: there were various Welsh identities within some common sense of nation (see Cloke and Milbourne, 1992):

> There is a Valleys' character. If you went to west Wales, you'd find the Welshman is different, it's a land-working Welshman. Here you have the industrial, south Welshman who is totally different to the north. There is a division between north and south and mid-Wales. We are such an influx of people into the area. I've been doing some research on my relatives, some come up from Bristol and come from the Forest of Dean. I suppose if you look back, the majority of us around here, perhaps 75 per cent, are really Welsh or Welsh stock. (M/60s/manager)

More locally, many recognize rural–industrial differences in character. 'In this area now we've got the agricultural area just over the top there. And in my opinion there's a difference in the people there and in the Valleys. A different character you know' (M/retired/70s). Again, this local difference may decline as the physical environment is improved and if the economic and social divide with the industrial southern coastal belt increases. A younger man, reflecting on the increasing 'greening' of the area, commented on the difference to the people of the south brought by industrial decline and restructuring, and said the changes, 'gave a greater affinity for the countryside' (M/30s/white collar).

Welsh language

Boundaries are recognized by locals as arising from the different ethnic mix and the distinctive bases of life in the various areas of Wales. As previously stated, there is very often a spontaneous reference to language when asked to define Welshness. The attention given to the language question is a significant indicator of the searching for a new basis for identity. The language issue is keenly felt and has gained increasing prominence in recent years, especially in the schools. The question raises ambiguities at the heart of Anglo-Welshness. Expressions of pride in being Welsh are commonly accompanied, in the same breath, by an admission of being non-Welsh-speaking. As one respondent very bluntly stated, 'Well, not Welsh-speaking. I was born in Wales, nationality Welsh' (M/70s/ex-steel worker). In fact, very few people have been Welsh-speakers in the valley for at least a hundred years. In 1911 only around 10 per cent of the local population were counted as being Welsh-speakers. Yet the language issue is a major topic of discussion and some revival of the language seems to be under way. In September 1991 Ysgol Gymraeg Brynmawr, very close to Blaina and Nantyglo, opened – the first Welsh-language primary school in Gwent (formerly a Welsh unit at the old Brynmawr Infants, King Street) with 198 pupils (*Gwent Gazette*, 12 September 1991).

A clue to the importance of the language question came early in the research through a passing discussion with a group of unemployed men. The conversation turned to the Welsh language. When asked why the language was now a topical issue one young man, an ex-miner, instantly replied, 'Well, it's our language isn't it. We didn't have it at school, we had French, but not our own language. I might not have been interested – *but it wasn't offered!*' (M/20s/unemployed). This reply both shows the sensitivity of the issue and gives an indication that interest in the language is not confined to the older age groups or the better off. The interest should not be dismissed as merely due to people having more time on their hands or in search of a diverting hobby with a local flavour. Also, what is important is not the numbers attending courses but the generally positive attitude towards the language. However, being a 'language learner' does not necessarily evoke positive regard. Like the 'new-comers' in the area, the 'language learners' symbolize the wider changes in personal and community identity and in the future social cohesiveness of the valley.

The following view summarizes the general feeling on the language question. Some of the hostility towards rural Wales is due to the perception that the valley community is not accepted as true Welsh and, therefore, lies outside the boundary of the 'Welsh community' and nation. 'It's a feeling of pride, although I can't speak Welsh. It's a thing I would have liked to have done but I never seem to have got round to it. People particularly in west Wales don't recognize you as Welsh. I like to see Welsh people doing well in everything you know' (M/40s/factory worker). There is a general awareness that the language has been badly treated in the past. A definite strand of people is keenly aware of the community in historical perspective. They have a strong historical consciousness, which informs their understanding of their identity in the community.

> Well Scotland have always had an interest in their culture haven't they. Almost all countries have got an interest in their own culture. Well Wales at the time they used to speak Welsh was downtrodden by the English. Welsh was barred in schools. The books were burned, everything like that. We got a good history – we got a good culture. (F/40s/factory worker)

This understanding of the history of the language, which was echoed by a number of others, has a powerful message and appeal. The new use and interest in the language recalls and *imagines* a distant (and part remembered) past, the early days of industrialism when the area was still Welsh-speaking. The language issue shows two processes: first, the perception of an exclusion and closure between Welsh communities (S4C, the Welsh-language channel, is a daily reminder of 'another' Wales) and, secondly, at the same time, the renewal of 'Welshness' (including the language) may be creating another boundary within the villages according to the degree of new Welshness being created by local groups.

The issues surrounding language and nationality raise deep sensitivities and confusions: Welsh nationalism is often equated locally with political extremism (bombings and other violence) and Welsh-language use with exclusivity and ostracism. At the same time, the language is valued and traditions are fondly remembered (for example, chapel walks) and some are being revived (for example, the local carnival). In summary, there seems to be an emergent, stronger sense of cultural nationalism rather than a discernible trend towards national self-determination as a political demand.

Nationalism and Independence

The prevailing view is that political independence for Wales is just not possible – 'The Welsh economy is not strong enough' is a frequent comment – so it cannot even be an aspiration. This would appear to fit the 'regional consensus' view (Rees and Lambert, 1981) of an identity within Welsh Wales associated with the industrial Valleys – a cultural nationalism within a British context. The recent influx of English newcomers represents a different possible future for the area – as British Wales with a different political and social outlook (Cloke and Milbourne, 1992: 367). The extent of the influx does not seem great. In any case, it is the visibility of newcomers and what they are seen to represent which is more important than their numbers as such.

The reformation of social images which provide the boundaries of identity is, perhaps, more cultural than overtly political at the present time. Even so, it is the more politically active, such as local councillors and Labour Party members, who seem most keen to revive local cultural organizations, celebrate past events and give recognition to the Welsh language. Plaid Cymru could prosper if it became a focus (through 'community politics') for disenchantment with local Labour councils unable to deliver services and a conduit for perceptions of regional disadvantage and uncertainties surrounding local and valley identity.

While the economic basis for independence does not seem possible, nevertheless, there is strong support for retaining some cultural difference. When more specific questions are asked, for instance on the benefits of a Welsh Assembly, views become rather more mixed and confused. For one ex-miner, unemployed, the issue was clear. 'Independence won't work. It's a complete waste of time. It's not viable. It's alright to have nationalism in a way, you can all shout for your country, like with football, boxing and other sports. That's as far as it should go' (M/50s/ex-miner/unemployed). And another older resident: 'Oh, ridiculous, we're not financially well enough off, for independence' (F/80s/retired). Independence would only cause further problems: 'Economically we have got to be part of Britain. It could create more trouble and more questions than you could get answers' (M/60s/retired clerical). A minority could not see any merit in thinking of change and firmly believed in a union within Britain.

But, generally, the ambiguity persists: between a perception of secondariness when compared with (mainly) southern England, but also a sense of secondariness, or at least difference, from the Welsh coastal belt and areas close to England *and* Welsh-speaking Wales. 'That's probably why there's a surge perhaps to learn to speak the language. They are thinking more of being independent probably. More so now because of this government. A Welsh Nationalist? Home Rule? I don't know the answer to that actually' (F/50s/small business). Interestingly, while there is a general support for the Welsh language, with most saying that they wish they could speak it or wish to learn it, those who actually are learning feel they are looked on with some suspicion: 'So, you've become a nationalist?', 'I suppose you're for independence?'. What these reactions show is again a sensitivity (and anxiety) towards shifting identities and boundaries both in the local community and its wider relations. Beneath the questions of independence and language are concerns regarding the image local people have of themselves and about their future.

Conclusion

Within the Valleys a reshaping or 're-formation' of Welshness is taking place, drawing in part from symbols of the past – language, festivals, and events in local social and political history. For most this is (as yet) merely registered as a series of questions and uncertainties. However, among a strong segment of the community there is a deeper historical consciousness, which is taking from the past (for some in a more directly political way) to meet the challenges of the present. This process is a reassertion of distinctiveness – a way of life rather than a tradition as a cultural possession, and expressed occasionally. Also, it can be distinguished from a commercial 'heritage Welshness', as found in the tourist industry, although this can also find local representation.

I have argued that an understanding of the process of 'ethnic reformation' – the reconstruction of social identity and its boundaries and relations – can be aided by reference to 'social images'. As Francis argues,

> Perceptions, symbols, and images may well serve to reduce the complexity of the 'worlds' we live in to a range of discrete and contrasting defined units, which can then be used for a diversity of social, political, and ideological purposes. These units may well exaggerate the sharpness of *boundaries,* the uniqueness of resident populations, the *'identity'* of neighbourhoods, and the like, but as representations they are an integral aspect of wider patterns of thought, knowledge, and organisation. (Francis, 1983: 139; my emphases)

In accounting for the reshaping of ethnic identity analysis we must also take cognizance of a number of areas of cultural change which we have not been able to discuss fully: the impact of consumerism on social consciousness, changes in work life and identity, and the patterns of distributional struggle, including community, sectional and class closure (Adamson, 1988; Francis, 1983; Eyles and Evans, 1987; Marshall *et al.*, 1987).

Social identities, in my view, are composed of patterns of social images which can encompass conceptions of social situation, including class, gender, ethnic, local and organizational position. They incorporate boundaries that are produced by processes of inclusion and exclusion. I have argued that conceptions of class radicalism and traditions in the south Wales Valleys require re-examination (both in historical and contemporary terms). Such a conception, which has been the main referent for discussion of social imagery, social identity and social consciousness within sociology, according to this perspective needs to be related to actual experience and seen as realized in its local context and specific social division. Class allegiance and outlook can be shaped by a whole range of factors, including spatial organization of labour and residence; the sexual division of labour; religious, ethnic and racial position; the membership of trade unions, professional and other organizations; the generational position of individuals; and wider ideological formations (Urry, 1981; Francis, 1983; Giddens, 1984; Eyles and Evans, 1987).

It has been our limited intent to argue that 'Valleys Welshness' is composed of a range of coexisting and interrelated social identities. Class outlook has been more varied and complex than sometimes realized and the specific construction and expression of the 'ethnic' dimension of 'Valleys Welshness' (and its relation with class) has been relatively ignored. There is a need for a more sophisticated analysis of social identities in the area, including research into the changing balance (which our study suggests) between the components of class and ethnicity.

In summary, from our research in the south Wales valley containing Blaina and Nantyglo, we found that the 'imagined communities' (for example, place, valley, nation) forming local identity are being redefined. However, we must remember that social boundaries are never fixed but continuously lived and interpreted: images are set in a process of 're-formation' which includes affirmation and redefinition. In our example, boundaries and imagery can be seen to be subject to increasing fluidity and reassertion through internal and external social and economic pressures. The final 'disappearance' of the mines and the 'greening' of the Valleys is an important symbolic moment for the shaping of identity. Sources of individual and group meaning are being re-evaluated. In this context, we can say that the ethnic dimension of social identity draws on the past to meet the challenges of the present and the uncertainties of the future. Such a reconstruction by a group is not performed without reference to perceptions of the social identities and perceptions of other groups. 'Valley Welshness', as one form of Welshness, is keenly aware of its relations with the British Welshness of the peripheral coastal and border areas and the 'Welsh Welshness' of the rural hinterland (Cloke and Milbourne, 1992). It is, in part, defined through these relations while these other forms also represent possible futures for 'Valley Welshness'.

Notes

1. This article was originally published in *Contemporary Wales*, 7 (1995), and is based on part of a paper 'The re-formation of ethnic identity: Welshness in a former mining valley', BSA Conference 1993 'Research Imaginations', University of Essex. The research was supported by ESRC Award R000232060 'Social and Economic Change and Life Courses in a Welsh Community', 1990–91.

2. The recent literature on the theme of identity, ethnicity and nation is considerable: see also Bauman (1992a); Connor (1990); *Feminist Review*, 1993; and Kellas (1991).
3. The research included eighty in-depth interviews from a 'rolling sample' (with allowance made for gender and generation), a postal survey, first-hand observations, and census material and other official data. Questions were loosely framed according to certain themes: Welshness, gender and generation; family life, work community involvement, and perceptions of the future.
4. The two wards, Blaina and Nantyglo, are high on indicators of ill-health and deprivation for Gwent (GHA, 1990). The local borough, Blaenau Gwent, ranks high (alongside the industrial valleys – Cynon Valley, Rhondda, Merthyr Tydfil) on indicators of social disadvantage when compared with the rest of Wales (Morris and Wilkinson, 1989).
5. In the interview extracts, F refers to female, M to male respondents, and numbers refer to ages.

7 Nation, Community and Conflict: Housing Policy and Immigration in North Wales

Ralph Fevre, John Borland and David Denney

Introduction

The death of Enoch Powell in 1998 occasioned a general reassessment of his significance in British political life. One of the questions that emerged from this reassessment was whether Powell's intervention in the politics of race and immigration from 1967 onwards should be described as racist or nationalist.[1] Given the importance of Powell to the course of British politics, and the fact that his speeches were supposed to give voice to the views of millions of Britons, this is no mere semantic question. Instead it focuses our attention on the search for the source, the system of ideas and beliefs, which gives rise to the periodic 'racialization' of British politics. For a long time those who opposed Powell had no doubt the single source was racism (and some, like Stuart Hall, see no reason to change their minds now). When interpreting the words of Powell, and later on, others in the Conservative Party like Margaret Thatcher, who used similar words when speaking about immigration, they were forced to add the qualification that this was *cultural* racism'. Nevertheless, the suspicion grew over time that even this term was inadequate and that there were important elements in the discourse, elements which clearly had great appeal to the British people, which had a different source – in the ideas and beliefs of nationalism.

Nationalism began to figure alongside racism in the writings of social theorists on immigration and racial conflict from the 1980s onwards. But by the time Powell died, some politicians and political commentators were suggesting that Powell's views on race arose from, and were part and parcel of, his nationalism. This chapter will consider the possibility that the 'cultural racism' of the 1970s and the 'new racism' of the 1980s were simply the preliminary conceptual moves that social theory had to make before recognizing that this virulent strand of populist British politics actually had nationalism rather than racism at its core (and it was this that appealed to so many of the British public). This possibility will be explored by considering the role of nationalism in a case where racial politics appear to be absent altogether: the reactions to large-scale migration from England to Wales in the 1980s, and especially to the Welsh-speaking parts of Wales in the north and the west. In doing so we will necessarily confront more orthodox treatments of this subject which tend to see nationalism as the product of immigration. In our view such treatments misunderstand the direction of causation in the relationship. The characteristics of nationalism – in particular, its relationship to place and territory – ensure that immigration acts as a sort of disclosing agent. Reactions to immigration show just how mistaken social theorists are if they neglect nationalism. They also expose the various ways of defining national identity – including those that rely on racialization – that underpin nationalism.

In the late 1980s, the rate of immigration into Welsh-speaking parts of Wales from England accelerated. This was apparently the result of spiralling property prices throughout the UK. The immigrants were finding that houses in Wales were still considerably cheaper than in much of England and that the rising market offered them capital gains which could be converted (as long as they migrated to Wales) into a superior property and perhaps even an income of some kind. It subsequently became clear that the peak of this migration from England to Wales was reached in the summer of 1988 (as the rise in Welsh house prices accelerated) and that immigration then rapidly declined as the bottom fell out of the whole UK housing market. At the 1989 National Eisteddfod the Director of Education for Gwynedd County Council (the region with the highest percentage of Welsh-speakers in the 1981 census) was able to report with equal measures of caution and satisfaction that it appeared that the influx of people from England had slowed down significantly (*Bangor and Anglesey Mail*, 11 October 1989).

In the first half of 1988, before the immigration from England abated, a third of the houses on sale in Gwynedd had been bought by people who did not live in Wales (*Bangor and Anglesey Mail*,

11 October 1989). Some of the voices raised in alarm at such developments were more strident and more extreme than others. There were, for example, the Free Wales Covenanters who became especially vocal in their resistance to English immigration and what was perceived as increased English influence. Nevertheless, in the mainstream, the official voice of Welsh nationalism was far from silent. Plaid Cymru MP (and later President) Dafydd Wigley went on television (BBC2 Wales, 28 October 1988) to say that 'we need to protect our own people' against the influx from England. According to Dafydd Wigley, the problem was the sheer numbers of these immigrants which far outweighed any sensible level of immigration. An acceptable level for the English presence was something like 10 per cent of the population. A week earlier Dafydd Wigley told the local press in Gwynedd that such large numbers of immigrants were bound to produce hostility in the local community which would lead to troubled (and perhaps violent) community relations between natives and immigrants:

> What is going to happen is that the tension between the local community and those who move in is going to be terrible – those non-Welsh speakers already here should realise this as they could find themselves in a very awkward situation. (*Bangor and Anglesey Mail*, 19 October 1988)

Dafydd Wigley's solution to the problem was to make immigrants pay more for their houses. In order to avoid the 'very awkward situation' he suggested that people moving into Wales should be forced to pay twice the going rate. This suggestion was not, in fact, as wild as might be assumed. This and similar policies were frequently proposed by nationalists throughout Welsh-speaking Wales at this time and in the same week that Dafydd Wigley made his contribution his party failed by just a single vote to change the rules to prevent ex-council houses from being sold to people moving into Gwynedd (*Bangor and Anglesey Mail*, 19 October 1988). Activists like Dafydd Wigley were, of course, not aware that the peak of English immigration had already been passed in the autumn of 1988, and nor were the more extreme nationalists. Earlier in the year the long-running arson campaign against holiday homes in Wales had been extended to estate agents in England and Wales who were 'accused' of selling Welsh homes to English immigrants. In mid-

October the group which claimed responsibility for these attacks, Meibion Glyndŵr, fire-bombed businesses owned by English immigrants in Welsh-speaking areas. There were also a variety of non-violent interventions by activist groups like Adfer and Cefn, and Cymdeithas yr Iaith Gymraeg, the Welsh Language Society, carried on a highly visible campaign proclaiming that 'Wales is not for Sale'. These were not, however, the concerns of activists alone. In September 1988 an opinion poll reported majority support in Gwynedd for 'keeping out English influence and preserving Welsh culture' (*Bangor and Anglesey Mail*, 26 October 1988).

The Causes of Nationalist Resistance to English Immigration

The height of hostility to English immigration to the Welsh-speaking areas of Wales may have been reached after the peak of that immigration had been passed, but it is possible to argue that this hostility was caused by the immigration that preceded it. Thus, if resistance to immigration continued to rise after the summer of 1988 this was only because there was no way of knowing that immigration had indeed abated for some time afterwards. So, in October of the following year, a local councillor in Dwyfor, in the west of Gwynedd, could still claim that 'Wave upon wave of people are rolling into Dwyfor, and we're totally defenceless' (*Bangor and Anglesey Mail*, 11 October 1989).

In this way circumstantial evidence would seem to implicate English immigration, along with other manifestations of increasing English influence in Welsh-speaking Wales, in the growth of Welsh nationalism itself. This was certainly what many thoughtful observers have concluded:

> The resurgence of nationalism and ethnicity began in the opening years of the 1960s as concern mounted for the declining use of the language and the increasing threat to Welsh culture and life-style posed by industrialization, English immigration into Welsh-speaking areas and the growing cultural-imperialism of the English-language media. (Adamson, 1991a: 170)

Gwynedd had three nationalist MPs by 1987 so it would be impossible to identify the large numbers of immigrants in the first six months of 1988 as the cause of nationalist voting. Nevertheless there was immigration, albeit at a lower level, into the areas which returned nationalist MPs earlier in the 1980s and, as Adamson points out, there were other ways (than immigration) in which increasing English influence could be detected. The argument that considers English immigration to be an important contributory cause of nationalist feeling is, however, as yet weakly theorized. Most importantly, we are left to wonder why English immigration should produce a particularly *nationalist* reaction since nationalism presented only one of the many channels through which resistance to immigration might be expressed? One possible way of theorizing this link in the argument in a more satisfactory way involves the use of the notion of 'community'.

As in most writing on nationalism we follow both Anderson (1991) and Gellner (1983) in asserting that the 'community' that interests us is not the real community of a settlement or locality. It is rather the *idea* of community that plays an important part in the way nationalism is generated. Thus Anthony Cohen (1985) tells us that 'community is largely a mental construct'.[2] Cohen then goes on to argue that nationalism is a predictable response when people feel that this mental construct is under threat because it (nationalism) represents the symbolic assertion of a boundary – *symbolically* uniting people in the face of threats to the 'structural forms' of their community. Nationalism is thus a consequence of the importance people attach to the idea of community. People turn to nationalism, according to Cohen, in order to express their resistance because it is community that is felt to be under attack and nationalism represents the obvious symbolic assertion of community.

To do justice to Cohen's view we must describe it in a little more detail. Cohen sees communities as 'worlds of meaning': behaviours and structures may not vary on either side of a community boundary but meanings will (1985: 81–6). Not only do people derive meanings from community, but they also find a medium for self-expression in community (1985: 107). In order to keep functioning in this way – providing meanings and permitting self-expression – communities need symbols, and people are required to express community in a symbolic way. This need not mean that communities are any less adequate media for self-expression because 'the sharing of a symbol is not necessarily the same as the sharing of meaning' (1985: 16), and

> Symbols are effective because they are imprecise . . . the symbolic repertoire of a community . . . continuously transforms the reality of difference into the appearance of similarity with such efficacy that people can still invest the 'community' with ideological integrity. It unites them in their opposition, both to each other, and to those 'outside'. It thereby constitutes, and gives reality to, the community's boundaries. (1985: 21)

According to Cohen, the symbolic construction of community is especially likely when the community's 'structural forms' are under threat: 'Indeed the greater the pressure on communities to modify their structural forms to comply more with those elsewhere the more they are inclined to reassert their boundaries *symbolically* by imbuing these modified forms with meaning and significance which belies their appearance' (1985: 44). Already it is clear how this argument might translate in the case of nationalism in Wales. Threats such as immigration are threats to 'structural forms' and in response to these threats *nation* is asserted as a symbol of community. Nation is the symbol which, as Cohen would have it, creates similarity out of difference. It is also the symbol that is increasingly asserted when a threat to community is perceived. That is, we would expect threats such as English immigration to stimulate nationalism in Welsh-speaking parts of Wales.

In fact we do not have to *interpret* how Cohen might apply his analysis in the case of Welsh nationalism because Welsh nationalism provides him with one of his many examples of the symbolic construction of community, and he uses the example of Welsh nationalism to illustrate the capacity of symbols to express a variety of different concerns:

> we can readily understand that the campaign for Welsh language rights, for the devolution of governmental powers, and for the restriction of English influence, might mean very different things to the Pembrokeshire hill farmer, the academic historian in Aberystwyth, the slate miner in Blaenau and the farm worker in 'Llan' . . . Yet they may all find in Plaid Cymru as an organization, or in Welsh nationalism as a cause, an articulate medium for their own inchoate sentiments. The movement and cause themselves become symbolic, condensing all the innumerable political grievances, ambitions, aspirations and propensities of its thousands of followers. It fills a vacuum; without it, these

feelings would only be expressed in a highly fractionalized and ineffective way. Indeed, they should probably not be heard at all. (1985: 108)

To summarize, the view of the relationship between community and nationalism we derive from Cohen is that nation is to be seen as the symbol which expresses community. This is particularly likely to happen (and nationalism will increase) as a symbolic assertion of boundary when community is threatened. Cohen would say the 1980s were just a case of the community asserting itself in some sort of symbolic (of unity) way in the face of threats to its boundaries.

We would emphasize once more that we are thinking of the idea of community here rather than real, locality-based community. For Cohen community is more-or-less synonymous with unity and so it has to be imagined because very little of this unity exists in reality. Reality is all about difference and lack of community whereas nation gives us a way of imagining the non-existent community. *This* is why nationalism arises when an imagined community is under threat – for example, when its symbolic boundaries are threatened. In this case nationalism will reassert those boundaries and hence the assert the idea of community itself. In the end, it seems that nationalism is particularly well-suited to the symbolic assertion of boundaries because it allows the appearance of unity where so many differences abound. People simply could not agree on any other symbol of community and imagined unity.

In one respect Cohen's argument is unimpeachable. The conclusion that the most important thing that nationalism does is to create the appearance of unity in the midst of difference and divisions has been reached by every useful theorist of nationalism since Max Weber (see Gerth and Mills, 1948: 922). Thus, for Benedict Anderson, nation 'is imagined as *community*, because, regardless of the actual inequality and exploitation that may prevail in each, the nation is always conceived as a deep horizontal comradeship' (1991: 7; emphasis in original). We want to suggest, however, that Cohen's argument takes us far beyond this common ground and that his explanation as to why Welsh people should turn to nationalism in order to express their resistance to English influence, including English immigration, is flawed. We would further suggest that it is flawed in exactly the same way that nationalist thought is because it performs the same sleight-of-hand trick (Gellner, 1983: 124). Furthermore, we wish to claim that, without the help of what we now suggest is flawed theory, the general explanation of increased nationalism in terms of causes such as English immigration remains undertheorized. We wish to argue that it will always remain so because this general argument is mistaken. We wish to offer an alternative version of events which starts at the same point as Cohen's theorizing but then develops in a different, and we hope more convincing, way.

In an earlier article (Borland *et al.*, 1992) we too described Welsh nationalism as a 'differentiated social movement' held together by the *idea* of community. This idea of community meant different things when it was operationalized, however. We identified four types of community which were constructed in Welsh nationalism: there was the 'open community' associated with one faction of the Welsh nationalist party, Plaid Cymru, and the 'racially-closed community' which we identified with the nationalist movement Adfer. Finally, there were two versions of the 'culturally-closed community'. A religious version was exemplified by the teachings of Professor Tudor Jones and a secular version – seen as the successor to the religious version – was found in the doctrine of Cymdeithas yr Iaith, the Welsh Language Society. In all four versions of community it was emphasized – by continually referring to the social *construction* of community, for example – that we were dealing with the *idea* of community.

Nevertheless, the four types of community were not simply rhetorical devices. They were also mobilizing concepts, mobilizing people into action. When people (perhaps different people in each case) perceived a threat to one of these sorts of community they would react: as we put it, each of the four constructions of community was a potential site of conflict and resistance. Some things – English immigration, for example – might well be seen as threats to more than one of these sorts of community. We must remember that these were not 'real' face-to-face communities but nevertheless they did have geographic referents – hence our continued emphasis on locality, for example. Thus our earlier paper was primarily concerned with electoral support for Plaid Cymru in Gwynedd and the activities of nationalist fire-bombers. But in the conclusions to that paper we also said that the ideas of community we had discussed:

have important social and economic effects in terms of the privileges the people of the place can claim in relation to that place. For those who are of the place, of the community, are seen to have a greater 'right' to the goods of the community – its jobs, houses, and educational provisions – than those who are not of the community. Those who are of the community have a greater 'right' to speak for the locality than those who are not; and those that are of the community have an 'ownership' of that community that is not available to those who are outside. Thus the question 'who appears to be of this place?' is not only fundamental to the nature of legitimate political action within Welsh nationalism, but also fundamental to the legitimate distribution of goods and rewards between individuals within the locality. (Borland et al., 1992: 66)

If we are right to consider community a mobilizing concept, there can be little doubt about what it is mobilizing: nationalist feeling. Nations *are* imagined communities – this is where nationalism derives its power to move people (Anderson, 1991) – and it is therefore little wonder that the rhetoric of community features so prominently in all the ways that they can be imagined. This was what we found in our four Welsh constructions: all four rely on the idea of community but all four are also ways of imagining the nation. They are, indeed, different versions of, different ways of doing, Welsh nationalism.[3] The consequences of this observation are crucial.

Since community comes into play in the mobilization of nationalism then it is hard to see how the imagined community could be understood to be under threat of attack prior to the generation (or even the expression) of nationalist feelings about this threat. There could be nothing yet constructed to be under attack without the prior process of mobilizing nationalism which brings imaginings of community into peoples' minds. It is therefore quite wrong to suggest that nationalism is the outcome of the threat to community and it makes more sense to argue that nationalism actually contributes to the perception of this threat (because nationalist feeling is necessary to create the object, community, that is to be threatened). To reinforce this point we should perhaps investigate exactly what the perceived 'threat' actually means in relation to those imagined communities we have identified. To do this we must begin with the geographical reference implied in our use of the term 'of the place' in the quotation above. It is the fundamental effect of any sort of nationalism that it *gives an identity to a place* (see also Williams and Smith, 1983; A. D. Smith, 1996b). Indeed there is no other way to give a place a national identity than by the attachment generated by nationalist feeling – military conquest and legal pronouncement are powerless in this regard.

Thus it would be foolish to argue that the Welsh-speaking areas of Wales are Welsh because they lie inside the recognized geographical boundaries of Wales rather than because of the identities they derive from Welsh nationalism. Indeed the nature of the Welsh identity of the places you travel through changes as you journey through Wales (especially if you travel from the south to the north). This happens because the nature and prevalence of Welsh nationalism is not the same in all parts of Wales. The nationalism that flourishes in the Welsh-speaking areas where resistance to English immigration has been most vocal is most frequently mobilized through the construction of (the secular version of) the culturally closed community identified in our earlier paper. This nationalism gives a culturally closed identity to its places and so in the Welsh-speaking areas Welsh identity most often means that the place belongs to those whose first language is Welsh. This is how national identity is conceived in those parts of Wales.

We want to suggest that 'threat to community' can also be understood as 'threat to the national identity of the place'. This is the logical conclusion we wish to draw from the argument we have presented above but it also makes sense of the sheer virulence of the reaction to English immigration. Only this sort of identity, this *level* of identity, can produce such extreme reactions. It is, of course, this potential for extreme feelings that sets nationalism apart (Anderson, 1991: 7, 143–5). Once we understand that the real threat that is being resisted is to the national identity of the place, we can also understand why arguments in support of this resistance so frequently centre on the sheer number of English immigrants and the size of the cultural and linguistic differences between those immigrants and the natives of the Welsh-speaking areas. Typically, it would be argued (in the autumn of 1988, for example) that there were too many immigrants and that they were too different (and too little prepared to change and accept the culture of the areas to which they had migrated) for small communities to bear. It would then be suggested that anyone could see the justice in this argument, yet both the apparently supernatural significance of numbers and the laboured (but perhaps exaggerated) cultural differences are only really important in the world of national identity.

If the Welsh identity of the place is being defined in terms of the Welsh language rather than, say, from finding the place within the borders of Wales, then this identity can indeed be threatened by immigrants who might lower the proportion of native Welsh-speakers in the area. In these circumstances the numbers of immigrants, and especially their percentage of the population, are obviously legitimate causes of concern for worried nationalists. Now it becomes obvious why Dafydd Wigley thought 10 per cent of non-Welsh-speakers constituted an upper limit (see above) and why other nationalists used the language of military conflict and natural disasters to describe the dangers of immigration. Similarly, the importance of emphasizing the degree of cultural difference (even where such differences may in reality be minor) is explicable in terms of the national identity of the place, since if differences were allowed to be minor then how could the argument for a separate identity be supported? This is something Max Weber was particularly keen to point out:

> Common cultural values can provide a unifying national bond. But for this the objective quality of the cultural values does not matter at all, and therefore one must not conceive of the 'nation' as a 'culture community'. (in Gerth and Mills, 1948: 178)

> The significance of the 'nation' is usually anchored in the superiority, or, at least the irreplaceability, of the culture values that are preserved and developed only through the cultivation of the peculiarity of the group. (Weber, 1968: 925)

For Weber (1968), significant cultural difference or peculiarity does not underpin nationality; nevertheless, he claims that nationalists value very small or imagined cultural differences because they believe that a mission has been given to them by providence.

At this point it might be objected that we have lost sight of the more mundane (and in fact more important) reasons for expressing resistance to English immigration. For example, was not nationalism 'just' (as Anthony Cohen might have said) providing a voice to those who saw immigrants moving into homes they might have lived in and simultaneously ensuring that house prices in Wales spiralled upwards so that poorer natives might as well forget for ever their dreams of having a home of their own? Any effort at a close examination of evidence for the links assumed in this argument will, however, quickly reveal some weaknesses.

Let us begin with the effect of immigration on the availability of council housing (and the resulting need to limit immigrant access to this housing). At the peak of the English immigration into Wales in 1988, people in Anglesey, in the heart of Welsh-speaking Wales, waited an average nine months for houses – not very long compared with many places in England (*Bangor and Anglesey Mail*, 19 October 1988). In the following year the number of people on the waiting list increased by 400 from 1,000 to 1,400 but of course this large increase happened after immigration into Anglesey had peaked. Both numbers on the waiting list and the average length of time spent on the list might in fact have had more to do with the overall reduction in the availability of council houses (down by 1,000 between 1980 and 1989) as a result of the Conservative Party's policy of selling council homes throughout the UK (*Bangor and Anglesey Mail*, 31 May 1989).

Turning to the private sector (as analysed by D. Thomas, 1989), Gwynedd had the smallest change in average house prices in Wales during the year of peak immigration in 1988 and kept its place at the bottom of the house-price league for Wales (interestingly, Gwynedd was not at the foot of the average income table). In fact all but three of the Welsh counties were ranked amongst the twenty UK counties with the lowest house prices. Nothing much had changed so far as relative house prices in Gwynedd (and the other Welsh counties) were concerned a year later (*Bangor and Anglesey Mail*, 5 August 1989).

All of this might go some way towards explaining why nationalists, who were so deeply concerned about housing shortages, could mount implacable opposition to plans to build new houses without any apparent anxiety that they might make the supposed housing shortage worse. Thus, in one of many similar campaigns, Cymdeithas yr Iaith resisted plans to build 150 new homes in Felinheli in Gwynedd on the grounds that 'These houses are completely unneeded and will be very harmful to the local community' (*Bangor and Anglesey Mail*, 5 August 1989). It is not at all convincing to point out that the nationalist objection was being made to higher priced houses which did not answer local need for lower priced starter homes since, in Gwynedd as elsewhere, starter homes became available as the families that occupied them grew (and earned larger incomes), but such families needed larger houses to move to and if such houses were not available then they had to be built.

In fact the contradictions of nationalist housing policy only make sense in terms of national identity. *The* point of all nationalist pronouncements on the subject is that the houses of Gwynedd and other Welsh-speaking areas should remain in the hands of people whose first language is Welsh because Welsh-speaking defines the national identity of the localities in question. This is why Cymdeithas described house building as 'very harmful to the local community' and why other new housing developments were resisted by nationalists, but it also explains why the more extreme nationalist groups were prepared to resist a variety of attempts to bring economic development to the Welsh-speaking areas. In 1989, for example, plans were announced for a £50 million leisure complex in a derelict slate quarry in a Welsh-speaking area (near Llanberis in Gwynedd) which might create 600 jobs. These plans had the support of the local authorities but the development company was English and the plans were opposed by nationalist groups including Adfer, Cefn, Cymdeithas yr Iaith and Padarn (the latter suggested reopening the quarry as an alternative way of boosting economic development – *Bangor and Anglesey Mail*, 31 May 1989). As with nationalist reactions to housing developments, resistance to economic development only really makes sense in terms of national identity: jobs might be sorely needed (the unemployment rate in parts of Gwynedd was amongst the highest in Wales) but were not wanted by nationalists if they threatened the national identity of the area in question.

Nationalism and Anti-Immigration Movements in England and Wales

We have argued that those, like Anthony Cohen, who would suggest that nationalism is the effect (or, perhaps, the means of expression), rather than the cause, of resistance to English influence in Wales (and in particular to English immigration) are mistaken. We conclude that nationalism must pre-exist for resistance to take the form it did. Thus the upsurge in all sorts of conflict and resistance in the 1980s was caused by what nationalists perceived to be threats to the Welsh identity of the Welsh-speaking parts of Wales. Increased conflict and resistance (even some increased nationalist voting) was a response to this perception of threat but the existence of any threat at all depended on people feeling strongly about the national identity of the places in question. Such feelings would not have been present without nationalism.

We will now attempt to apply this insight into the importance of nationalism (and the resulting significance attached to the national identity of places) for the generation of anti-immigration movements to the recent history of resistance and hostility to immigrants in England. The possibility of drawing a parallel between the hostility expressed towards migrants from the Caribbean and the Indian subcontinent to England in the 1960s and the hostility towards English migrants to Wales in the 1980s was not lost on some of those who went into print in the local press in Gwynedd in the late 1980s. Thus, goaded by some of the more extreme pronouncements of the Free Wales Covenanters in the summer of 1988, 'Immigrant (but not English)' wrote:

> Enoch Powell strikes in Wales! Let's dig out his speeches of the Sixties on immigration and feed them to the Free Wales covenant.
> In England the word immigrant is no longer used and I feel it is dangerous to print such racist language in a local paper.
> However in Gwynedd anything goes in the name of the Welsh language – rampant national socialism.
> Why not in fact start by giving all the immigrants a yellow star – or a red rose or a Scottish thistle before putting them in cattle trucks . . .
> (*Bangor and Anglesey Mail*, 15 June 1988)

Of course in Gwynedd – as in more serious conflicts elsewhere – accusations of racism and comparisons with the policies of Nazi Germany flew in both directions. The Covenanters themselves were later to compare the upgrading of the main road-link between north and west Wales and England with Hitler's development of German autobahns (*Bangor and Anglesey Mail*, 6 March 1991).

Throughout the 1980s Cymdeithas yr Iaith were prone to expressing their solidarity with the African National Congress and to drawing parallels between the situation of Welsh-speakers in Wales and that of the oppressed black population of South Africa which was still subject (then) to apartheid (see Williams, Chapter 4 above). Similarly, the term 'white settlers' was used to describe English immigrants by the Covenanters and others while Meibion Glyndŵr also made frequent mention of English colonialism and English racism against the Welsh. Nevertheless, before we dismiss the comparison of Welsh-speaking Wales in the late 1980s with England in the late 1960s as just another example of rhetorical invention, let us remind ourselves of the content of those Enoch Powell speeches that the correspondent to the *Bangor and Anglesey Mail* referred to. Powell's interventions began in the early months of 1967. The key points that were made in the speeches that followed are summarized below (for more details see, for example, Miles and Phizacklea, 1984).

Powell, then a leading Conservative politician, told audiences up and down England (but especially in those areas with a large immigrant presence) that the immigrants were strangers in our country and brought with them an alien culture (in part characterized by loyalty to their homeland and anti-British attitudes). He went on to conclude that Britain could only digest so much of this immigration – so many people who were so different to everything that being British stood for – and predicted both the total transformation of Britain and horrendous violence. With his notorious, classical allusion to the 'Tiber foaming with much blood', Powell underlined the connection he saw between the numbers of people (who were so culturally different) coming in, the hostility that they would therefore inevitably encounter, and the unavoidable descent into the sort of violence American cities had already experienced in the 1960s.

We do not have to look to the extreme Free Wales Covenanters for evidence of very similar arguments being made about English immigration to Wales but only as far as the views of the leadership of the mainstream nationalist party which were described at the beginning of our chapter – views which we are led to believe had considerable support in the Welsh-speaking areas. Here it is worth pointing out that Bagley and Verma (1979) claim that hostility towards immigrants to England peaked in the three years after

Powell's April 1968 'Rivers of Blood' speech and that Powell himself (rather than immigration) was the catalyst. On the other hand, contemporary surveys reported that Powell was only saying in public what very many people thought in private and were very grateful to him – alone amongst mainstream politicians – for expressing.

Powell was of course edged out of the Conservative Party in later years and eventually lost his place at the centre of the anti-immigration stage, but by this time many more politicians were happy to take up his role. Thus in the 1976 Immigration Debate Conservative MP Ivor Stanbrook told the House of Commons that 'The average coloured immigrant has a different culture, a different religion and a different language. This is what creates the problem. It is not just because of race.' While Bagley and Verma blame the explosion in hostility between 1968 and 1970 on Powell, they also note that levels of 'prejudice' in the population at large stayed high and possibly increased from the mid-1970s onwards (as did electoral support for the extreme National Front). We might have thought that if anti-immigration feeling were caused by immigration then the reduction of immigration to a trickle by 1970 would have led to a reduction in hostility. This is not what happened. In fact we might now observe that the argument that blames immigration for hostility and conflict seems to be more-or-less identical with the claims made by Powell in his 'Rivers of Blood' speech and elsewhere: if such large numbers of people who are so culturally different come in this will inevitably produce a hostile reaction and conflict.

There is no doubt that these views retained their appeal (see, for example, Cashmore, 1987) and that their rehearsal by Margaret Thatcher in a TV interview in January 1978 did much to help her win the general election in the following year. In that interview she said:

> If we went on as we are, then by the end of the century there would be four million people of the New Commonwealth and Pakistan here. Now that is an awful lot and I think it means that people are really rather afraid that this country might be swamped by people with a different culture. And, you know, the British character has done so much for democracy, for law, and done so much throughout the world that if there is a fear that it might be swamped, people are going to react and be rather hostile to those coming in. So, if you want good race relations, you have to allay people's fears on numbers.

Again the association is made between the sheer numbers of immigrants who are culturally different and the inevitable hostile reaction and subsequent conflict, but social scientists who sought to understand the appeal of anti-immigration rhetoric in England in the 1960s or 1970s took this sort of argument as the starting-point of their analysis, not its conclusion.

It is worth pointing out that few, if any, social scientists looked at the speeches of Powell or, later, the Thatcher interview, and concurred with these politicians that immigration was indeed leading to hostility and conflict. Fewer still looked at the immigration figures or the cultural endowments of the immigrants themselves and concluded that the numbers were 'too high' and the cultural differences 'too big', yet these are exactly the approaches taken in Wales in the late 1980s by some geographers and sociologists. Just as they never took seriously accusations that immigrants from the New Commonwealth and Pakistan were 'stealing' houses or jobs from English men and women – see, for example, the work of the geographer Ceri Peach (1968) on settlement patterns or Cohen and Jenner (1968) writing on jobs and immigration – so social scientists looked on the pronouncements of anti-immigration politicians as phenomena that required explanation not explanations which should simply be accepted. Thus Robert Moore (1975) took the argument about numbers (see his chapter 'Politicians and the number game') and the extent of cultural difference as the phenomenon to be explained and concluded that the explanation for this phenomenon must be found in racism – the racism of both politicians and the population they spoke to (the next chapter is entitled 'Keeping out the blacks').

Moore was not alone in reaching this conclusion (see, for example, Centre for Contemporary Cultural Studies, 1982), but in reaching it he and others were obliged to regard some of the components of the messages preached by Powell and those who followed in his footsteps as either disingenuous or as coded messages. What Powell had to say about cultural difference, for instance, was to be read as an allusion to racial difference. By the mid to late 1980s social scientists (see, for example, Barker, 1981; Duffield, 1984; Gilroy, 1987; Miles 1987a, 1987b) were less happy to draw this sort of conclusion, however. In essence the view that was expressed by these writers was that we should not dismiss those messages – such as Margaret Thatcher's fear of being swamped by a different culture – as smokescreen or cypher. Instead such messages were perhaps evidence of a new sort of racism which had rather more to do with nationalism.

We could go on to agree with the basic argument that those writers made. We could even agree with those amongst them who wondered exactly how new all this was and whether what had really happened was that social scientists had neglected the significance of nationalism all along – from Powell's first interventions in 1967 and perhaps even before he took the stage. In fact, we wish to go further than this and, on the basis of our parallel example from Wales, to suggest that, the role played by nationalism in the politics of immigration in England has been much greater than is usually allowed, even in the mid-1990s. Consider, for example, what Margaret Thatcher had to say about the British character and how closely this recalls Welsh nationalist eulogies to Welsh language and culture (see, for example, Borland *et al.*, 1992). Consider also how both examples cannot fail to recall the quotation from Weber (reproduced above) concerning the 'superiority, or . . . irreplaceability, of . . . culture values'. In our earlier work (also see Denney *et al.*, 1991) we have suggested that racism has not played an important role in Welsh nationalism but we would now like to add to this that the importance of racism in the anti-immigration politics of the UK has sometimes been overemphasized to the exclusion of nationalism. The fact that such close parallels can be drawn between anti-immigration arguments in England and the reactions to English immigration into Wales is strongly suggestive, in fact, of the necessary and important role played by nationalism in generating both sets of reactions (and in any consequent hostility and conflict).

The anti-immigration politics of the period after the halting of black (primary) immigration to the UK was characterized by a shift of emphasis from immigration control to 'induced repatriation' (Sivanandan, 1978) in which those migrants already settled in the UK were told that their *presence* here now constituted a problem. After the summer of 1988 English immigration into Welsh-speaking parts of Wales halted (and probably went into reverse) and Welsh nationalists shifted their attention to 'those non-Welsh speakers already here' (see the quotation from Dafydd Wigley above). The biggest impact of this attention was in employment where access to jobs for non-Welsh-speakers was restricted, first by the policies of public bodies and later by statute (see Fevre *et al.*, 1997), but nationalists were also active in the housing field as well. For example, in the spring of 1989 local councillors in Gwynedd attempted to restrict the renting of council homes to those who had lived in Wales for at least ten years and had spent at least five of them in the predominantly Welsh-speaking borough of Arfon itself (*Bangor and Anglesey Mail*, 31 May 1989).[4] Perhaps the lowest point in the history of immigration to Welsh-speaking parts of Wales was actually reached four years after that immigration was acknowledged to have come to an end when Meibion Glyndŵr renewed their fire-bombing campaign and threatened five named 'English colonists' to leave Wales or have their homes burned (*Independent*, 10 November 1992).

Nationalism makes the identity of a place sacred in some sense and so the focus of serious conflict and resistance when that identity is threatened. It is not the scale of immigration or the size of any real cultural differences between immigrants and natives but the strength and popularity of nationalist feeling in and about the locality in question that makes for conflict and resistance. This may be something that has been partially overlooked in the effort to dissect the arguments of those who opposed immigration, including those on the far right such as the National Front and the British National Party. In fact the centrality of nationalism in the far right's anti-immigration rhetoric was explicitly recognized by the National Front when it praised Meibion Glyndŵr and expressed the belief that both organizations were engaged in the same sort of enterprise (*Bangor and Anglesey Mail*, 19 October 1988).[5]

Conclusion

The violation of national identity in England by immigration was signified by race. It was race that alerted nationalists to the threat to the national identify of the place. In Wales it was not race but language that signified the same sort of violation. We do not mean to imply that race was important in the Welsh case or that race was not a major factor in the Powellite anti-immigration movement of the 1960s and 1970s. We do, however, conclude that race only became significant because this movement was grounded in a nationalism which contemporary commentators largely neglected to analyse. We have learnt this by looking at the Welsh example from the late 1980s – where, perhaps because of the absence of racialization, the nationalist tenor of anti-immigration rhetoric is easier for everyone to see. We do not think this makes the Welsh example a special case, but it does allow us to expose the nationalist roots of all such social conflict and to explain better other anti-immigration movements. We conclude that, without nationalism, the views of Powell and, later, Margaret Thatcher would have seemed incoherent and would have lacked their apparent popular appeal.

Notes

An earlier version of this chapter was given under the title 'Nation, Identity and Immigration in England and Wales 1967–1989' at the annual conference of the American Sociological Association, Toronto, August 1997. We wish to thank all those who have commented on that version; however, any mistakes which remain are entirely the responsibility of the authors.

1. See for example the remarks made by Denis Healey and John Biffen (*The Times*, 19 February 1998).
2. Cohen does, however, find it difficult to stick to this point in practice (see, for example, 1985: 44). We, in contrast, are quite certain that the only 'real' communities-as-social-actors which are of interest here are in fact status groups. It is amongst status groups that we find the 'carriers' of nationalism – and these are not necessarily locality-based (see Fevre *et al.*, 1997).
3. In practice they are not always separated out in the way we describe, although (as we showed in Borland *et al.*, 1992) they can be, especially for the purposes of internal nationalist politics.
4. These attempted restrictions were rather more stringent than those residency qualifications operated by English local authorities in the 1960s and 1970s which had the (sometimes unintentional) effect of keeping black immigrants out of council accommodation (see Rex and Moore, 1967; Henderson and Karn, 1987).
5. At this point we might also remember that Enoch Powell joined the Ulster Unionists in the later stages of his political career.

8 Prospects of Wales: Contested Geographical Imaginations

Pyrs Gruffudd

> Wales is a process . . . a process of continuous and dialectical historical development in which human mind and human will interact with objective reality. Wales is an artefact which the Welsh produce; the Welsh make and remake Wales day by day and year after year. If they want to. (Williams, 1982: 200)

These words by Gwyn Alf Williams place Wales firmly in the realm of the imagination. In post-structuralist times we might challenge the notion of an 'objective reality', but these words still help us to see Welshness as constructed and multiple, not given and singular. We might also add – as did Williams himself, of course – the observation that Wales has also been made and remade by peoples other than the Welsh; Welshness has usually been constructed in relation to Britishness. But Williams's work forms a central part of that relatively recent understanding of how the nation in general, and a 'Welsh nation' in particular, might usefully be viewed as 'imagined' – as an idea rather than a material entity (for example, Anderson, 1983; Curtis, 1986).

This chapter considers the role that territory and landscape play in this process of cultural imagination, focusing mainly on the period between the two World Wars. The terrain of Wales has long been contested both materially and symbolically and the multiple interpretations of landscape illustrate Wales's ambiguous position – within the British state yet on its margins; and furthermore imagined and represented as separate by some of the Welsh. Within geography there is a long tradition of theorizing the relationship between ideology and space. Nationalism can, for instance, be read primarily as a territorial ideology – one that gains its legitimacy from the mobilization of identity within a specific, and active, geographical context. Williams and Smith (1983) identify eight major dimensions of national territory: habitat, folk culture, scale, location, boundaries, autarchy (self-sufficiency), the idea of 'homeland' and processes of nation-building. Attempts may be made to 'solidify' or 'confirm' national space. These can be material acts – the extension of a communication network, for instance – or symbolic ones such as the changing of place-names from an earlier phase of occupation. Clearly, though, the boundary between what is 'material' and 'symbolic' is blurred, and perhaps necessarily so. In any case, such acts serve to harden the identity of that piece of land and to deny the claims of others upon it.

Landscape and the geographical imagination (Gregory, 1994) are important in this process of national socialization. As Stephen Daniels (1993: 5) puts it, 'Landscapes, whether focusing on single monuments or framing stretches of scenery, provide visible shape; they picture the nation. As exemplars of moral order and aesthetic harmony, particular landscapes achieve the status of national icons.' The idea of national landscape, even specific physical features (mountains, rivers, forests), can become emblematic of national identity and can offer cultural relationships through which a people make *a* land *their* land (see Schama, 1996). This process almost inevitably draws on an awareness of history:

> The nation's unique history is embodied in the nation's unique piece of territory – its 'homeland', the primeval land of its ancestors, older than any state, the same land which saw its greatest moments, perhaps its mythical origins. The time has passed but the space is still there.
> (Anderson, 1988: 24; see also Smith, 1986, 1991b)

In many cases, rural landscapes are imagined as the 'real', 'authentic' essence of the nation. Daniels (1993) argues that the gentle, pastoral lowlands of southern England – and paintings of them by artists like John Constable – have come to symbolize 'Englishness' and have been used at times of social tension (the two World Wars, for instance) as emblems of national identity. This idealization also extends, as I will argue below, to the people – or 'folk' – living within them in idealized, organic communities.

In Search of Wales

The whole notion of landscape is one that has, arguably, been politicized in Wales. Mainstream academic readings suggest that 'landscape' in Wales begins with the Picturesque and Romantic movements of the eighteenth and nineteenth centuries through which Wales achieved the heights of aesthetic fashion and was reconstructed as the location of an idyllic rural existence (see, for example, P. Morgan, 1983, 1986a). But recent writings on this period have revealed a complexity through which we can see in landscape the whole process of national imagination. The art historian Peter Lord, for instance, has attacked the historiography of landscape art − even of landscape 'awareness' in Wales − by highlighting an indigenous visual tradition predating Richard Wilson (the Welsh eighteenth-century artist reputed as being the first great landscapist) by some 150 years (Lord, 1992, 1994). He exposes a continued English high art convention that culminated in a sociological narrative (in which the Welsh themselves were complicit) of the 'non-visual Welsh'. At the same time, we can also see different − even resistant − readings of Romantic landscape in Wales. The Welsh themselves constructed moralized discourses of landscape and rural life by echoing the aesthetics and the narratives of English antiquarians to create a subtly different geographical imagination (perhaps illustrating what Mary Louise Pratt (1992) has called 'transculturation'). From this indigenous concern with landscape, continued into the national revival of the later nineteenth century, we eventually see emerging the romantic idea of the *gwerin* − the 'folk' or the common people of Wales − as rural, Nonconformist, moralized and Welsh-speaking; an idea that would be used in opposition to Anglicization and to the imposition of an urban-industrial Britishness on Wales.

If the Romantic movement was responsible for establishing a dominant way of interpreting Wales amongst the nineteenth-century intelligentsia, in the twentieth a widespread form of neo-Romanticism did the same, creating a strange, moralized landscape. Memorably defined by David Mellor (1987) as being a fusion of King Arthur, William Blake and Picasso, neo-Romanticism found its sense of place largely on the western ends of Britain. In St Ives, for instance, artists lauded the retired fisherman Alfred Wallis for his unmediated, experiential view of

Figure 1: 'Baptism in the River Ceiriog' by Mildred Eldridge, from *Recording Britain*, Vol. 3 (Palmer, 1948)

landscape. In Wales, David Jones transferred both Arthurian legends and biblical tales to Capel y Ffin on the borders. Graham Sutherland was drawn to rural Pembrokeshire in Wales – 'a country, a part of which, at least, spoke a foreign tongue, and it certainly seemed very foreign to me, though sufficiently accessible for me to feel that I could claim it as my own' (*Sutherland in Wales*,

1976: 11). In addition to the elemental forms of nature and the marks of earlier civilizations – elements of what he called the 'exultant strangeness of the place' – Sutherland was motivated by the inhabitants. Their life, he noted in 1934, was complete, content and 'almost biblical in its sober dignity'. That sober dignity is expressed in John Piper's 1937 series of paintings of Welsh Nonconformist chapels, and echoed in Mildred Eldridge's watercolours of open-air baptisms, peat-cutting and humble cottages for the Second World War (though unpublished until later) *Recording Britain* volumes (Figure 1). Of the open-air baptisms the accompanying text notes that 'The scene is to some extent a reconstruction, a feat of memory, yet these outdoor ceremonies lasted down to 1939 at least' (Palmer, 1948: 102). The theme was picked up after the war in Gwyn Jones's (1948) text and Kenneth Rowntree's drawings for *A Prospect of Wales*. Of the chapels, Jones said, 'to-day their power weakens, but for three Welshmen out of four the gleam of a varnished pew, the smell of polished linoleum, the ecstatic rustle of a rising congregation, and maybe the taste of a hymn-book cover, are unforgettably part of those childhood years when in sensuous innocence we stood a rung nearer heaven' (Jones, 1948: 24).

Much of the construction of Wales as a spiritual zone was based around its consumption through travel (we might even say pilgrimage). Texts added to the notion of the Celtic Fringe as the spiritual reservoir or conscience of Britain. In 1905 Edward Thomas (1983), like George Borrow a couple of decades earlier, found Wales to be a land of cultured, God-fearing peasants and found its hills imbued with mythology. He was followed by an increasing number of travellers in the inter-war years. In 1935 Edmund Vale argued that the touristic construction of Wales – or, indeed, its lack of visible symbols of nationality – denied a deeper spirituality:

> May I urge that Wales is something more than a landscape? It is a world. But unless you have the key to unlock the enchantments which hide this world within the fold of its own scenery it will appear to be merely a landscape, a sweet superficies, a pleasaunce wherein to walk, to bathe, to climb mountains, to motor, to take photographs. (1935a: p. ix)

None the less, the whole of Wales 'is pervaded by an invisible essence which issues from invisible sources and which we may call

Figure 2: 'A Vanished Generation'; the frontispiece to H.V. Morton's *In Search of Wales* (1932)

Welsh atmosphere' (Vale, 1935b: 161). He employed the modernist metaphor of electricity to describe the contribution of Welshness. He could imagine no better thing happening to England 'than an awakening of a more perfect understanding with the people of Wales. Just now West Britain is an accumulator of imaginative forces standing at full charge, waiting to be put into circuit' (1935a: p. x). Vale imagined himself in the role of the educated, didactic conductor for Wales remained, in his opinion, a secretive land. The travel itinerary thus became a crucial indicator of discernment, the reaching of remote villages and communion with their natives a ritual feature if not a matter of honour.

David Matless (1998) discerns this ethical attitude in the work of H. V. Morton, a professional travel writer whose *In Search of Wales* was first published in 1932, reaching its tenth edition only six years later. The book's frontispiece muses on the fluctuating stereotypes of Wales, women in Welsh costume somewhat mournfully labelled 'a vanished generation' (Figure 2). But Morton's tour is a humorous and sensitive interpretation of Wales and the Welsh in a state of balance between tradition and modernity. His tour took him along the border and coast of the north east, then criss-crossed Gwynedd before heading southwards to Pembrokeshire and then into the industrial south. This descent into what he called 'Black Wales' set Morton's book apart from the countless other Welsh travel books as being willing to engage with the landscapes and peoples of industry. His historically layered and insightful narrative is littered with chance encounters such as that with Mr Evans the mid-Wales farmer ('a vivacious, elderly little Welshman with quick, humorous, grey eyes', 1932: 167), and with Miriam the Penclawdd cocklewoman ('young and salted as a Bismarck herring. Her eyes were as soft as a doe's and her forearms were those of a warrior', 1932: 231). Through these interactions and his appreciation of landscape and of history, Morton sets up a sympathetic resonance between the enlightened traveller, as opposed to the vulgar tourist, and the spiritual Welsh peasantry:

> It is amusing to sit in a corner and watch some worthy man, whose life has been spent among crowds in Manchester or Birmingham doing his best to cultivate the native . . . He talks to a man who can see corpse-lights as if he was talking to a mechanic in his factory. (1932: 135–6)

Morton's book begins by recalling a railway journey to north Wales:

> The train rushed through the hot night, and I remember getting out at cool wayside stations, conscious that I was in a strange, new land, a land of mountains and mad streams. I could hear water falling and running over stones, and I could see the shadow of great hills, like arcs of black velvet blotting out the summer stars. (1932: 2)

It is surprising how frequently this form of transport offers the writer some form of cultural leverage in their reading of Wales. Eiluned and Peter Lewis's *The Land of Wales* (1949, originally 1937) begins by noting that 'The traveller who buys a ticket at Paddington or Euston should be warned that he is about to travel backwards as well as westwards, for Wales is a storehouse of the past' (1949: 1–2). Wales is constructed for the reader in terms of its wild topography, its layered history, its mysterious and rich folklore and its complex sociology. The writing of the book is as much creation as it is representation; one chapter includes this footnote: 'While this chapter was being written, fairy music was heard near a lake in Montgomeryshire. The writers spoke to a farmer nearby, whose daughter and grandchildren had heard the strains at dusk . . .' (1949: 11). The authors impart a sense of harsher realism by evaluating the impacts of the industrial revolution, and the prospects for Welsh nationalism. *The Land of Wales* thus offers the reader a frame for correct, ordered appreciation. What emerges from this gaze is the spirit of Wales – the quest of the enlightened traveller – a spirit characterized by 'a keeness of comprehension, the understanding heart as well as the ready tongue, an interest in spiritual and intellectual matters that characterises even the casual occupant of a third class railway carriage, west of Offa's Dyke' (1949: 111).

Interpreting Rural Wales

This understanding of rural Wales was also reflected in academic research. Employing the view from the railway carriage, the Aberystwyth geographer H. J. Fleure – in *The Blue Guide for Wales* – noted that

> The visitor approaching Wales feels he is nearing his destination when the hills begin to crowd upon his path, when the views from the train window or the motor are of the fair valleys that run among the hills, and the conversation of the people who come into the railway carriage at the little wayside stations takes a new tone and begins to deal with matters unfamiliar to dwellers on the open plains or in the industrial districts of England. (Fleure, 1922: p. xi)

He later noted that 'as one travels from England to rural Wales the talk in a railway compartment changes from betting to chapels, or from horse racing to the eisteddfod' (Fleure, 1940: 883). Through anthropological research – including physical surveys of Welsh types – Fleure elevated the Welsh rural population to a position of sociological importance, manifested in the subtle moral message of the railway-carriage conversation (Gruffudd, 1994). In his opinion, the Celtic Fringe in general and rural Wales in particular was 'the ultimate refuge in the far west, wherein persist, among valleys that look towards the sunset, old thoughts and visions that else had been lost to the world' (Fleure, 1926: 1). The spiritual qualities of the peasantry – poetry, oratory, religiosity – were of importance in combating the materialism of unbridled *laissez-faire* and its destructive social effects. Industrial civilization, Fleure suggested in 1921, was facing collapse and society's one hope of avoiding collapse was to have a stream of supply from the remote corners where the treasures of ancient thought survived, imparting to urbanites those spiritual values, discernment and creativity that Fleure felt were the possession of rural society (Fleure, 1921). The cry was for a new vision of the future that could only come from those who retained their rural roots. He rejected the blind attachment to 'Progress' and its effects, as he saw it, on personality – enforcing specialization and dependence by contrast with the rich variety of peasant life. In this way, Wales was conceived – as in the case of the enlightened travellers – as 'a fount whence may well up streams of inspiration refreshing to the jaded and overstrained business life of our perplexed modern England' (Fleure, 1922: p. xi).

Fleure's colleague at Aberystwyth, the plant scientist George Stapledon, likewise sought to promote rural life. A mystic, he had read Henri Bergson 'and was deeply imbued with the feeling that an evolving Spirit of Life was immanent in Nature' (Waller, 1962: 74). This spirit, however, was being denied by a modern, urban life that was one-sided in its appeal to the mental, as opposed to the pre-mental, aspects of character exemplified by the intuitively wise peasantry of places like rural Wales. Harmony and understanding could only come through the contemplation of nature. In addition, Stapledon feared the physical degeneracy caused by city life and is, as such, linked to the eugenics movement, a movement that promoted the quasi-science of 'racial planning' (see Searle, 1979).

The 'country stock' was, he argued, sounder than the urban; the countryside of Britain 'carries in its population the genes, unsullied and uncontaminated, that maintain and perpetuate our national vigour and national characteristics' (Stapledon, 1944: 231, originally 1935). To alleviate this general waning of the influence of the rural on British life (a lower 'coefficient of ruralicity' as he called it), Stapledon was a vocal campaigner for National Parks and for the inculcation of rural values through the schools and universities. More dramatically, though, he argued for the wholesale revival of upland Britain: 'Let rural Britain die completely and the whole superstructure will totter to ruin. It is just and only just not too late to stop the rot, but only heroic endeavours will suffice' (Stapledon, 1943: 94). Drawing inspiration from Mussolini's land-reclamation programmes, Stapledon urged that scattered rural hamlets in mid-Wales be joined into new upland communities, well-designed and serviced by roads, social and entertainment facilities, in order to reinvigorate rural life for the sake of British society as a whole.

Nationalism and Ruralism

This writing and theorizing, whilst apparently elevating Wales to a position of moral strength, still served to commodify Welshness for the sake of Britain. Wales was constructed as the remote, spiritual hinterland of Britain's core, located in metropolitan, industrial England. To the Celtic Fringe, travellers and artists could come for inspiration and moments of enlightenment. To the core were exported poets, visionaries and teachers. But the emergence of a formalized nationalist political party in Wales would draw on this ruralism in markedly different ways, and would lay different claims to these Welsh cultural topographies. Plaid Cymru (the Welsh Nationalist Party), formed in 1925, used this rural version of Welshness to counter Britishness. In this, of course, Wales was far from unique. Throughout Europe nationalist movements – of both left and right – studied, idealized and sought to protect and ultimately enlist their rural nationals. In Ireland, for instance, the linguistic and geographical character of the Irish-speaking *Gaeltacht* made it the focus of Irish cultural aspiration (Nash, 1993). Denmark was widely viewed as a society that successfully modernized without losing touch with its peasant traditions. Fleure noted how 'Denmark has been a laboratory of experiments in the modernisation of peasant life without setting the peasants adrift, while using methods that promoted individual initiative within a frame of collectivity that was prepared to recognise government by discussion rather than by dictation' (Fleure, 1943: 61). Denmark was frequently referred to as a model for Wales (for example, Bowen and Fleure, 1930).

During its first twenty years, Plaid Cymru was essentially a cultural and educational movement which sought to resist and reverse all those trends that were assimilating Wales into England – continued industrialism in the south, tourist industries in the north, standardized educational regimes, the BBC (D. H. Davies, 1983). The version of Welshness that Plaid Cymru sought to defend and to re-establish was traditional, organic, Welsh-speaking and rural: the Wales of the *gwerin*. As party president Saunders Lewis put it, agriculture should be Wales's main industry 'and the foundation of its civilisation'. Furthermore, south Wales should be de-industrialized 'for the moral health of Wales, and for the moral and physical benefit of its population' (Lewis, 1985: 16, originally 1938). Here, then, rather than being some politically neutral moral reservoir to be drawn upon by writers, artists and travellers, the *gwerin* and its rural world becomes both symbolically and actually that which is threatened by English-speaking metropolitan culture. The *gwerin* was a storehouse of a specifically Welsh rural identity and as such was explicitly politicized. In the following section I will consider two ways in which this nationalized idea of the *gwerin* and of rural Wales were deployed – one in defence of national territory, the other in an attempt to build nationality.

A persistent theme in Plaid Cymru's campaigning was the defence of Welsh territory but Wales's lack of autonomy was demonstrated dramatically in the later 1930s by large-scale land requisitioning by the military authorities. The location of training areas was particularly controversial as they posed immediate threats both to the organic rural communities that served as the nationalists' definition of the nation, and to their ideal of national territorial control. One proposed requisitioning provided a defining moment in Welsh nationalist history when plans were announced in May 1935 for the establishment of an aerodrome at Porth Neigwl on the Llŷn Peninsula, an area represented as the heartland of Welsh culture. Plaid Cymru's 'geographical imagination' of Wales – an amalgam of moral and territorial stances around the notion of 'the rural' – served to define their response to this and other claims made on Welsh territory (see also Gruffudd, 1995b).

One of the key definers of the *gwerin's* contribution to Welshness in the inter-war years was the geographer Iorwerth Peate. Peate had been one of Fleure's first students at Aberystwyth and would later become the first curator of the Welsh Folk Museum at St Fagans (Gruffudd, 1995b). With Peate, Fleure's moral geography became explicitly politicized. In a fruitless attempt to rouse the preservationist body the Campaign for the Preservation of Rural Wales into action, Peate claimed that the Llŷn Peninsula's population was 'an excellent example of . . . an unsophisticated peasant community. It seems to me to be a heinous sin to introduce any kind of camp into that area' (Peate, 1935a). Opposition to the scheme was immediately defined in terms of threats by an 'alien civilisation' to the cultural and geographical integrity of the Welsh nation. Peate claimed that the peninsula was 'virgin ground almost completely unaffected by modern building and the effects of tourist and English influences' (Peate, 1935b) and as such it had become, like other western European peninsulas, a storehouse of the Celtic tradition. An essentially modern folk-life offered vital knowledge to sociologists and ethnographers, and most of the peninsula was over 90 per cent Welsh-speaking with a significant monoglot population. It was 'imperative that the peninsula should maintain the unsophisticated purity of its native tradition' (Peate, 1935b). In these ways, the topographies of Welsh identity – of rural cultural continuity, of folk wisdom and spirituality – were politically mobilized. The Porth Neigwl case thus came to symbolize for Plaid Cymru the struggle to define and defend a particular Welsh national identity. Plaid Cymru's president Saunders Lewis argued in *The Listener* that the aerodrome, proposed exactly 400 years after the Act of Union, would be

> an English garrison set up in an area where the Welsh language has ever since the fifth century been established and undisturbed, where Welsh speech has moulded a countryside rich in intelligence, noble in the purity of its idiom, and with its native culture harmoniously developed through fifteen centuries of unbroken tradition. (Lewis, 1936a: 915)

This geographical imagination and rhetorical pattern was repeated elsewhere – most notably on Epynt in mid-Wales, and on the Preseli Hills in Pembrokeshire. In the case of the former, Iorwerth Peate – in his capacity as folk-culture curator at the National Museum of Wales – visited the Epynt mountain to record the vernacular architecture before its destruction by the military. In a powerful, poetic evocation, Peate mourned the destruction of a community:

> I walked to the front of the house. There I saw an old woman of eighty-two. I'll never forget her: she pulled an old chair to the far corner of the farmyard and sat there like a statue, staring at the mountain-side with tears pouring down her cheeks. She was born there, and her father and her grandfather before her. She leaves today and here she is compacting into her last minutes one rich contemplation of the old mountain or remembrance of her lifetime in the old farmstead. (Peate, 1941: 184)

These schemes and incursions were also interpreted strategically. In the same way as studies of the Welsh language (for example, D. T. Williams, 1936) had highlighted linguistic 'fortresses', 'divides' and 'frontiers', so nationalist politicians adopted geo-political discourse to represent the struggle between English and Welsh culture over the western and upland strongholds. According to Saunders Lewis 'Whilst Llŷn was Welsh we did not need fear for the Welsh nation', but 'this threat by the Air Force aims straight and true at the heart and life of our language and literature and culture and existence as a nation' (1936b: 6). Welshness was understood in profoundly geographical terms, as illustrated in a remarkable letter to the press by a group of prominent nationalists:

> the advance of Anglicising influences along the seaboard, powerful and disturbing though they were, could still be regarded with a certain qualified equanimity, so long as the mountains of Snowdonia offered a barrier behind which, in the profoundly Welsh peninsula of Lleyn, the forces of defence, and ultimately of counter-attack could safely rally. The value of Lleyn . . . is absolutely irreplaceable in our national life, and any blow to the security of Welsh culture here is a mortal blow. The establishment of the bombing school here will do for modern Welsh culture what the occupation of Anglesey by Edward I in the thirteenth century did for Welsh political independence – destroy it by cutting its communications and vital supplies. (*Western Mail,* 24 March 1936)

This letter's geopolitical imagery and rhetoric clearly illustrates the power of the geographical imagination in Welsh cultural and political discourse between the wars. In this one scheme the process of diffusion by which Wales had been steadily Anglicized for centuries was replaced by a form of internal colonialism, and the mountains, Wales's traditional protectors, were defeated. In Epynt too the strategic implications were grave:

> By dispersing the *gwerin* of Epynt Mountain, one of the last solid parts – of any meaningful size – of Breconshire's Welsh culture has been destroyed. And though it may be possible to re-populate the area when men return to their senses from the present madness, it will not be with the *gwerin* of Epynt Mountain, not with men and women with their roots in the area for centuries, and with the native language on their lips, but rather with newcomers. And it will take centuries for those to root in the land as had the community murdered in 1940. (Peate, 1941: 185)

Back to the Land

The other strand of Plaid Cymru's geographical campaigning relied on the renationalization of territory through planning and the process of nation-building. The party – locating Welshness amongst the *gwerin* and arguing that agriculture should be the economic cornerstone of Wales and the foundation of its civilization – instituted a 'back to the land' policy, calling for the de-industrialization of south Wales for the sake of the physical and moral health of the population. This, again, was a policy beloved of a range of political and national movements, especially during the late nineteenth and the early twentieth centuries. On the left, for instance, the Danish co-operative movements influenced the work of Plaid Cymru, as did the romantic socialism of the Arts and Crafts Movement (see Gould, 1988; also Bramwell, 1989). In Wales, such a cultural and material shift was meant to unite a culturally and geographically divided nation by bringing the industrial proletariat back in touch with their Welsh-speaking, rural roots. As the leading nationalist Ambrose Bebb put it, 'one of Wales's greatest needs today is not only to keep her sons on the land, but to bring back from the city to the land the masses who

Figure 3: 'Back to the Land'. Source: *Y Ddraig Goch*, 108 (1936)

flowed there during recent years' (quoted in D. H. Davies, 1983: 91). In addition to providing cultural legitimation for the nation, this process had an economic logic. Resettlement on the land was to provide an economic foundation for political independence from England. A cartoon from *Y Ddraig Goch* (Figure 3) represents in visual form this ideological stance. The physical dignity of the peasant farmer contrasts abruptly with the aggressive awkwardness of the capitalist who urges him 'For the sake of the free market

– don't become self-sufficient'. Whilst the farmer stands before a prospect of quiet fields traditionally farmed, the capitalists' domain is the polluting wirescape of industrialism.

This does not suggest, however, that the 'back to the land' ideology was entirely nostalgic. Indeed, in Wales there was a marked fusion between tradition and modernity in the writings of some of the more thoughtful commentators on the national scene. Iorwerth Peate, rapidly alienated from Plaid Cymru because of the party's presumed lack of social radicalism, in particular denied any simplistically romantic reading of a stable organic countryside. In 1943 he criticized the Scott Report on *Land Utilisation in Rural Areas*, published in 1942, which conceived of the countryside as an 'amenity' area dependent upon the towns, and thus continued to see rural Wales as some kind of spiritual, and in this case aesthetic, resource for urban England (Peate, 1943). The report thus established a division that Peate claimed was alien to Wales, a country where rural and industrial activities were historically integrated, and it thus denied the vital role of the rural in Welsh national identity. The 'national character' had emerged in part, he argued, from the co-operative patterns of rural industries – wool, woodworking and so on – combined with agriculture. He had long sought to revive this dual foundation on the basis of new technologies like electrification:

> We cry for the old methods in vain, we attempt to revive the dead in vain, but on the grave of the old methods we can build new factories and keep – in the sound of the machines of our age – the spirit of the rich culture given to us as an inheritance by the old craftsmen of Wales. (Peate, 1929: 8)

In this sense, Peate (and others like Fleure) appeared to be expressing a form of what Paul Rabinow calls 'techno-cosmopolitanism' which

> claimed that health, productivity and efficiency (an orderly modern society) could be achieved only through a reordering and reactivation of essentially healthy sedimented practices – society depended on history. (1996: 59–60).

Wales, Plaid Cymru argued, needed a national plan calculated to revive the depopulated rural areas and to give a territorial basis to

Figure 4: The 'TVA Way'. Source: Welsh Nationalist Party (1945)

Welsh national aspirations. 'Planning or the lack of it', a representative argued, 'is very closely linked with the political and cultural survival of our nation' (R. Lewis, 1949: 1). But in Plaid Cymru's opinion the state continued to treat Wales as a peripheral region of Britain, and the management of territory kept Wales firmly in a broader British space. For Plaid Cymru, these concerns were heightened by the government's reconstruction proposals of the 1940s, themselves part of a discourse of British nation-building. The existing planning system was therefore politically and culturally defective both in failing to recognize the Welsh national unit and in failing to address the role of industrialism in Welsh life. Plaid Cymru, sustaining their location of Welshness in the countryside, looked to the Tennessee Valley Authority (TVA) for inspiration. Its comprehensive revival of rural life was seen as an attractive model of state-sponsored self-determination (for example, Matthews, 1949). In a debate prompted by large-scale hydro-electric developments in Wales in the 1950s a number of nationalists saw potential parallels between Wales and Tennessee. Plaid Cymru called for a Welsh TVA to generate and control electricity supply. It would use the financial surplus from the sale of electricity for promotional activities and for research and development. Centralized food-processing plants, demonstration farms and incentives like subsidized fertilizers could stimulate agriculture, while light industries could be established in the rural areas. Electricity was seen as a revitalizing force that could resurrect the old rural social order on a new (and national) foundation (a process that Bill Luckin (1990) has called 'techno-arcadianism'):

> [Electricity] can transform our country, not only from the economic but from the social point of view. Properly applied it can make us into a happy, prosperous, self-reliant nation, proud of being something more substantial than *Gwlad y Gân* (the land of song). (Welsh Nationalist Party, 1944: 1)

The utopian possibilities of such a scheme are clearly represented in the cartoon shown in Figure 4.

Conclusion

The landscapes of Wales have frequently been contested and their inhabitants drawn into a variety of moral, aesthetic and political discourses. There is a long historical tradition of 'peripheral' places like Wales being represented as a spiritual, moral and environmental resource for the metropolitan cores. That tradition of constructing 'moral geographies' – arguably begun in Britain in the eighteenth century – was continued well into the twentieth, where it coloured a variety of artistic and intellectual activities. Whilst placing Wales in a spiritually or morally superior position, this tradition arguably represented Wales as a pre-modern 'other' to be preserved – so Peate (1943) said of the Scott Report – for amenity. But these geographical resources were also jealously nationalized within Wales and deployed not as a complement but in outright opposition to metropolitan England by an indigenous cultural and political movement seeking to sever the spatial and intellectual linkage between Wales and the rest of Britain. The aim was to re-establish the rural as the cornerstone of a modern Welsh civilization and by so doing to build a nation again.

The interesting paradox that lies at the heart of this national construction of modern Welsh geographies is the fluid relationship between tradition and modernity. For the neo-Romantics, Wales's traditional and ancient virtues were most powerfully represented through modern art. For H. J. Fleure, sensitive to national tradition and to Welsh culture, the rural might form the foundation of a better modern society for the sake of civilization as a whole. For Plaid Cymru, and for individual writers like Iorwerth Peate, the reconciliation between rural and industrial significantly echoed the Janus-headed character of nationalism. This 'techno-cosmopolitanism' (Rabinow, 1996) is instructive in that it treats national identity as a dialogue between several dimensions, and sees the nation as a process and not as an artefact.

9 Spatial Restructuring in the Capital: Struggles to Shape Cardiff's Built Environment

Huw Thomas

Introduction: Capital Cities and Spatial Structure

During my teens I visited Cardiff only three times. The first occasion was to see the Snelling Sevens, as they were then called, at Cardiff Arms Park; the second to see an FA Cup tie against Arsenal at Ninian Park. Exciting times, but nothing different in kind from a trip to St Helens or the Vetch in Swansea, the usual destination for a Port Talbot boy. The third visit was wholly different. I had an interview at Glamorgan County Hall, and at sixteen saw Cathays Park for the first time. Now here was something qualitatively different from anything I had experienced before. It was a summer's day and I was overwhelmed by the grandeur of the majestic white-stoned buildings, so formally arranged, by the red tarmacadamed avenues, the gardens, the sense of importance. For me Cardiff came alive as a capital city that day, and so it should – the design of Cathays Park was intended to produce such an effect (Wilson, 1996). But while the symbolism of grand buildings and stately malls may be straightforward to interpret, why that symbolism should be felt appropriate (by the producers and the audience) in Cardiff's case requires exploration. There are, after all, many different kinds of capital cities, with a variety of different relationships to their countries (Taylor *et al.*, 1993). The effectiveness of Cathays Park in underlining Cardiff's legitimacy as capital of Wales can only be understood in the context of a political project which constructs Welsh nationality in a certain way and provides a role for a city such as Cardiff within it. This project will be discussed in this chapter, but only as a prelude to an examination of episodes of reshaping Cardiff which are more recent than the construction of Cathays Park. It will be suggested that these, too, are 'culturally encoded' (Jackson, 1989), in as much as a full understanding must relate them to political projects in which specific cultural roles, and images, for the city were (and are) being developed (roles and images which were and are by no means uncontested). A particular interpretation of Cardiff's status as a *capital* city has been central to these projects; though, it will be argued, in recent years this conception has become particularly thin, or shallow. The introduction discusses the significance of capital-city status and its relationship to the built form of a city, concluding with an analysis of some episodes of spatial restructuring in Cardiff over the last forty years.

The most cursory review of capital cities worldwide reveals that there is no single universal reason why a settlement becomes a capital city – there is no essence to be discovered, nor can we speak sensibly of 'true' capitals as opposed to 'nonauthentic' ones (Taylor *et al.*, 1993). The formal designation of a capital, then, will gain its significance within the politics of a particular country or region; the precise kind of capital city being designated will vary according to the politics of the place though the designation of a capital is always part of a project to create or underline some kind of unity among people living in a given territory. Yet if generalizations are perilous it is plausible to suggest that remaining a capital city for any length of time always requires more than simply being designated as such – it requires acknowledgement and acceptance on the part of the populace at large, or at least significant portions of it. Such acceptance can (at a minimum) amount to no more than a recognition of the legitimacy of a government which has its seat in a particular city, but more often a capital city will be expected to provide an appropriate symbol of the country of which it is capital. It need not be *typical* of the country, but it must, in some sense, be *worthy* of its special designation. If it is not a seat of government, then this worth will tend to be expressed in cultural terms.

Anthony King (1993) has claimed that those capital cities which are also 'world cities' have a central role in sustaining a cultural hegemony which extends at least within their own territorial boundaries and often beyond. This hegemony privileges values, mores and ways of life which are followed by and/or help to justify the position of, powerful social groups. He suggests that there are specific mechanisms through which these cities play their part in this process; of particular interest to the theme of this chapter is his contention that the development of their built environment simultaneously expresses and helps constitute a cultural order. The spatial structure of the city, he points out, 'not only represent(s) a given social order, but, in [its] physical, spatial and symbolic forms actually participate[s] in the construction of social and cultural existence' (King, 1993: 263). Such construction, though, is not uncontested, and the development and the use of the built environment is a focus for the clash of material interests and cultural outlooks. This is a plausible interpretation of what occurred in Cardiff Bay in 1996 when ambitious (and expensive) proposals for a new opera house, to be designed by an internationally renowned architect and supported by members of the Welsh social élite, were characterized in the local media as élitist and 'out of touch', and failed to gain widespread public or (local) political support (Harris, 1996). The latter swung behind a different kind of 'flagship' project – the development of a multi-million-pound sports stadium as the national rugby ground, a proposal with its own set of socially, economically and politically influential supporters, and one which underlined a central strand in a conception of Welshness which is widely acknowledged within and outside the country.

Set-piece confrontations of that kind may steal headlines, but the cultural encoding of places is a process which continues day to day; for as Harvey (1989), among others, has pointed out, a particular configuration of buildings in space is open to a variety of readings, and can be used in a variety of ways. For example, Sibley (1995) points out the ways in which young people might wish to use shopping centres as spaces where they can just hang around, idly socializing, and how this use of space is contested by the owners of shops and shopping centres whose security guards move young people on if they are not obviously consuming. Shopping centres are places in which a certain pattern of behaviour, underpinned by a set of attitudes towards individual consumption, is encouraged, and is appropriate. If you are not able or willing to indulge in such consumption then you are to be made to feel out of place. In Cardiff, for reasons which are not entirely clear to the non-participant, some of the paved surfaces around the National Museum of Wales have become (in 1997) a favoured spot for young skateboarders, a use which is hardly compatible with the early twentieth-century vision of the marquess of Bute and city councillors who planned the quasi-colonial layout of Cathays Park with its ensemble of civic buildings clad in Portland stone. For the moment, the deviant use continues unchecked, and an alternative interpretation of what that space is for, what it means, is made available to passers by.

These differences (and conflicts) over use and meaning are the more complex in the case of *capital* cities because national identity – which at least some groups will want to see embodied in the city's structure – is itself a socially contested idea. As Penrose (1993: 28) puts it:

> the socio-cultural-political units which are commonly referred to as 'nations' are not immutable 'givens' but the product of human thought and action. The existence of nations is not a truth that human beings have *discovered* but a conceptualization of the world that we have *created*.

Social constructions of nationhood will incorporate what H. Moore (1994) has described in relation to gender construction as 'fantasies of power' – ideas about the 'proper' or 'appropriate' power (and other) relations between the nation being defined or constructed and other nations, or (more generally) any person outside the nation. They will also, typically, contain ideas about appropriate power relations *within* the nation – about the role of women, for example (the 'Welsh mam', as Beddoe (1986) notes, is an extraordinarily resilient component of a particular conception of Welshness). Promoting a particular sport as a national sport is not exempt from those relations of power. Rugby – both in its idealized form as an expression of individual athleticism, dexterity and courage combined with team spirit and in its somewhat brutalized reality of endemic violence and boozy off-field camaraderie – embodies particular conceptions of manliness, of masculinity and, by implication, femininity. The material underpinning of the sport, through the provision of a national stadium, reinforces these values and power relations. Where national identity is a focus for contemporary political conflict, and where cross-cutting such conflicts are struggles over racialized, gendered and class-related inequalities, debates over the development of a built environment appropriate for a new, and insecure, capital city will be complex and multi-layered. The remainder of this chapter provides at least a preliminary analysis of that process and some of its outcomes. It begins with a reprise of the fragility of Cardiff's status as capital, of why – in the phrase of an iconoclastic local MP – it remains at best 'half and half' a capital (R. Morgan, 1994).

Cardiff is a very new capital city, and its status is subject to conflicting interpretations. It was only in 1955 that it was designated as capital, fifty years after it had been accorded the status of city. Both these honours were bestowed by monarchs of a country (Britain) created – in practice – by submerging Welsh (and other) identities. The inevitable whiff of colonialism associated with a capital city's being *created* in the middle of the twentieth century reinforced long-standing resentments and suspicions elsewhere in Wales of Cardiff's right to some kind of symbolic leadership of the country simply because of economic pre-eminence based on an extraordinary spurt of demographic and economic growth in the latter half of the nineteenth century (Daunton, 1977). Whereas Edinburgh's status as capital city has never been questioned, however vibrant the economy of Glasgow (Hague and Thomas, 1997), Cardiff's claim to being capital largely rested on its being the largest settlement in the country – it played no significant role in the tortuous political history of Wales before the nineteenth century, and has no special cultural or religious significance to the Welsh population (J. Davies, 1993). Moreover, its sphere of economic influence in Wales has been considerably smaller than, say, that of London in England, or Paris in France: Cardiff has not historically been a financial or administrative nerve-centre because Wales has never been a coherent political unit. As a political project, then, Cardiff's designation as capital, and actions taken to bolster this status have been open to radically different interpretations. For bourgeois civic leaders becoming a capital city might represent a vital episode in a story of municipal self-assertion which began in the late nineteenth century with the weakening of the influence of the aristocratic Bute estate over city politics (J. Davies, 1988; Evans, 1985a). This story continued with bids for national institutions (the National Museum, the university college), and city status, and – in the 1990s – has included the proclamation by the city's political leaders of Cardiff's status as a major European city (Hague and Thomas, 1997). In the early stages of this process – in the confident south Wales of the turn of the century – the grandeur of Cathays Park was precisely the kind of symbol which would emphasize Cardiff's claim for preeminence. In later years, influential members of the labour movement in the city – such as those who were so suspicious of the rationale and need for city-centre redevelopment in the 1960s (see below) – have seemed (at times) to view the whole idea of being a capital as a potential diversion from major political tasks to be tackled, namely housing the working class and (especially from the late 1960s onwards) providing replacement sources of employment for declining manufacturing and heavy industry (N. Evans, 1985b; Imrie and Thomas, 1993).

We might speculate that Cardiff's Welsh-speaking middle class – most of them immigrants from elsewhere in Wales – might have their own distinctive perspective on the city's being a capital.[1] For the many working in the media, the university and the other public agencies, being a capital is the city's basis for their having employment of the kind they have. Some might view a strategy of Europeanization as potentially a dilution of that status; on the other hand, in a 'Europe of the regions' regional capitals would have an enhanced status (Harvie, 1994).

There have also been a variety of perspectives from outside the city. Rees and Lambert (1981) have analysed the way in which promoting Cardiff as a capital city has featured in the strategy of a broad-based regional coalition which, in the post-war period, has pressed for (UK) government (and, latterly, EU) financial assistance for economic development in the face of economic restructuring. Stoker and Mossberger (1994) have argued such coalitions need a common sense of purpose, and an ideology which can provide a common vision and obscure (or play down) differences of interest. Rees and Lambert (1981) argue that a construction of Welsh nationality, of Wales, as a significant economic and political unit with shared concerns, largely fulfils this role of providing an ideology for a coalition of interests which cuts across class – and Cardiff's physical development as a worthy capital city for a modernising country has symbolic significance within Wales. In practice, the conception of Wales (and of its capital) to which Rees and Lambert refer is one which stresses the centrality of the relatively recent industrialization of (primarily) south Wales, in particular the Valleys, and the distinctive communities which have developed there (Evans, 1996; Rees, 1997). The institutional expression of this coalition has had at its heart, for well over fifty years, the labour movement and its grip over local politics and agencies of governance. But the remarkable consensus over the desired trajectory of the Welsh (and, especially, south Wales) economy (and, with it, the kind of society to be created) has extended to other institutions, and other tiers of government: the Welsh Office's relations with local government, for example, have been noted for their lack of conflict over matters of principles, irrespective of party politics (Hambleton and Mills, 1993).

The survival of the Wales referred to above has been seen as depending on the capacity of the Welsh economy to modernize, to restructure sectorally and – to a limited extent – spatially. Cardiff has an important role in this strategy, for if manufacturing and heavy industry are being superseded as sources of employment by service-sector jobs, then what better flagship for the modern, service-led Welsh economy than a city in which service-sector employment has always been disproportionately important by national (UK) standards (H. Thomas, 1989). To be sure, a booming Cardiff must be balanced by a revitalized Valleys to which have been attracted clean, modern manufacturing, and successive Secretaries of State have tried to share state support between these competing objectives, but as long as there are no perceptions of gross injustice, this analysis and vision has been enough to sustain support across different classes and political parties for boosting Cardiff. And, within this vision, Cathays Park, while important, is less significant than a city form which functions effectively as an economic unit.

There are competing constructions of Wales, though. In particular, the notion of Wales as having a distinctive cultural identity, with the Welsh language playing an important (perhaps central) role in bolstering this, has remained politically potent in rural Wales, and has periodically been part of a political programme which has provided a refuge for the disaffected in labourist heartlands (though it is doubtful whether it is the cultural vision which has attracted supporters in these areas – Adamson, 1991a). From this perspective Cardiff's role is an ambiguous one – clearly the most likely Welsh town or city to impress as a modern city in the latter part of the twentieth century; but hardly a city which typifies or symbolizes the cultural distinctiveness of the country. If Laponce (1993: 411) is right and 'Bilingual capitals are sometimes at their most effective when they do not speak . . . [but unfortunately, too often] cannot be mute', it is difficult to see Cardiff as speaking anything other than English. With only 6 per cent of its population able to speak Welsh, and a cosmopolitan population quite different from that of the rest of the country, Cardiff must be as alien a city as Liverpool or Birmingham to many of those brought up in Welsh-speaking areas of Wales (Cardiff City Council, n.d.).

These concerns are little more than irritants for those committed to boosting Cardiff as an increasingly prosperous and attractive capital city. They rarely ruffle the Labourist, south Wales construction of Welsh nationality referred to earlier, and have little resonance in the city's local politics. It would be foolish to ignore them entirely, but more pressing for those involved in promoting the city has been the tension between developing the city's regional role (and aspirations to be taken seriously as a capital) and the rather more mundane need to deliver the goods to key constituencies within the city. It is the management of this tension which provides the immediate context for the shaping of the city's spatial structure. Unfortunately, in the absence of an authoritative account of post-war city politics, the discussion of the city's recent urban development must, inevitably, be somewhat speculative; though the author can draw upon interviews with prominent local and national politicians, some published autobiographies, as well as preliminary analyses of trades council archives, and selective accounts of some episodes of redevelopment.[2]

Redeveloping the City Centre: from the 1960s to the 1980s

In 1945, Jim Callaghan found the major concerns of the electorate of Cardiff were housing and reconstruction following wartime damage (Callaghan, 1987). In the mid-1970s, and through the 1980s, ensuring a steady supply of affordable housing (specifically in the form of peripheral housing estates) remained a major local authority concern; but it had been joined (arguably, even eclipsed, in importance) as a town-planning issue by city-centre redevelopment and enhancement (E. Davies, interview). This reorientation of political and professional interests initially owed little to local political pressure: the local labour movement was indifferent to, and periodically suspicious of, city-centre redevelopment throughout the 1960s and 1970s, while the Chamber of Trade also expressed reservations about ambitious plans in the late 1960s which would have disrupted existing business in order (in effect) to create better trading conditions for new competitors who would be attracted to the city.

The push for change came from the regional arm of central government, and increased in intensity in the early 1960s as momentum picked up for considerably more substantial devolution of governmental administration and policy-making to Wales than had hitherto been the case (Griffiths, 1996). In the latter years of the Conservatives' period in office, and into the mid and late 1960s, the idea took hold of a need for coherent regional responses to economic restructuring and development. In Wales, the creation of the Welsh Office and the production of *Wales The Way Ahead* was one manifestation of this (Griffiths, 1996; Rees and Lambert, 1981). So was central government's decision to fund perhaps the best known planning consultant of the day (Colin Buchanan) to produce a study of the capital city, which – in the words of Alderman H. E. Edmonds, chairman of the Public Works and Town Planning Committee – was

> a probe into the future of our city . . . [the consultants] . . . have looked at the likely growth of Greater Cardiff up to the year 2000. Within that setting they have looked at the changes that they think will be necessary to achieve a new city centre. A centre not only worthy of the citizens of Cardiff but also to serve adequately the needs of South Wales and indeed of the whole principality . . .
>
> We have a tremendous opportunity to create a worthwhile environment that will help us and especially our children to live in a fuller, richer manner; and we have a great responsibility to Wales to ensure that the centre of Cardiff is capable of providing the service expected of a capital city.
>
> This study is therefore put into your hands; I hope that all those who care for the beauty and prosperity of this City will read this and feel that they can contribute in their own way to the creation of a better and yet more prosperous Capital City of the Principality. Your City and mine. (Foreword to Buchanan and Partners, 1966)

Buchanan's so-called Probe Study (Buchanan and Partners, 1966) proposed a spatial expression of these sentiments. For the regional spatial coalition for which the Welsh Office was, at that time, a voice, visible commercial prosperity was a key criterion for an effective capital city of a modernizing region (or nation). Buchanan suggested a reorganization of the city centre which would create an efficient transport network (public and private) as it simultaneously defined orderly development areas for high land value uses – usually shopping and offices – by sweeping away (and reorganizing) the street patterns of areas of so-called obsolescence (typically, older working-class housing and warehousing on the fringes of the city centre (Dumbleton, n.d.)). The civic and national dignity of the city was emphasized: it proposed a national theatre, an opera house and major expansions of both the university college and the National Museum in Cathays Park and its environs (schemes which involved, *inter alia*, obliterating Park Place with its Victorian villas). This was decidedly a plan which gave priority to Cardiff's role as capital city – the grandeur of Cathays Park took precedence over the domestic simplicity of Park Place, the centre of gravity of shopping was to move decisively east from the locally owned department stores and small arcade traders of the St Mary's Street/Castle Street area, and small warehouses (and smaller houses) were to be replaced by offices and exhibition centres. Typical of the apparent lack of sensitivity to local sentiments was the study's proposal to relocate the Roman Catholic cathedral to an unspecified alternative location where it would not stand in the way of an efficient, rational (and profitable) redeveloped shopping area.

Buchanan's ideas for city-centre development were 'condensed' (Cooke, 1985: 219) into proposals agreed by property developers Ravenseft and the City Council in the late 1960s: the so-called Centreplan. Though the precise terms of the agreement changed as interest rates fluctuated and prospects for profit varied (Cooke, 1985), the main thrust was that the City Council would use its powers of compulsory purchase (subject to Welsh Office confirmation) to assemble sites and develop infrastructure, which could create conditions for profitable redevelopment by Ravenseft. Civic uses such as a national theatre were no longer included. The proposed redevelopment involved a physical restructuring of the city centre, and this was promoted as a strength of the scheme. An enormous wooden model, built to scale, was exhibited in the city centre, with new developments picked out in lighter wood. As if to emphasize the transformation, illustrations of the scheme portrayed an angular, futuristic townscape of high-level walkways, rushing traffic and modern materials (glass, steel, concrete).

In the event, Centreplan foundered in the property slump of the early 1970s. But while developers could walk away (albeit after the payment of compensation), the City Council was left with the task of redeveloping sites it had assembled through compulsory acquisition. Of necessity, a more cautious, piecemeal, approach had to be taken, with individual redevelopment packages being agreed for each major city-centre site, incorporating grants from the Welsh Office and the local authority as necessary (Hamilton, 1988). It was the late 1980s/early 1990s before the final major sites were redeveloped. The result has been a less radical visual transformation of the core shopping areas of the city, but the accomplishment, nevertheless, of significant changes in land use (as Buchanan originally envisaged) and a highway (and parking) network more attuned to car-borne shoppers and commuters.

Overall, the city centre has less design coherence than it would have had if Centreplan succeeded, and, to that extent, it is less impressive as a statement of civic pride and capital status. But it works: in the 1980s and 1990s retail turnover and rentals have been buoyant and office rentals – if not high – have not been embarrassingly below those of (say) Bristol. Cardiff can, just about, claim to be a part of the fabled M4 corridor west of London (see, for example, *Estates Gazette*, 1988). However, the redevelopment has been in essence the creation of a subregional centre, not unambiguously a capital city. A comparison with, say, Nottingham (a city of similar size) finds that both cities have similar mixes of shops, offices and leisure uses. This does not show the irrelevance of nationality, and being a capital, in Cardiff's redevelopment, but rather the *thin-ness* of the particular conception of being a capital which has political salience. Cardiff has enjoyed the consistent attention of the Welsh Office because it is the capital city: the status has also been an important element of local boosterist strategies. But for both these constituencies, being a capital has amounted, in effect, to being some kind of alleged economic motor for the subregion and the eventual pattern of Cardiff's city-centre redevelopment bears witness to this.

Even so, redeveloping the city centre has been a long and uncertain process demanding (and enjoying) a remarkable degree of consistent *local* political support as well as Welsh Office assistance in the form of grants, loan sanctions, confirmation of compulsory purchase orders and supportive planning decisions. The latter has been forthcoming throughout, for the strategic regional significance of Cardiff's modernization has never been questioned. The former has issued, in part, from the financial stake which the City Council has developed in the city centre, but it has also been consistently cultivated: for example, by ensuring that other local political concerns – notably housing and latterly economic development – have also received serious attention from planners, and by encouraging a perception of the city centre as a historically significant area, a perception which complements the modernizing strand in planning policy. Between 1974 and 1980 three conservation areas were designated in the city centre. Their boundaries carefully drawn so as not to impede realistic prospects for major redevelopment, these designations signalled to businesses outside the areas of greatest physical change that they were not being overlooked by planning policy. Some (relatively modest) material rewards have followed in the form of Welsh Office grants to help with refurbishment and external building works, with around £1 million in grant aid having been given by the late 1990s. Less tangibly, but no less importantly, the designation of conservation areas, the production of town trails of the historic city centre and the proliferation of blue plaques on historic buildings – all innovations in the city's planning in the late 1970s and early 1980s – resonated with the keen interest of apparently large numbers of residents of the city in local history. The remodelled city centre of the 1980s is touted as one worthy of a modern capital city, but care has been taken to create points of reference and a sense of ownership for a local audience.

Johnson has emphasized the significance of public statuary for shared meanings. He has argued persuasively that 'the space which . . . monuments occupy is not just an incidental material backdrop but in fact inscribes the statues with meaning' (1995: 348). The attempt to create a townscape which can simultaneously be interpreted in local *and* regional/national terms is perhaps nowhere better illustrated than by the statue placed in the St David's shopping centre, the flagship redevelopment of the new Cardiff, a Cardiff pre-eminent in Wales for its spaces of consumption, not spaces of culture or antiquity. Here we find Gareth Edwards, renowned Welsh rugby player from Wales's recent golden age. From its origins, rugby union has been a sport which (in Wales) recruited adherents across classes and whose growth in the nineteenth century coincided with and became an expression of Welsh nationalist sentiment (Smith and Williams, 1980). Thus the statue, in the St David's Centre, underlines the city's status as capital. But Edwards (whose roots were in west Wales) was, for many of his glory years, a player for Cardiff Rugby Football Club where he was the mentor of his successor, the decidedly homegrown Terry Holmes, and, as a consequence, the statue's impact is simultaneously national and local. This same requirement to manage the local and the national has also shaped the redevelopment of Cardiff Bay and here, too, we shall see that the shallowness of the construction of Cardiff's role as capital city has been exposed through struggles over the shaping of space.

Buchanan's studies and the ambitious sets of comprehensive redevelopment proposals to which they gave rise can be read as illustrations of the complex relationship between the state and a particular fraction of capital, namely that which organizes and depends upon the financing of development (Cooke, 1985). There can be little doubt that a vital strand in the story of Cardiff's city-centre redevelopment has been the need for the state to create profitable investment opportunities for property developers and commercial operators of particular kinds (notably, retail businesses, hotels and office users). Local authorities and central government worked together from the late 1960s to the late 1980s to appropriate land, subsidize risky development and share commercial risks in order to facilitate private investment, largely by national and internationally mobile capital (Cooke, 1985; Hamilton, 1988; Imrie and Thomas, 1993). But too intent a gaze on the pressure of capital on the state to facilitate development and the dependence of the state on private finance distracts attention from political choices (sometimes subtle) which are made about the *form* of development, and the need for complex political management to secure consistent state support.

In the case of Cardiff's city-centre redevelopment, the regional political coalition which envisaged Cardiff as having a key role in a modernizing Wales – whose point of view was expressed by Alderman Edmonds – saw a prosperous city centre (as measured, in part, by the rental levels, land values and spending by shoppers) as an important criterion of a modern regional capital. But this approach to restructuring space in the city was (at times) opposed by locally organized groups. Foremost among these were residents whose houses were to be adversely affected by parts of the ambitious Buchanan vision. Their protests met with mixed success. Working-class housing, often rented, close to the centre was swept away along with low-cost warehousing generally owned by local firms (Dumbleton, n.d.). Their continued presence was considered entirely incompatible on financial and symbolic grounds with the kind of modern city centre Cardiff was to have. On the other hand the plan for the notorious Hook Road – an inner distributor road – managed to offend both suburban and inner-city residents as it cut a swathe through the east of the city, largely affecting owner-occupiers. In the face of sustained opposition which was evidently going to translate into hostile votes it was the future Conservative leader of the council, Cardiff born and bred and a self-employed businessman, who bit the bullet and buried the road scheme (Hill, 1974). Councillor Watkiss was described by a one-time editor of the *South Wales Echo* as a 'Good Cardiff Boy' (H. Thomas, 1994), by which was meant that he was one of a smallish group of men influential in the city's public life who had roots in the city but were also attuned to the city's national role – they were senior councillors, members of boards of quangos, and editors of local newspapers such as himself. He implied that by virtue of their backgrounds and aspirations they internalized and managed a tension in the city's politics of urban development between delivering benefits to local residents and creating a city which could fulfil a significant material and symbolic role as a capital city. We have seen how in the city centre that process of management has helped influence the built form of the city – has underpinned conservation, for example – even if the major determinant of the centre's structure has been a particular conception of what modernization involves.

Regenerating Cardiff Bay

The Cardiff Bay urban development area is a tract of 2,700 acres in the south of the city. Since the late nineteenth century this has been a place of heavy industry, working-class housing and an economically and socially distinctive commercial and residential enclave associated (originally) with Cardiff's port (H. Thomas, 1989). In brief, this has been a poor and neglected part of Cardiff – an industrial area in a service-based city, and nineteenth-century residential areas in a city of peripheral expansion. Cardiff Bay Development Corporation (CBDC), set up in 1987 as a Welsh Office initiative with which local authorities reluctantly acquiesced (Edwards, interview – see n. 2), has a remit to change the Bay by promoting a spatial and physical restructuring which will facilitate its economic and social transformation. The corporation's *Regeneration Strategy*, adopted in 1988, envisages the development of three million square feet of new office space, 6,000 new homes (75 per cent owner-occupied) and a complex of leisure facilities of national significance (CBDC has adopted a target of attracting two million tourists annually to the Bay by the year 2000). Central to achieving these kinds of targets is a physical transformation of the area between the city centre and the city's waterfront, labelled in the strategy as 'the core', known to officialdom as Butetown, and to others by a variety of names (many referring to subtly different portions of it): Tiger Bay, the Docks, Rat Island, to give a few. For many people this strip of land, some mile or so long and less than that in width, is Cardiff Bay. The Cardiff buses which have 'Cardiff Bay' as their destination do not go to the fringes of the inner-city areas of Splott or Adamsdown but to Butetown. The renamed Cardiff Bay railway station is in Butetown. And if the corporation is to achieve one of its key objectives of 're-uniting Cardiff and its waterfront', then something radical must be done about the housing and industry in Butetown which has hemmed in the city centre to the south for a century.

It has been argued elsewhere that the Cardiff Bay project has been promoted as the latest phase in the modernization and boosting of the capital city (Thomas and Imrie, 1993a), this time attempting to project the city as a capital ('Europe's youngest') on an international stage. In interview, local government officers and local councillors have made it clear that promoting offices, leisure development and (preferably up-market) housing in the city's docklands was perceived as the only feasible response to a changing world – a world in which most footloose, private-sector investment was only interested in such developments and, as a corollary, where developments of such a kind were a mark of any serious engagement with modernity and progress. But the aspiration to create a city with European credentials has faced a stumbling block: the tract of land which is at the core of the 'new Cardiff Bay' has been the subject of stigmatization for a hundred years; it has been portrayed as 'dirty, violent diseased and immoral [while also] a mecca of racial harmony' (Jordan, 1988: 53).

Physical redevelopment, radical restructuring of space, has had the twin objectives, therefore, of first creating a pattern of infrastructure and land ownership which will facilitate profitable development (a long-standing function of state land-use planning – Fogelsong (1996) – and the task undertaken largely by local government in the redevelopment of Cardiff's city centre), and, secondly, recasting the image of the area, the old Tiger Bay and Docks, by reshaping its spaces. Central to Cardiff Bay Development Corporation's approach to this task has been a major restructuring of the spaces of Cardiff Bay. In most cases this has meant the creation of new kinds of space – for example, the new arc of entertainment on the waterfront includes Harry Ramsden's (family) fish and chip restaurant, the Techniquest hands-on science exhibition and a craft centre; swept away are the North Star club and other down-at-heel establishments of dubious repute. The waterfront is being reshaped to play a part in promoting Cardiff as a European capital, and the tiny dives are remnants of a time when (most of) respectable Cardiff chose not to visit the area. Their removal not only marks a change in the kinds of people for whom the Bay is to be a place of leisure; it also sweeps away the subversive potential for respectable values of racialized and sexualized popular music (Gilroy, 1987; Valentine, 1995). The Bay is being reclaimed for a modern Cardiff, fit for European exposure.

Yet the resident population of the area remains a population long constructed in popular stereotypes as different (and potentially dangerously so) from the remainder of Cardiff and Wales. If visitors and investors are to come to the Bay, then, they must be shielded from this population; this is a major function of the area's new highway network. Roads connect locations but, like features of the natural environment, can also be useful ways of delineating territory. Access to the new commercial and leisure attractions of Cardiff Bay is going to be swift, and direct. New dual carriageways already whisk visitors through the area without sight of Butetown.

They are safe corridors, spaces for visitors. The new roads are justified as essential underpinnings for increasing the area's commercial attractiveness: they are aimed at convenience, it is argued. There is much in this point, but convenience is compatible with territorial delineation, and in one spectacular instance it is evident that the latter is considerably more significant than the former. This is the plan for Bute Avenue, a £60 million tree-lined dual carriageway which is to be built between the city centre and the waterfront. The avenue is complex technically, inasmuch as preparatory work involves demolishing a railway embankment as well as relocating scores of small businesses. Considerable officer time at CBDC and in the local authorities has also been devoted to ensuring that the two ends of the avenue (in the city centre and the waterfront) will make connections of appropriate grandeur and dignity (H. Thomas, 1995). Grandeur and dignity is central to the project, for its necessity as a corridor for vehicles is not at all obvious. There already exists a dual carriageway link from the city centre to the waterfront, built in the late 1980s at a cost of £15 million; moreover, another existing road – Bute Street – runs in parallel with the line of the proposed Bute Avenue. Bute Street will remain, but as a service road for the Butetown housing estate; Bute Avenue will barely connect with Bute Street, and will allow visitors to enter the new Cardiff Bay without the need for contact with the old Tiger Bay. The scale of the new road is out of proportion with the amount of traffic likely to use it, which suggests that its development is more about making a statement about the new kind of place Cardiff Bay is going to be (and the kind of people who will be welcome there) while simultaneously cordoning off the potential embarrassment of visitors' first view of the area being a poor, multiracial council housing estate.

The Bute Avenue project is tantamount to a rejection of Cardiff Bay's history and the reality of contemporary disadvantage and discrimination. It illustrates that where the promotion of Cardiff as a Eurocapital demands an unambiguous symbolism from the built environment then the sensitivities of people who remain relatively powerless even within the city's politics, let alone Welsh politics, will be brushed aside. However, it appears that in the 1990s, as in the 1960s and 1970s, there remains a need to bolster political support for city boosterism, and the ensuring spatial restructuring, by providing some tangible benefits for working-class residents of the city. The *Regeneration Strategy* states that 25 per cent of all housing will be social housing, and the depressed housing market of the early 1990s has ensured that the proportion of social housing built to date in Cardiff Bay exceeds that target. The *new* social housing, however, is located on the fringes of the development corporation's area, well away from the 'core', and in marked contrast to the pre-1987 development of housing association flats for rent a stone's throw from the 'arc of entertainment'.

The development corporation has also recognized the impossibility of completely segregating or removing the resident population of Butetown. Two approaches have evolved as it attempts to reconcile its creation of a new Bay and what must appear to it to be the recalcitrant reality of the old; the delineation and definition of space is central to each. The first approach has simply been to provide tangible community benefits.[3] Whether these are in the form of training schemes for local residents (among others), a Youth Pavilion, or meeting rooms for local groups, they are – unambiguously – in marginal spaces. Thus the training centre and youth centre are in Dumballs Road, an industrial zone in which the corporation has declared itself unwilling to intervene – this will remain an area of small firms in low-rental premises and as such is clearly peripheral to the new Cardiff Bay.

A different approach has been to try to exploit the area's image, or at least some dimensions of it. It is plausible to speculate that the name 'Cardiff Bay', a coinage of the late 1980s, is designed to trade on the familiarity of Tiger Bay while simultaneously distancing itself from the latter's lurid reputation. Similarly, the area's maritime past has been referred to, in sanitized forms, in names of new housing and commercial development, such as Admiral's Landing and Windsor Quay (Thomas and Imrie, 1993b).

On at least one or two occasions, the corporation has attempted to develop this strategy beyond simply naming places. As with place-names, the strategy has been to try to exploit a sanitized, safe version of Butetown's racialized population. This approach was adumbrated in a chapter of the *Regeneration Strategy*, which contained an illustration of a street scene in the vibrant new multi-ethnic community which was to be created. In it, a number of visibly minority ethnic people were shopping in the Butetown Bazaar. This was an imaginary development and the illustration was intended to re-present the area's population – long stigmatized and racialized and the victims of acknowledged discrimination in the labour market – as a colourful, interesting ethnic mix, the kind of portrayal of ethnic diversity as spectacle which has become a staple global tourism product (Robins, 1997). In this case, and perhaps unsurprisingly, the representation was not sympathetically viewed by third- and fourth-generation non-white Butetown residents, who considered themselves *Welsh* people, not bazaar dwellers. No proposals for a bazaar have ever been produced – nor perhaps were the ideas ever more than flights of fancy, but they represent a skirmish in the campaign over the meaning of Butetown to outsiders and residents, and, incidentally, a skirmish over the construction of Welsh nationality (C. Williams, 1995).

A few years later, a similar approach informed the corporation's dealings with the Butetown Carnival Committee. This informal (and changing) group of local people organized an annual carnival, essentially as a local entertainment, though (as Jackson, 1989 points out) carnival is also an expression of popular control and enjoyment of particular spaces. CBDC became interested in grant-aiding the event, but only if it became a significant visitor attraction. Committee members were encouraged to look to London, Bristol and elsewhere as examples of the potential of the event. Very modest financial support was accompanied by attempts to force the organization to become considerably more formal and entrepreneurial; faced by local recalcitrance, CBDC hired a multicultural arts project from outside the area to run workshops for local children (with expertise imported from Latin America) on aspects of carnival (costume making and so on), a move which is most plausibly interpreted as an attempt to change the meaning of the carnival and of its claim to space (Thomas *et al.*, 1996). After a few years, the development corporation ran out of patience, and the carnival committee felt it preferable to retain control, albeit with a smaller budget: a modest attempt by CBDC to reinterpret some of Butetown's spaces had failed.

The way in which the corporation's attempted restructuring of the dockland spaces has sometimes successfully appropriated and reinterpreted Butetown's history of ethnic mix, racialization and conflict (Evans, 1980; Sherwood, 1991), is demonstrated by the fate of the Norwegian church. Originally a modest galvanized steel structure built to minister to the Norwegian sailors who frequented the port, the church had fallen into disuse and decay by the 1980s.

It stood in the path of the new peripheral distribution road, but the personal intervention of the then county council's director of environment saved it from destruction – it was removed, and stored. After considerable efforts by that individual and others the development corporation agreed to refurbish and relocate the church at a prominent position on the waterfront. In practice, the church has been largely reconstructed (albeit of Norwegian or otherwise authentic materials). It stands now a spruce, picturesque tea-room, exhibition space and meeting room; there is a persistent suggestion that a Roald Dahl museum be established in it. Taken from its spatial and historical context the Norwegian church helps re-present Butetown as a multi-ethnic mix which is palatable for middle-class tastes, the accident of Dahl's birth in Cardiff (of unusually prosperous Norwegian parents) a godsend to the marketing people.

Conclusion

There are no essential characteristics of capital cities; the content of the idea is shaped by the particular political circumstances in which it is used. The significance of episodes in which the idea is used to justify the restructuring of the built environment can only be understood, therefore, by setting them within their local political and cultural context. In the case of post-war development in Cardiff particular forms of redevelopment have been justified as being essential for the creation of a worthy capital for a nation whose economy is in the process of radical restructuring, and, in particular, is modernizing. This latter notion, in practice, involves an acceptance of an economic trajectory which is largely dictated by the requirements of capital, an acceptance that there is a single, modern path for the global economy which, therefore, it is imperative that regions like south Wales, or Wales as a whole, fit into, or risk being bypassed and, presumably, plunged into penury. This concern for modernizing, with its supplication to (supposed) international trends, drains the notion of national specificity, and of being a capital city, of a great deal of its significance. The result is that the rhetoric of being a capital city is used to help sustain political support for restructuring the built environment in ways which are not especially distinctive. This conclusion needs to be qualified a little. In certain cases (for example, the regeneration of Cardiff Bay) the project of reconstruction has faced difficulties caused by popular stereotypes of the nature of the area to be redeveloped. An understanding of the regeneration strategy must take full account of these popular constructions of place and the attempts being made to reshape them. We have seen that redevelopment proposals have been contested and that their implementation has been accompanied by initiatives which contrive to create meaningful spaces for potentially disaffected groups – notably, local residents. We have also seen how the interests of these groups have not been allowed to jeopardize the achievement of key elements of the restructured built environment. Similarly, in the city centre there have been attempts to create places which simultaneously strike national and local chords, and, it is argued, these manœuvrings are explicable only if the cultural encoding of the built environment is taken into account.

Notes

1. Speculation is the best that can be done because the role of Welsh-speakers in the life of Cardiff – economic, social and political – is largely unresearched.
2. Minutes and papers of Cardiff Trades Council are lodged with the library of University of Wales, Cardiff. Interviews cited in this chapter are with: E. Davies, City Planning Officer, Cardiff City Council 1974–87, and Nicholas Edwards (now Lord Crickhowell), Secretary of State for Wales, 1979–87.
3. The significance of the budget for community schemes varies, from year to year, but has generally been between 1 and 3 per cent of the corporation's budget. The material which follows draws upon research conducted with Sue Brownill, Konnie Razzaque and Tamsin Stirling on an ESRC-funded project, L311253060.

PART III　　　　　　　　　HERITAGE

10 Great Little Trains?: The Role of Heritage Railways in North Wales in the Denial of Welsh Identity, Culture and Working-Class History

Dave Marks

Introduction

The impetus for this chapter arose from my wider research into the slate heritage industry in north Wales. I observed that although apparently similar organizations were prominent players in the development of the heritage sites in both England and Wales, the portrayal of working-class history was usually approached in a quite different way. For example, in Wales there was usually a powerful notion of struggle. This was much less evident in the representations in England, where the working class were often represented in a more sentimental and benign way. The slate museums of north Wales arguably reflect both the Welsh and the (dominant) English traditions. The particular discourses presented in the heritage sites are argued to be strongly related to the history and economic development of the particular site and the way the new layer of economic and cultural development has interrelated with the old. All the representations in the slate heritage sites do, however, acknowledge the Welsh dimension in some way (Marks, 1996).

A striking exception to this Welsh presentation are the narrow-gauge heritage railways – the Great Little Trains. The history of slate, for example, arguably the most Welsh of Welsh industries, seems to have disappeared. The railway appears to have been removed from its particular industrial and cultural history and re-packaged and reconstituted as an ahistoric, acultural and apolitical heritage experience – a ribbon development of Englishness winding its way through a heavily Welsh-speaking, culturally nationalistic region. In this chapter I shall demonstrate how the present debates about the meaning and role of heritage can provide insights which illuminate the process and character of the heritagization of two slate transport networks, the Llanberis Lake Railway and the Ffestiniog Railway. Such insights are needed to explore the implications of these processes for Welsh culture and working-class identity and to assess the possibilities for the reclamation of the history of this industry and this region by its people.

Theoretical Issues

Clearly all places have a history and the passing on of shared histories through living memories (Samuel, 1994), such as stories, poems, songs, paintings and embroideries, can be seen as part of a positive interpretive tradition (Uzzell, 1989). The development of heritage sites can be argued to be the institutionalization of this tradition. Heritage centres, museums and environs can be argued to fulfil two roles, on the one hand as an interesting or fun day out, and on the other, as an educational experience. It is not always easy to separate these roles, as Walsh (1992) has noted. In the case of the slate railways, though, the problem has been side-stepped – the educational dimension is yet to begin.

The growth of commodified heritage attractions is a development that Bennett argues to be as significant as the transition of the semi-private museum to the state-controlled institution: 'dedicated to the instruction and edification of the general public' (1988: 63). Today most heritage attractions have an entry fee and more and more forms of heritage and culture are bought and sold like any other commodity – part of the 'cultural logic of late capitalism' (Jameson, 1991).

Hewison (1987) has argued that the positive values of past heritage myth-making – stewardship, scholarship and identity – are subverted by this commodification. The commodification of heritage and culture can also be argued to be part of the process that fragments local people and separates them from their history (Bennett, 1988). In the case of north Wales, *cultural* commodification has a further dimension. English approaches to heritage may alienate local Welsh people because of the particular way their local history and culture are represented in these discourses or, in the case of the slate railways, not represented. Welsh industrial history may have been subordinated by particular discourses related to other agendas. This ethnic dimension may result in the marginalization of Welshness and lead to a subliminal acceptance of the Welsh being part of England.

So the transition from history to heritage and from heritage to heritage industry is problematic. Uzzell (1989) suggests that it is through interpretation that history becomes heritage, that memories become alive. But interpretation is not a neutral process. There are power relations in the selection of heritage and in the creation and interpretation of the history it represents. Samuel (1994 and 1995) argues strongly that in the end power lies with the people and their capacity to reinterpret and subvert the heritage representations, but others cited here are more doubtful.

Power, it can be argued, still lies in the hands of those who hold the material, those who research it and those who decide how and if it should be represented – which stories should be told, whose stories should be told. Though it may elicit different responses from the audience, the script in the theatres of memories are written by the producers. Given the inequality of the relationship between the producer and receiver, and the potential utility of heritage as an instrument of social control, the danger is that heritage becomes not an opportunity for people to recapture their past and through it understand their present, but rather the 'handmaiden of oblivion' (Wright, 1995). The ideological function of heritage in maintaining stability – and the existing political power structure – and the use made of it by those in power is strongly noted by many of the protagonists in this debate. Bennett argues that the whole way in which working-class culture is represented is 'often so mortgaged to the dominant culture that "the people" are encountered usually only in those massively idealized and deeply regressive forms which stalk the middle class imagination' (1988: 64).

The representations found at industrial heritage sites inevitably contain discourses of history offering a variety of interpretations of working-class life and also frequently the more traditional insights into bourgeois achievements. Those at the slate mines of Gwynedd, however, are somewhat more complex to unravel because there are also contrasts between the Welsh cultural background of the quarrymen and that of the quarry management who were linked directly to English social and cultural structures. This results in a division of labour which frequently has both a cultural and a class dimension. The ethnic dimension is revealed to be even more complex in Blaenau Ffestiniog where there appear to be different ways of presenting the history of the same industry at the two different heritage sites there (Marks, 1996). It would seem that different cultures expressed through different ownership legacies may have had an effect on how the industrial heritage of the same place is represented. This will be shown to be particularly pertinent in the heritagization of the slate railways.

There are some clues offered in the above discussion as to why it is industrial heritage in particular that has been the focus of the heritage industry's development. It is no longer the secure age of village communities that is longed for. The hardships, injustices and insecurities of such past lives are prominent in the representations of the heritage industry. The new golden age is that of industrialism. The time when jobs were secure and the futures of those who were members of a leading manufacturing nation known and predictable. Thus Hewison argues that heritage can be best conceptualized as a replacement industry. The industrial workplace and its associated community is disappeared by the death squads of multinational companies and neo-liberal politicians and philosophers – to be replaced by – a museum. A nice little earner for a few, a job for a few more and a desperate search for roots, for identity, for something firm by the masses. In this search the past is written and rewritten and a protective illusion created. So a new imagined community, a new social cohesion arguably, may emerge from the shared consumption of the cultural and material products of the heritage industry.

Thus the industrial heritage industry may be part of the recipe for a crumbly and elastic cement, specially designed for the fragmented individuals of the postmodern age. In the case of the slate railways though, it will be argued that their industry is not represented at all. The comfort here may come from a closely (very closely in the case of some of the tiny railway carriages!) shared and enjoyable experience, a taste of a bygone age of steam when the pace of life seemed retrospectively more human. In other words a communal participation in nostalgia, a communal withdrawal from the 'bad things in life' and, perhaps, a distraction from engagement with the process of changing them (Brecht, 1990).

Clearly then, in north Wales as elsewhere, a heritage site does not only consist of the formal museums. It also incorporates a particular heritage environment. The slate heritage industry is part of a spectacle in which the individual sites could be considered as separate attractions by both the visitors and the operators. The mountains and coast of north Wales are holiday destinations, so the heritage attractions are promoted as part of a day out when on holiday rather than as a heritage destination in themselves. The Great Little Trains are both a heritage spectacle in themselves and a means of viewing the wider spectacle, and participation is as real passengers as well as participating as the voyeurs or actors associated with the customers of most heritage attractions.

Spectacular Snowdon

Arguably then, it is the whole environment that is the heritage spectacle. Nowhere is this more apparent than in Snowdonia. In Llanberis, the once industrial village at the foot of Snowdon, there is little immediate evidence that a major industry was once located in the vicinity. Nature has reclaimed the slate tips and transformed them into a beautiful 'natural' environment, a haven for trippers and tourists. Nevertheless the village has not been 'beautified' and 'made picturesque'. It has not been subject to the 'heritigization of space: the reduction of real spaces to tourist space' (Walsh, 1992: 4). The main street does not consist of craft shops but the shops and facilities of everyday life: Co-op, library, schools, butcher's, and so on. It is still possible to live out a life there, and the Welsh language is still important – useful enough to be spoken by the owners of the Chinese takeaway, if not the English-owned businesses!

Yet the old slate industry is no longer welcome. A recent proposal to reopen old quarry workings on the western slopes of the village met with local as well as wider resistance in spite of its potential for creating much-needed skilled jobs. This is an interesting separation of picturesque tourism from industrial work which puts the past firmly where it belongs – in the museum. This reinforces the point Walsh makes that:

> Since the nineteenth century representations of the past have, perhaps unwittingly in most cases, contributed to a form of institutionalised

rationalisation of the past. As people have been distanced from the processes which affect their daily lives, the past has been promoted as something which is completed, and no longer contingent upon our experiences in the world. (Walsh, 1992: 2)

Massey in her consideration of place-bound identities makes a similar point. She argues:

> traditions do not only exist in the past. They are actively built into the present also. The concept of tradition which sees in it only nostalgia understands it as something already completed which can now only be maintained or lost. It is already something from which we feel ourselves inexorably, inevitably distant. Talking of places as 'unspoilt' evokes just this notion. (Massey, 1995: 184)

The Llanberis Lake (Padarn) Railway represents an interesting example of just such a nostalgic way in which the past heritage of the slate industry is being reworked and reconceptualized economically and culturally. This railway is presently owned by Rheilffordd Llyn Padarn Cyfyngedig (Ltd.), though Parc Pardarn is managed by Gwynedd County Council. The discursive unpacking of timetable and information leaflet produced by the company to promote the railway provides some interesting insights into this heritagizing process. The leaflet shows a photograph of happy-looking children hanging out of the windows of a narrow-gauge steam train, on its front cover. Inside is the timetable, prices and more happy children. The short text promotes a sight-seeing trip: 'From your seat in the comfortable enclosed coaches you can enjoy spectacular views of Snowdon and the surrounding high mountains.' English pronunciations are given in brackets following the Welsh place-names, which is an interesting contrast with the English-dominated Ffestiniog Railway which will be considered later. The back pages contain mainly a colourful illustration of the train's route, showing some of the attractions that can be viewed and visited from it. While the Welsh Slate Museum is listed among these attractions, no indication is given that the slate industry and railway are historically connected. The original railway was an integral part of the old slate industry and was built by the Dinorwic Quarry to transport finished slates to its own port near Caernarfon, Port Dinorwic (Felinheli in Welsh). Its slate past has however been reconstructed in the present heritage industry.

In this case it is not the slate past that is being presented and represented but a romanticized *timeless* idealization: 'Nothing evokes more nostalgia than the age of steam. Steam engines, travelling at a snail-like pace through the countryside for a mile or two, drawing passenger-laden coaches, provide a romantic picture of "the good old days"' (Jenkins, 1992: 57). Connections can be made here with Gramsci's idea of folklore being 'studied as a "picturesque" element' (Bennett, 1988: 63) thus removing the visitor from the seriousness of the original article thereby suppressing history and its associated political and collective identities (Jameson, 1991). It may also remove the visitor from the 'alien world' of the present (Turner, 1990: 149) and by concentrating on 'the good things of the past' prevent engagement that might change 'bad things of the present' (Brecht, 1990). But *purpose* may be part of the 'full meaning' (Baudrillard, 1983) of this 'wilful nostalgia' (Robertson, 1990) and the purpose of this discursive formation may have ideological and cultural dimensions which both transcend and articulate with the profit imperative of late capitalist society.

Interestingly, though, in this renaturalized environment strewn with the abandoned and overgrown relics and ruins of the old slate industry, the lake railway is the only representation of the past at Padarn to be taken out of its original context. This reconceptualization has happened in a number of ways. Although the railway runs on part of the trackbed of the original industrial slate railway, that is the only similarity with the past. The railway was completely rebuilt in a smaller gauge, using small engines and new carriages, and runs to a picturesque picnic location at the lakeside, rather than the original Felinheli harbour. Heritage here could be considered as 'a place where men make videos and women are left holding the baby' (Crang, 1994: 350).

A further aspect of the enterprise differs from the organization of the other slate railways. When the enterprise was set up an agreement was reached to employ paid labour rather than volunteer labour. This arrangement also exists on the Snowdon Mountain Railway (built and still used purely as a tourist railway), but differs from the other Little Trains of Wales which rely heavily on volunteer labour. Interestingly, I observed on a visit to the Snowdon Mountain Railway, while all the manual staff appear to be local Welsh-speaking, talking amongst themselves in Welsh, the management (two men in grey suits) were obviously English. They communicated with the employees in English. I witnessed exactly the same phenomenon at Llechwedd Slate Caverns. Clearly further research would be necessary to confirm these observations, but they would seem to show that the cultural and class dimensions of the division of labour that existed during the English ownership of the slate quarries and railways (R. Merfyn Jones, 1982), are mirrored today. Though, as Giggs and Pattie point out, 'links between class and ethnicity and language in Britain have been under-researched' (1992a: 273).

A Ribbon Development

From the beauty and romance of Padarn and Llanberis the contrast with Blaenau Ffestiniog could hardly be more stark. Here is a town which has not escaped its slate-industry past – only the relative economic prosperity it brought has gone. Here the whole town is a living museum to slate. Mountains of grey slate debris surround it, looming threateningly as the coal tips once did in Aberfan. Slate dust seems to seep through its pores, be dissolved in its grey rain and reflected in its grey skies. The greyness is all pervasive. Everything seems to be built of slate – buildings, walls, streets, pathways – even the mountains themselves. This is not a tourist town.

Yet tourists come here. At least they come to the formal museums on the outskirts of the town and they come via the Ffestiniog Railway to the town centre. Like the Llanberis Lake Railway, the Ffestiniog is an example of how part of the history of a place can be marginalized in the reconstruction of that place in the heritage spectacle. Again the information leaflet and timetable make interesting reading. It is promoted as 'The Oldest Independent Railway Company in the World' and the logo is a steam locomotive. The front-cover illustration is strikingly similar to that of the Llanberis Lake Railway, except that it is the engine driver not children who are visible. This leaflet could, therefore, be making an appeal not only for the paying customers who will ride on the train, but also for volunteers for its unpaid workforce. The opportunity is being offered to every steam-age (modernist!) schoolboy to fulfil his childhood dream of becoming an engine driver.

Like the Padarn leaflet, the inside also describes the journey and the attractions on route. There is no help with the Welsh pronunciations here though. The Welsh language is still visible, however. I was told that it was 'policy' to have some Welsh on the leaflet. 'Tourists like it' was the explanation. This is still a predominantly Welsh-speaking area and it would seem that the living local language is being reduced into a quaint text of a fairy tale, part of the romanticized spectacle of a historic-train journey separated from history. There is little acknowledgement by the Ffestiniog Railway of the importance of language as part of cultural heritage or as communication and certainly no acknowledgement of its 'close association with certain institutions'. As Jones (1952) cited in Pryce (1986: 33) argues: 'the significance . . . of language can easily be underestimated . . . Welsh remains the indispensable medium for expressing Welsh cultural values.' Wright's 'handmaidens of oblivion' may have been busy here!

The leaflet's brief text makes no reference to the railway's history. The map of the route shows the forests, lakes and mountains and the villages that the train passes through. Once again it is the journey, landscape and the comforts offered on the train which are promoted. Only the more dedicated railway enthusiasts will endeavour to seek out the railway's slate past. This may not always have been the case. There was no free leaflet at the time, but the 1957 map was readily and cheaply available. It was produced by the same railway company and shows the same route passing through the same places, but here it is not the features of the landscape that are marked but the quarries and the inclines which linked them to the railway. Particular parts of the map are enlarged insets. Porthmadog is featured in both publications. On the 1995 leaflet it is illustrated by a photograph showing the train steaming through the natural environment as it approaches the town and by a sketch of the town centre locating the station, car park, supermarket and petrol station. The 1957 inset featuring Porthmadog also locates the station, but the other features located are the many slate wharfs, the timber yard, weighing building and the railway turntables. The other stations and 'attractions' featured on the earlier map all illustrate the railway's industrial use. On the 1995 leaflet the only reference to the slate past is nostalgic railway-buffery, Victorianized under the banner of SPECIAL TRAINS: 'Victorian Excursion Trains . . . Take the opportunity to travel on The

Ffestiniog Railway's unique collection of Victorian rolling stock. Gravity slate trains will be run. Period costume'. The back page promotes the other activities of the company – literature, gifts, holidays, restaurants as well as an appeal for those interested to join the Ffestiniog Railway Society and give financial or volunteer support to the railway. Clearly there has been a discursive change in the representation over the last forty years.

There are further interesting issues here. The first concerns the way the railway today may be seen in a completely different light by the tourists and railway enthusiasts who visit it in droves, to its original *raison d'être*. It seems probable that the majority of passengers see the railway as one way of viewing the scenery in the Snowdonia National Park, or as a rather quaint ride on a small steam train. Certainly this is how it is commercially promoted. There is a dichotomy between the present 'heritage trains' and the original purpose of the railway. The presentation of the railway is aimed at steam-railway nostalgia and landscape heritage rather than industrial heritage – which could have been conceptualized as 'a quarryman's journey', for example. This story is told, but only on special heritage occasions. In its re-presentation the railway has become a separated attraction from the rest of the slate heritage industry though it was an inseparable part of the actual industry. This is a further example of 'the disappearance of the original and real historical referent' (Lash and Urry, 1987: 298) to which Jameson (1991) and Lash and Urry (1987) refer. An analogy could also be made here with West (1988: 67) and his point regarding artefacts at Beamish being removed from their social context: 'the tendency is for them (artefacts) to be severed of such associations and to serve, instead, as vehicles for the nostalgic remembrance of sentimentalized pasts'.

This railway is, however, inseparable from the history of the slate industry, the people who worked in it and the communities sustained by it. It was built in 1836 with the sole purpose of transporting slate from the mines at Blaenau Ffestiniog to the purpose-built harbour at Porthmadog. Later on, the railway was used to convey the quarrymen to their various places of work. It was never conceived as a tourist railway, although passengers were carried when the slate industry went into decline and the Company sought additional revenue through diversification. The railway closed completely soon after the Second World War and was revived on a partial basis by a group of railway enthusiasts in the early 1950s.

During this period, the slate past may have been closer to enthusiasts' interests, but the language of the industry was not, and this has not changed. In the quarterly journal sent to the Ffestiniog Society's members, the magazine is titled: CYFNODOLYN RHEILFFORDD FFESTINIOG RAILWAY MAGAZINE. In all other references in the journal the English spelling Festiniog is used and this is the 'normal' spelling in other publications. This is not accidental. The original railway was opened by an English company who spelled the name in the English way. It is argued by the society that this spelling is maintaining the historic connection. It is interesting that the society is anxious to maintain this particular historic connection while all other 'historic connections' are annihilated. In references to the railway in Welsh publications, such as those produced by the local authority, Ffestiniog is spelt the Welsh way within English-language texts. Either could be conceptualized as historically correct.

The railway is sustained through the support of a very large railway preservation and conservation movement whose members offer financial support and give their time and labour free of charge. There is a further interesting dimension here. This concerns the involvement, or the apparent lack of involvement, of the local Welsh-speaking community. This is the dimension where there is a dramatic difference from the way that the Llanberis Railway is organized. Although the Ffestiniog Railway runs through one of the largest Welsh-speaking area in Wales there is rarely any Welsh heard on the railway. The small number of full-time staff employed on the railway appear to be mainly English and the volunteer labour, provided by the Ffestiniog Railway Society, are also drawn predominantly from the English regions. Of the thirteen officers of the three organizations associated with the Ffestiniog Railway – the Society, the Company and the Trust – whose addresses are listed in the railway journal, only two have a Welsh address. Neither live in north Wales. Surnames that are obviously Welsh are remarkably absent from the very long list of named officers.

No local support group is listed in the journal – the only Welsh group identified being situated in Cardiff. A member of the Ffestiniog Railway management told me that he thought this lack of interest in Wales was a legacy of the obsession of English men with playing trains. Where Welsh volunteers do take part they are obliged to speak the dominant language in order to communicate. The dominant language of the region may be Welsh but on the ribbon of development that constitutes the Ffestiniog Railway it is without doubt English. This means Welsh railway enthusiasts and volunteers participate on English terms, if they participate at all. The lack of a local group of supporters and the inaudibility of the Welsh language does suggest that Welsh railway enthusiasts mostly choose not to participate in this venture.

A further aspect of this cultural separation can be found in the heritage displays, shops and cafés situated on the stations – stations which are usually geographically distanced from local centres of population, viewing and shopping. They are staffed and managed by the Society's volunteers so there is little articulation with the local economy or culture. It is as if the railway is a narrow swathe of English eccentricity, English people playing with trains, oblivious to or completely ignoring the Welsh industrial and cultural part of the railway's history. But the Ffestiniog Railway is just as much part of the slate heritage scene as the quarries and mines themselves, and the way it is used and perceived (commodified) within the leisure/spectacle rubric could be argued to be part of 'the history making business . . . through which it legitimizes its view of history' (West, 1988: 38). West was making this point in respect of Ironbridge Gorge Trust, but there is an extra cultural dimension here – the relationship of dominance and subordination between England and Wales, between the English and the Welsh. This has deep historic roots which are invisible in the heritage representation.

The slate museum at Llechwedd in Blaenau Ffestiniog is one place where one history of the railway can be uncovered. The surface attractions here include a small exhibition, 'Slates to the Sea', which considers the role of the transport systems that were involved in moving the slates, notably the Ffestiniog Railway which was connected to the Llechwedd slate mine. The presentation is interestingly dissimilar to the slick, Disneyesque 'postmodern' style of presentation in the rest of the museum. Just as the railway can be seen as a relic from another age so can the displays in this museum. This is a 'modern' museum and most of the exhibits are large (rather battered and faded) photographs with lengthy

(English) annotations. There is no spectacle here for immediate consumption. Only those visitors already sufficiently interested in the 'story' are likely to be exposed to the time-specific story being told. The rest walk in and out very quickly from this 'unspectacular' display.

Today the Ffestiniog Railway terminates in Blaenau town centre, rather than at the foot of Llechwedd's haulage incline and buses convey tourists to the heritage mine, so it is still an important part of production – but heritage not slate production. It no longer transports slates to the sea; rather, it transports an already captive railway clientele through the turnstile at Llechwedd!

The story of the railway and its heritagization still continues. It has recently received grant aid from the Welsh Office of around £500,000 for improvement to facilities, including major developments at the Blaenau end of the line which it is hoped will entice some of the tourist traffic which passes along the A55 Conwy Valley corridor. This is the same traffic flow that the two slate mines rely on. This development and grant aid is part of a broader package of improvements for Blaenau Ffestiniog and other initiatives are being coordinated by the local district council. The main impetus has come from the closure of Trawsfynydd nuclear power station, which employed 600 people and was the largest employer in the area. The intention is to encourage alternative economic initiatives in the area. One such alternative is tourism based on the area's past. The industrial and cultural legacy is therefore an important component of regeneration. The Ffestiniog Railway will therefore compete with the slate mines in Blaenau for tourist trade, but without any significant local Welsh participation. It seems that the English still control a major part of Welsh history without involving the Welsh or even acknowledging that they were ever involved, a point reinforced by Gwyn Alf Williams who noted that a 'great deal of Welsh history has been Welsh history with the Welsh left out' (1982: 26).

A further project may be about to continue this process. The sum of £4.4 million has just been received from the Millennium Commission to facilitate the rebuilding of another railway with its history in slate. Presently the remnant of the Welsh Highland Railway consists of half a mile of track at Porthmadog. The proposal is that the rebuilt railway will run all the way to Caernarfon. When it was part of the transport infrastructure of the slate and copper industries it ran only as far as Rhyd-ddu (the station inevitably was given the English name of South Snowdon) near Beddgelert. It was eventually extended to Porthmadog in 1923, but by then the slate industry was in decline. It was then promoted also as a tourist railway but did not prove successful and closed in 1937 (Baughan, 1980). Thus this railway also has an important, if short-lived, tourist heritage. The Ffestiniog Railway Company have won the right to build and operate this railway. It will be interesting to see which history, if any, is promoted.

The Other End of the Line

Another town which was a major centre of the old slate industry is Porthmadog. It has taken yet another path in its tourist development. Here it is the natural environment which predated the slate industry which is being promoted. Most vestiges of the old industry have been long cleared away. Holiday flats have now been built on the site of the old shipyards, where they built the famous Porthmadog Schooners that transported slate all over the world. Between 1826 and 1913, 259 ships were built here, but the harbour is now filled mainly with pleasure craft. The Ffestiniog Railway is a notable survivor of this clearance but, as described above, its heritage role has been reorientated and reworked.

There is also a small museum devoted to the railway. This is situated at one end of the café in the Harbour Station. Here the presentation is largely photographical and the displays, like those in the 'Slates to the Sea' exhibition at Llechwedd, are reminiscent of those usual in the 1950s and 1960s. However, there are some interesting aspects to be noted. In contrast to the other museums of the north Wales slate industry, here, like the railway, the displays are largely removed from their social context. This, arguably, mirrors the organization of the Society which operates the railway and the interests of the Society's members and volunteers. Hence much of the emphasis here is a technocratic one. There are lots of photographs of steam engines annotated with a wealth of technical details. There are other artefacts and mechanical devices connected with the railway, engineering details of how the line was constructed but little about the industry it served or the workers and communities affected by it. This is very much a technocentric discourse. Great men also figure largely in this history. The museum is a male domain where bored accompanying females allow their menfolk to indulge their eccentricity or where the female members of the family opt out of heritage in favour of the consumption of food and drink in the adjacent café.

This is altogether a very male discourse and a very powerful one, but it is not the only discourse in this interesting little museum. While the slate history of the railway is acknowledged by two large photographs and a truck in one corner laden with the last load of cut slates to be transported, the innumerable other exhibits refer only to the line's historic role as a *tourist* railway. That this was a small part of the line's function is not discernible. Many of the exhibits are advertising memorabilia which describe the line as a 'faery railway' or a 'toy railway'. It is unlikely that the cold, wet quarrymen travelling in its very basic carriages would have described it as such! But their story is absent. The past and present are not being completely disassociated or de-historicized – there was a tourist past but it was insignificant to the railway's industrial function. Nevertheless it is the story of this tourist past that has been selected to be told and it is in this stated continuum with the present that the railway is being de-historicized and de-politicized.

A further interesting aspect of the displays is that not a single Welsh word invades them. Every piece of memorabilia – promotional leaflets and posters, official correspondence, and so on – is written in English. This is still a predominantly Welsh-speaking area, but at the times contemporaneous with the exhibits there would be few, if any, local people who did not speak Welsh as their first language and many who did not speak English at all. For example, in 1891 in the Ffestiniog district, 21,500 people spoke only Welsh, 4,200 were bilingual (mostly women in service with English families) and 700 spoke only English (R. Merfyn Jones, 1982). Imperialism would seem a useful word to sum up the relationship of dominance and subservience between the English and the Welsh during the historical period covered by the museum. In this still predominantly Welsh-speaking area all the exhibits were annotated in English. How much has changed?

Concluding Remarks

Place – and its history – is the outcome of a multi-layered power struggle. It is clear that place-based culture and identity does not refer only to places on a map but to places in time and space: 'constantly shifting articulations of social relations through time; and to think of particular attempts to characterise them as attempts to define, and claim coherence and a particular meaning for, specific envelopes of space-time' (Massey, 1995: 188). The places associated with the historic slate industry and present slate heritage industry can be seen to be extraordinary culturally complex. The relationship between the English and the Welsh over a long period of time is a crucial relationship here and perhaps spills over into even the academic world. The heritage industry in north Wales may offer an opportunity to transcend this and make visible the lost history. But the constraints of the unequal relationship are arguably still in place and will be a factor which will influence how far Welsh people may try to do this, and the degree of their success.

The particular heritagization of the slate railways could be conceptualized as one outcome of this continuing power struggle. While other heritage representations have Welsh dimensions of varying strength (Marks, 1996), the history of the slate railways belongs as surely to the English bourgeoisie as did the original transport system. So far this history has not been reclaimed by the Welsh men and women who made it. The railways are now an anachronistic English heritage phenomenon which the critiques of the heritage industry discussed here have helped to illuminate. The railways have, though, provided a vehicle for the examination of the complex cultural factors relating to Welsh ethnicity and the historic power relations between the English and Welsh. These add a further cultural dimension to the debates about the commodification and industrialization of heritage which I have only begun to explore in this chapter.

11 Territoriality and Heritage in South Wales: Space, Time and Imagined Communities

Bella Dicks and Joost Van Loon

Introduction

In this chapter we consider how the cultural category of 'community' – germane to the question of 'Welsh identity' – is constructed and mediated through representational forms. We want to interrogate how a community (a 'common-unity') of social, spatial and temporal elements is imagined at sites of public representation, and how this unity appears in different guises: the nation, the region, the locality. We argue that national as well as local collective identities are organized through symbolic forms. These symbolic forms are created and disseminated by a wide range of technologies of representation.

Focusing on a south Wales heritage centre as a particular ensemble of representational technologies, we appropriate the term *territoriality* to describe the way in which collective identities are imagined. Territoriality operates through the fixing of cultural boundaries. This fixing takes the form of myths that are imposed upon and come to stand in for (hence supplement) the divergent histories and geographies of 'places'. Territorializing myths turn the conflicting, diverse and heterogeneous fields of local social life into narratives of *identity*. They depend on the establishment of boundaries, which position the Other as a spatio-temporal differential to be colonized by the Same.

Territoriality has a double function: differentiation and integration. Differentiation spells out relations of difference, both as the external exotic Other and the stranger within. Integration, on the other hand, seeks to cultivate particular qualities as universal – to become an expression of collective 'identity'. 'Community' is thereby constructed not only through boundaries drawn between it and 'the outside', but also through internal distinctions which specify what is/is not 'its' identity. Both forces presuppose each other and operate in a dialectical relationship, since identity depends on the specification of both difference (what does/does not belong) and similarity (what it is that is shared).

We shall begin with a brief but critical account of the way in which space and time have been configured in theories of nations and nationalism. This provides us with a theoretical apparatus for understanding the mythical figurations of community which anchor historical narratives into a timeless obviousness. We will pay particular attention to the significance of 'marginality' in establishing the cutting edge of territorialized identity formations. Following Said (1978) and Bhabha (1990), we argue that 'national identities' always-already entail a spatio-temporal *residue*, which cannot be fully absorbed by the homogenizing force of (symbolic) representation.

In order to substantiate our argument, we apply the notion of territoriality to a discussion of the modes of representation implied in local heritage centres. Unlike national-collection museums, which seek to historicize the nation through displaying its cultural antiquity and inheritance (Anderson, 1991), local heritage sites represent another form of collective identity, the 'local community'. They are primarily concerned with the ordinary everyday, working and domestic lives of people living in a designated locality. However, these local identities are often articulated in particular ways to wider (regional and national) formations. The question we want to raise here is: how do heritage sites configure this relation between the local and the national? This is particularly pertinent in the case of the contested 'identity' of Wales, since the question arises of how narratives of *local* identity reference the wider collectivity of the fledgling nation-in-waiting.

We are also interested in what this can tell us about the mechanisms through which various forms of collective identity come to be naturalized in symbolic forms. We argue that community-as-nation and community-as-locality are constructed through the same processes of spatial and temporal differentiation, since the specification of *nation* always implies the other levels of the *sub-* and *supra*-national. However, the very coexistence of both national and local heritage sites (for example, the National Museum of Wales and the Rhondda Heritage Park) suggests that there is a sense in which each is making different cultural appeals.

We shall endeavour to unpack what this difference might comprise in the second section of this chapter. There, we present a concrete case-study of the Rhondda Heritage Park (RHP) in south Wales. This site provides an authoritative account of a local identity-formation which references a wider formation of 'Britishness' as opposed to 'Welshness'. This Britishness manifests itself in two modes of territorialization: empire and welfare state. These two modes endow a particular meaning onto the category of 'the Rhondda' as imagined community, and we shall explore what kind of identity is thereby secured for the ex-coalmining Valleys of south Wales.

Territoriality and Community

In his acclaimed *Imagined Communities*, Benedict Anderson (1991) argues that nations are actively constructed communities with finite boundaries, in which the face-to-face mode of human interaction has been displaced by an imaginary simultaneity of existence, disseminated by print-media such as the novel and the newspaper. This imaginary simultaneity consists of the impression, cultivated through public sites of mediation by successful ideologies of nationhood, that community members all share an awareness of each other's existence at any one point in 'empty, homogeneous time'. This impression is produced through countless narrative devices (from novels to maps and museums), which propose the notion of a shared 'meanwhile', granting a temporal unity to the imagined community. The members of imagined communities are engaged in different spheres of life and will never meet all the other individuals that make up the community face to face; yet through these sites of mediation 'they' are all represented as partaking of the same past, present and future. What unites this past, present and future is the identity-construct of 'the nation'.

A clear focus in Anderson's work is the centrality of space and time, or in his case geography and history, as organizing principles for the actualization of imagined communities. Representation is itself a material practice; it takes place in an apparent reality because it spatializes and temporalizes the world in mediated forms. For Anderson, imagined communities are spatialized in symbolic forms because these always imply the articulation of a particular place (here) against a horizon of abstract space (there). Similarly, technologies of representation temporalize the universe because they articulate a specific time ('now') against a horizon of temporality that is at once past ('no-longer'), present ('meanwhile'), and future ('not-yet'). Technologies of representation — such as the map, the census and the museum — provide various ways of configuring this unity: the map through 'logoization' (the endless graphical representation of the nation's physical shape), the census through 'serialization' (the identification of community members as numbers in a particular series) and the museum through genealogization (the construction of an evolutionary ethnic inheritance).

A considerable strength of Anderson's work is that he shows how powerful discourses of community emanating from a symbolic centre (such as colonialist discourse) themselves generate counter-discourses in the form of nationalist ideology. This turns the 'them' of colonialist history into the 'us' of national identity. In the revised edition of *Imagined Communities*, Anderson shows how the 'grammar' of nationalism is provided by systems of representation set up by the very colonial regimes it was destined to overthrow: 'the state imagined its local adversaries, as in an ominous prophetic dream, well before they came into historical existence' (1991: p. xiv). In this sense, he understands how territorial identities are not pre-existent entities, awaiting their full representation through the arrival of the language of nationalism, but instead are brought into discourse through historical struggles and conflict which engender the means (and the motivation) for collective thinking in the first place. However, the consequence of this is that Anderson is forced to reduce difference into a 'fatality' of the human condition which vanishes as soon as it becomes consolidated in symbolic forms.

A second critical point we wish to make is that Anderson's interest remains tied to the ways in which symbolic representation *enables* community to be spoken by public discourses, and he subsequently neglects the *disabling* effects which these mechanisms also imply. He does not, for example, accept the connection between nationalism and racism, arguing instead that racism actually denies nationality by creating an overarching class discourse of physiognomy, 'breeding' and 'blood' rather than national identity (Anderson, 1991: 148–50; see Gilroy, 1987: 44–6, for a critique of this position). In his account, nationalism appears as a singular, reactive language, rather than as a field of power-relations established through ongoing struggles over its own boundaries and exclusions.

For Anderson, nationalism is to be understood principally as an anti-imperialist force, generated by mutual solidarity on the margins (Brennan, 1990). Whereas this certainly provides a useful antidote to all those accounts of nationalism as negative and destructive, it suffers from a certain blindness as to the logic of representing collective identity. This logic means that in any act of representation, a splitting occurs, in that an excluded Other is created which is *constitutive of* that representation. What is excluded can never be banished beyond the boundaries. It always remains as a residue, to unsettle – and yet simultaneously to confirm – the identity created through the act of representation. In other words, rather than a mere fatality of the human condition; difference is the generative force that constitutes the possibility of identification.

Anderson conceives of space and time only in terms of the particular symbolic forms in which they are actualized, namely geography and history. He thus conflates space to geography and time to history. That is, in lacking a conception of the modalities of territorialization (which are linked to the deterritorializing force of imperialism, capitalism and globalization), he has no conception of difference as *constitutive* of the principle of identity. He does not acknowledge the violence inherent in any technology of representation. The *imagined community* remains a purely descriptive category, without referring beyond the pragmatic narratives of geography and historiography. This has been summed up well by Homi Bhabha (1990b: 300):

> Counter-narratives of the nation that continually evoke and erase its totalising boundaries – both actual and conceptual – disturb those ideological manœuvres through which 'imagined communities' are given essentialist identities . . . Quite simply, the difference of space returns as the Sameness of time, turning Territory into Tradition, turning People into One.

In contrast to Anderson, William Connolly's (1994) critical reading of Alexis de Tocqueville's *Democracy in America* exposes the violence inherent in the formation of nation-states, including the work of technologies of representation. Central to his argument is the concept of *territoriality*. He argues that in the word 'territory', there are two meanings which are melted into one: *terra* (earth) and *terrere* (terror, violence). As Giddens (1985) has noted, following Weber, the nation-state is based firstly on the monopolization of violence and taxation, but expands into more cultural and ideological domains such as education and schooling and of course the media (also see Gellner, 1983). The nation-state is based on a violent conquest of land, either physically, such as in colonialism, or in more legal forms, via law and property rights. Alongside physical and legal violence, there is thus a second mode of conquest, often ignored by sociologists studying state formations, this is the conquest of the social, or better, the creation of a mode of regulation which appropriates the arteries of religion to constitute a micro-physics of power. This mode of governmentality is nationalism.[1]

> Central in the formation of a nation-state is the articulation of boundaries. Boundaries form indispensable protection against violation and violence, but the divisions they sustain in doing so also carry cruelty and violence. Boundaries provide preconditions of identity, individual agency and collective action; but also close off possibilities of being that might otherwise flourish. Boundaries both foster and inhibit freedom; they both protect and violate life. (Connolly, 1994: 19)

Connolly argues that the forgetting of violence is endemic to the nation-state. This echoes Anderson's observation that the new post-colonial nationalisms of the eighteenth and nineteenth centuries were involved in a simultaneous process of remembering and forgetting: remembering past events and granting them a central role in canonical narratives of identity, but also 'forgetting' that these events were embroiled in quite different, and often antagonistic, narratives that actually undermined this very identity (Anderson, 1991). Later in this chapter, we shall see how the heritage centre in the Rhondda that we discuss aspires to act as a 'reminder' to the centre (but to the British – not the Welsh –

nation) of its own 'forgetting' that the Rhondda was another centre in past times.

The notion of territory as the inscription of spatial violence in symbolic forms and technologies of representation is an integral part of what Edward Said described as *Orientalism*. Said appropriates the term *Imaginative Geography* to refer to the spatial ordering of the world via symbolic and imaginary associations of images to people and places, giving them a sense of here versus there and us versus them. Place and togetherness thus create a sense of belonging with which the world can be ordered, categorized and mapped-out in systems of classification which distinguish between groups in terms of superior–inferior, included–excluded. Orientalism is an 'imaginative geography' that has institutionalized an 'economy of objects and identities that make up an environment' (1978: 53).

However, although Said opens up a critical understanding of geography as distinct from space and place, he maintains a relatively uncritical understanding of time and temporality and – like Anderson – reduces these to 'history'. The Orient is, of course, more than merely a historical sedimentation of Western history, and is not merely the sum of its representations. The very act of representation opens up possibilities to contest the authoritative stamp of a singular history. Said fails to see that his own narrative is itself enabled by Orientalism (Clifford, 1988). Said's historiography does indeed allow us to see how the Oriental Other is a spatialized prerequisite for the very formation of an Occidental Self. He does not, however, fully pursue the consequences of this effect. He does not fully recognize the nomadic potential of difference and thus underplays the importance of the 'other' as a disruptive presence amidst; the Stranger within which breaks up the homogeneity of the centre (Kristeva, 1988; Bauman, 1990).

Homi Bhabha's notion of *Nation and Narration* allows us to see how spatial and temporal difference is not subsumed by geographical and historical representations. No subject is ever identical with its representation. The imagination of community requires an endless dissemination of multiple histories that add to the imaginative geographies of the nation, but they do not add *up*. That is, nationhood itself implies an Other, whose existence is presupposed and is therefore constitutive of the very identity by which it is displaced. It is not the same, but the different, which constitutes the existence of the nation. The narration of nationhood is itself a dissemination of traces, whose fabrication, for example in reinterpretations of histories, unsettles the institutional authority of official history (Ahearne, 1995).

It is through the dissemination of narratives that the idea of a collective identity (a nation, a place, a region) takes shape. When these histories of identity are brought into alignment with geographies of identity, collective identity becomes tied to place and thereby to boundaries. However, because the assertion of an 'us' also specifies an excluded 'them', the Other continues to haunt the imagined community – because representation cannot work without it. There is always a struggle occurring on the horizon between competing versions of 'who we are' and 'who they are'. This results in the constant and excessive production of new narratives of identity, shoring up the boundary anew by reconfiguring what is included and what is excluded. Thus, the 'content' of the imagined community may change, to accommodate historical shifts and flux, but the insistence on identity continues. In such an excess, the symbolic representation of collective identity becomes an ongoing site of (sometimes violent) struggle. It is at this point that territorialization-through-heritage emerges to contain the excess by elaborating public narratives of identity through the conventions of heritage display.

A Museography of Banal Nationalism

In order to concretize the way in which national identities are spatialized and temporalized in symbolic forms, we provide a specific 'museographical' case-study of the Rhondda Heritage Park (RHP). We shall examine how this heritage centre imagines the community of the Rhondda, by considering the technologies of representation through which it constructs a boundary around its subject. We shall also interrogate how this boundary is implied in wider territory formations – in particular *vis-à-vis* British and Welsh identity. We argue that heritage sites constitute a prime site of public mediation in which the 'banal' and everyday forms of collective identity are displayed and enacted (Billig, 1995). Billig argues that it is in these banalities that nationalism becomes such a persistent and pervasive force in the modern world. We could add that they also provide the stage within which the currency of subnational collective identities circulates. After a short excursion into Billig's argument, we will provide an account of how museography can be set to work to uncover what Billig calls 'the *deixis* of nationhood'.

In *Banal Nationalism*, Michael Billig seeks to explain the persistence of nationalism in a world marked by the disappearance of fixed boundaries and identities. Through being overly concerned with the excessive, exceptional and exotic forms of nationalism, Billig argues, most social scientists have not developed an adequate explanation of the ways in which the nation becomes 'enhabited' (Billig, 1995: 42 and 15–19). Enhabitation ensures that the nation acquires a silent omnipresence in discourses and practices of everyday life, that is, in routine forms of remembering without conscious awareness (Billig, 1995: 42). It allows the 'nation' to be at once universal and particular. Universal, because everyone 'has' a national identity; particular, because one always belongs to one specific nation (Billig, 1995: 24 and 73). The nation is 'flagged' in everyday language in rather mystified, mythological and uneventful ways (Billig, 1995: 105). Nationalism is primarily embodied in such banalities as the unwaved flag outside a public building, the organization of sporting events, the language used by media, politicians, weathermen and philosophers.

He describes in detail the mechanisms of this dialectics of remembering and forgetting via a pragmatic analysis of what he calls *homeland deixis* (Billig, 1995: 105). Here, the nation becomes signified in the smallest of words: the, this–that, here–there, us–them, now–then. These words *index* the nation: 'The homeland is made both present and unnoticeable by being presented as *the* context' (Billig, 1995: 109). This becomes most clear in notions such as '*the* country', '*the* prime minister' or '*the* economy', which index a particular situation as a self-evident context, beyond which nothing can be. In other words, the particular becomes universal – through the process of integration which we noted earlier. We could extend these insights into subnational collective identity by noting the common shorthand terms for localities: 'the Rhondda', for example – a nomenclature which suggests a natural commonality and cohesiveness to the numerous towns and villages in the two valleys of the Rhondda Fach and the Rhondda Fawr. We then have the quasi-anthropological extension: *'the people of* the Rhondda' or *'the people of* Wales'. Indeed, the word 'community' itself implies just such a project of unquestioned and natural unity.

A Note on Museography

'Community' is central to ethnographic museums and heritage sites, for they are primary loci for the public display of collective identity (Urry, 1996). They are territorialized configurations of space–time relations, in which the past is spatialized in a present, via the presence of artefacts, narratives, visual representations and performances. Museums, however, not only organize, order and classify the past, 'they are also expressions of the ordering of the social' (Hetherington, 1996: 155). That is, the relationships between past and present are 'already imbued with power-knowledge that derives from social context' (Hetherington, 1995: 155). For example, the particular reading-paths with which the public are guided through an exhibition imply authoritative interpretations. These interpretations transform a selective sequence of events into an 'official history'.

However, histories, even the official versions, are never without contestation. They always imply an Other that is an exteriority within. Indeed, interpretation not only engenders an Other, it presupposes it. As a result, the Other is always doubled into an explicit, exoticized Other (on display) and an implicit, residual Other (which allows the display to make sense). Like history itself, the museum is a contested space – a space of many places, a heterotopia (Foucault, 1986; Delaney, 1992; Hetherington, 1995). Museums provide possibilities for contesting interpretations because they imply a multiplicity of space–time configurations. The arrangement of artefacts through particular reading-paths does not foreclose on alternative readings. This is because space and time can never be completely incorporated by geography and history.

Heritage displays inscribe particular past events into a place-identity, thus marking out a boundary and setting into motion an infinite chain of differentiations. Museums operate to fix those boundaries in the timeless obviousness (always-already) of myth.

Myths embody attempts to eradicate the temporal and spatial residual of history and geography, which allows its object to resist the homogenizing force of symbolic representation. Myths present a world that is fully enclosed within itself. Thus, because the logic of public communication operates through texts which are essentially 'readerly' and closed, and do not leave much space for uncertainty, ambiguity or contradictions, heritage narratives 'fix' past events into a particular chain of interpretation. Analysing these allows us to uncover what is excluded and what constitutes the instability and silences of the texts in question.

Museography has to be a practice of demythification. The first step is to map out the myths which constitute the enclosure, the territorialization of the object. This implies a hermeneutic approach that can be further operationalized in (1) a semiotic iconography, focusing on how objects (including images, sounds, smells and/or texts) signify; (2) a pragmatic iconography, focusing on how the signification of objects are communicated to the public; and (3) a narratology, focusing on the ways in which the semiotic and pragmatic iconographies are structured and organized into specific reading-paths, often within a unified temporality.

However, such interpretations are not very useful if they ignore the ways in which people actually interact with these displays. Moreover, a museographical analysis remains theoretically impoverished if it ignores the social context of this process (both in the sense of the more immediate context of the 'production of meaning' and the wider context of more general socio-cultural transformations in which museums are situated). We would thus argue for an approach which integrates analysis of both encoding (the practices and contexts of constructing heritage displays) and decoding (the practices and contexts of visitors' interaction with them) – compare Hall, 1980.

It is clearly impossible to accomplish all of this within a single chapter. However, we recognize the inevitable shortcomings of a museography in which much of the context of production and interpretation is bracketed off. In terms of text, we shall offer a reading of the audio-visual presentations in the chosen heritage site. We shall not be able to address visitors' readings of these texts within the scope of this chapter.[2] In terms of context, we will limit our attention to one specific articulation of context, namely that of the so-called 'heritage industry' (Hewison, 1987), which has provided a new twist to the political economic 'restructuring' of many marginal regions throughout Britain and Europe. Central to this reconstruction of the past is the articulation between 'national identity', 'local identity' and 'consumer culture' (Urry, 1990, 1996).

Configurations of Space and Time at the Rhondda Heritage Park

This section examines how narratives of 'local community' also imply narratives of nationhood and wider collectivities. Heritage centres are particularly fruitful sites to study in relation to the representation of these two levels of collective identity. New principles of exhibitionary grammar at ethnographic 'living museums' and heritage centres self-consciously display the identity of the local and the particular realm of life, as opposed to that of the nation-state. They seek to cultivate a sense of recognition on the part of visitors – an identification with familiar everyday objects, stories and scenes. In national-collection museums, on the other hand, the traditional glass-case principles of classic curatorial displays invite a reverence for the 'aura' (Benjamin, 1973) of sacred or scientific objects. These objects illustrate the 'inheritance' of the nation: by displaying the *range* of human life and achievement over time and space, national collection museums present the visitor with a catalogue of objects – both familiar and foreign – which are displayed as the nation's possessions. They do not seek visitors' identification so much as their enlightenment.

It is true that new museum practice is increasingly embracing principles of dramatic narrative and enactment, yet most collection museums retain a special emphasis on the illustration of categories. They are not primarily concerned to enlist artefacts within a 'story', and eschew the kind of high-tech simulated spectacle that characterizes the heritage centre.[3] Many collection museums are funded publicly, reside in capital cities (like the National Museum of Wales in Cardiff) and are – as Anderson (1991) suggests – central arenas for mapping the nation. The new breed of heritage centres, on the other hand, are often part of a *local regenerative* strategy to attract tourists to a particular locality. There is an increasing number of local heritage centres which put on display a working-class history of *particular ways of life* instead of a range of life, and which often address a specific industry – such as coal, steel, shipbuilding and so on.

These enterprises seek to replace lost industry by re-presenting that history as tourist spectacle (Crang, 1994). Hence, at the RHP, the guides who show visitors around the colliery-as-spectacle used to earn a (much higher) wage from actually working in the local area as miners. The fact that heritage sites are part of the tourist and leisure industries gives them a particular inflection, in that their exhibitionary logic is usually driven by a need to provide spectacle, interest, entertainment, enthralment – above all, to capture and maintain the gaze of the visitor. The objective is to provide the visitor with an experience. This must be memorable, intense, captivating, different from everyday life (Urry, 1990).

These principles constitute the field of production in which the RHP tells its history. The emphasis in 'Black Gold' (the name for the three audio-visual shows telling the history of the Rhondda) is on the staging and dramatic presentation of sensory phenomena (such as the fleetingly illuminated tableaux of historical figures, dramatic soundscapes and lighting, audio recordings of the hustle and bustle of Rhondda streets at the height of the coal boom). Similarly, the spoken narratives in the audio-visual shows mimic the narratives of historical television drama – using a chronological unfolding of historical events interspersed with anecdotal human-interest stories to create suspense, hold attention and to generate momentum. These devices work to immerse the visitor in the concrete and sensory detail of a way of life – the identity of local community. They seek to involve the visitor emotionally by evoking memories and stories told by grandparents and relatives, and by the grandparents and relatives in soap operas and serials. They aspire to collapse the sense of 'critical distance' cultivated in the collection museum, and to replace this with a stimulating and engaging sensory environment. This environment 'is' the community, and this community 'has' a highly elaborated and colourful identity.

Signifying History

However, although the emphasis on spectacle and the prioritization of the gaze tend to rule out a historiography that can pause on the complex ideational controversies of history (the heritage site is not well suited to the elaboration of concepts, theories or debates), this does not automatically mean a slide into uncritical and complicit accounts of past events, or a tacky, sensationalist and intellectually useless treatment of local issues. If this were indeed the case, as several heritage commentators have argued it inevitably is in heritage centres as opposed to museums (Hewison, 1987; Walsh, 1992), there is no doubt that heritage sites would arouse much more comment, controversy and criticism from the local sphere than they actually do. If the RHP had portrayed a version of local history that played heavily on the sensationalism of mining disasters, for instance, then local opinion would have been so irretrievably alienated that it is unlikely the Park would have obtained the (albeit limited) degree of local acceptance that was necessary for its establishment and funding.[4]

The Rhondda is an area whose history is popularly associated with politically left-wing events, personalities and disputes, and where the Labour Party has for long had the local political monopoly on power. Moreover there has also been a widely acknowledged tradition of Communist Party activity (albeit less visibly displayed in the RHP). It would simply have been impracticable to present local people with a version of their own history that was significantly out of touch with these traditions. This points to an essential feature of heritage sites that is often overlooked: they are usually representing a specifically *placed*, local story. This means they have to engage with the canon of accepted local history and popular memories – unlike national large-scale museums. In fact, what the RHP presents is a form of historiography that is essentially *labourist* in character. It acknowledges, for example, a stark division of interest between miners and coal-owners. It is pointed out by the guides that the colliery managers attached greater value to their horses than to the colliers' lives.[5]

In the major historiographical audio-visual film that introduces the visitor to the history of the Rhondda from 1850 to 1958, the wealth of the ruling Bute family of Cardiff, and of W. T. Lewis the colliery owner, is explicitly contrasted with the poverty and suffering of Rhondda people. The deprivation and misery of the 1930s is contrasted to the lives of luxury led by the coal-owners. This contrast sets the stage for the presentation of the Miners' Federation leader, A. J. Cook, whose demands for justice on behalf of the miners are shown by means of a *tableau vivant* of Cook addressing a large crowd of enthusiastic supporters. The riots of Tonypandy in 1913 are encoded as a struggle for 'a decent living' and conditions, as are the strikes of 1921 and 1926. The emphasis on the dangers of mining, low wages and the constant threats of explosion and injury, elaborate a narrative that works to underpin, justify and *account for* the political agitation presented.

The RHP does not therefore present a hegemonic legitimation of capitalist relations. Nor does it present a banal, any-place version of 'Community World'. It does feature antagonisms and struggles; it does offer a locally recognizable historiography. Collective identity, however, is symbolized through the claims and silences of the representations: what is and what is not 'the Rhondda'. In fact, the 'Black Gold Community' represents a particular historical narrative that seeks to claim for the south Wales Valleys a collective identity which is labourist and transnational in character. The RHP's depiction of the 'Black Gold Community', which celebrates the virtues of hard manual labour and comradeship, which acknowledges the inequities of a traditional gender division of labour whilst insinuating its inevitability, which celebrates a local culture of self-improvement and individual achievement along with traditional socialist principles of collectivism, welfarism, support for nationalization, and so on, is perfectly in line with what could be termed a local 'labourist' political culture. It is, above all else, a narrative which banishes most of the images traditionally associated with the Wales of Welsh nationalism: land, language, song, wilderness, romanticism (P. Morgan, 1983). We shall return to the question of local community versus national community in the next section.

How is the collective identity of the 'Black Gold Community' constructed at the RHP? The audio-visual scripts point out that, before nationalization, colliery conditions were atrocious and miners exploited. Afterwards, things improved significantly. The chronology is organized thus:

1890–1920 – the coal boom and the Rhondda's hey-day;
1920s–1930s – the slump: depression and suffering;
1940–1950s – the coal recovery: return to prosperity.

In this trajectory, the recovery coincides nicely with the post-war

Labour government that set up the welfare state and nationalized the industry. The narrative does therefore acknowledge the inherent violence in the transformation of the sparsely populated rural backwater of the early nineteenth century into 'The Rhondda' – a place 'crammed tight' with people. After the war, the violence enacted in producing the Rhondda as a place of exploited labour is finally brought reparation, catharsis and healing. This act of reparation is accomplished by the process of nationalization, which is set up by the narrative as the antithesis to the chaotic, free-market excesses of the coal-owners. It is the nationalization of coal-mining under the British welfare state which thus provides the greatest territorialization of the mining industry itself by demobilizing some of the most nomadic elements of 'free-market capitalism'.

The year of 1958, however, is as far as the story goes. Although the 1984–5 strike is mentioned in passing, no explanation is offered as to why deep coal-mining in south Wales is now virtually extinct. In this sense, the RHP offers a historiography that is severed from the present. The next historical 'moments' – the mass pit closures of the 1960s and the diversification of the industrial base, followed by further decline and the elimination of mining in the 1970s and 1980s – are exnominated. Through this failure of nerve, this refusal to bridge the gap between past and present, the narrative presented is suffused with a sense of *loss*. This loss is the basis for collective remembering, and sets in motion a discourse of nostalgia – for it offers above all a wake for the past. That is not to say that the past is glorified or romanticized, but it is presented as a full, rich and multi-layered space – a 'heady mixture', as Neil Kinnock's voice describes it on one audio-visual. A vision of intensity and vibrancy is offered: great suffering but also great creativity. In this sense the RHP presents a past that is *more real* than the present, because it is more knowable, more elaborated, more visually dramatized (compare Huyssen, 1995).

As we have seen in the preceding section, the representation of community identity always implies an excluded other: an exteriority which is both temporally and spatially constituted. In the historical narrative presented at the RHP, one such exteriority is the 'now' of the Rhondda, which remains as a silence and a gap in the chronological sequence. Community identity, as in self-identity, can only make sense through the telling of a narrative that proposes an 'entity' moving through time and through historical vicissitude, but whose 'identity' (self-sameness) remains intact throughout. In the heritage narrative, 'the Rhondda' *then* is the same entity as 'the Rhondda' *now*, so the spectator is invited to see the qualities claimed for its past as also constituting its identity in the present/future. Thus, the particular (select traditions, certain qualities – all derived from the occupational culture of the collieries) is claimed as the universal (that is, consecrated as the 'essence' of the Rhondda as mining community *par excellence*).

But as this universalization is claimed for the Rhondda *as mining community*, what happens to the identity it confers when the institutions and occupational culture of the collieries are erased? How does the RHP 'manage' the silence of the present, which threatens literally to undermine the community identity on display? It is in this problematic that we can see the way in which 'history' is co-opted into the imagination of community. As with Anderson's recognition of the importance of historical antecedence in the constructions of nationalist discourse, so the assertion of community at a subnational level requires the simultaneous remembering and forgetting of the past. The RHP imagines a mining-community identity for the Rhondda by remembering certain traditions, events and origins and by forgetting their contingency, contestation or their embroilment in quite different narratives. Thus, in 'Black Gold', 'the Rhondda' was born at the moment of the discovery of coal, at which point all the Rhondda's public narratives begin. The past has become merely a repository for the 'old traditions', and has – thereby – become retraditionalized (Morris, 1996).

The discourse of the Rhondda-as-community is constituted from the symbolic content of what was frozen as its identity through successive waves of temporal change. At each point in the long decline of the mining industry, these narratives have remained intact and served to underpin calls for community activism, for community renewal, and for community survival (G. Rees, 1997). It is the identity of the *mining* community (the particular becoming universal), however, which has provided the imagery, the vocabulary, the signifying material, of the Rhondda's distinctive identity. This indicates how successive layers of mythologizing – the RHP is only the latest form of a long tradition of canonizing 'the Valleys' as coalfield communities – are essential to the assertion of community (both national and local), and how the term itself is particularly dependent on a backward-looking gaze, constantly destabilized by the contrary presence of the silenced 'now'. Bauman has captured this quality well in a memorable passage:

> Tönnies-style communities fall apart the moment they know of themselves as communities. They vanish (if they have not evaporated before) once we say 'how nice to be in a community'. From that moment on, community is not a secure settlement: it is all hard work and uphill struggle; a constantly receding horizon of the never-ending road; anything but natural and cosy. We console ourselves and summon our wilting determination by invoking the magic formula of 'tradition' – trying hard to forget that tradition lives only by being recapitulated, by being construed as heritage; that it appears, if at all, only at the end, never at the beginning of agreement; that its retrospective unity is but a function of the density of today's communal cloud. (Bauman, 1992b: 138)

In this way, the discourse of community imagines an entity progressing 'up time' towards the present (compare Anderson, 1991), endlessly constructing a 'retrospective unity' and a purpose which leaves in its wake only a cloud of residuality and silences.

The RHP and Territoriality

How can we relate this community identity of the local to the community identity of the nation? Here, we would like to offer some comments on the ways in which power is deployed spatially in representational practices (compare our earlier arguments about the – symbolic and actual – violence done by the drawing of boundaries through the twin processes of integration and differentiation). We have noted that the RHP offers a narrative of history which occupies an uneasy position in terms of wider hegemonic symbolic formations in Wales. 'Black Gold' offers the story of the 'people of the Rhondda' as a story of the heroism of ordinary working-class people in the face of exploitation and indifference. How does such a narrative relate to other narratives, particularly those which construct a territoriality which is wider than the local? In other words, how does the 'Black Gold' narrative relate to its Other – the narratives of Welsh and/or British identity?

As the earlier discussion showed, every representation of identity summons up immediately an 'us' and a 'them'. For Said, the enunciation of a 'we' presupposes a 'them'; however, as Bhabha points out, the 'them' is already part of 'ourselves'. The Rhondda cannot name itself without reference to its other: the centre of power, which is elsewhere (yet in-here). But the question is, which is the centre to which the RHP addresses its local identity? The answer, quite explicitly, is that the centre against which 'the Rhondda' is defined is either the subnational entity of Cardiff (stripped of its connotations as capital city of Wales), or the construct of 'Great Britain'. On the subject of the Welsh nation, the RHP is almost entirely silent. Indeed, this silence allows us to deconstruct the identity therein claimed for 'the Rhondda'. The RHP constructs the Rhondda as an imagined community – a 'here' as opposed to the 'there' of Cardiff or Great Britain, but it is also inscribed with the traces of an 'elsewhere': the Welsh nation. In what follows, we shall try to elaborate how 'the Rhondda' of the RHP constructs a territory. It does so by claiming back the space of the centre-which-is-Britain, but also by hitching 'Welshness' to the same space. It thus refuses to contribute to nationalist narratives predicated on a strong demarcation between the identities of Britain and Wales.

The Denial of Peripherality

One of the strategies of territorialization that the RHP deploys is the claiming of a role for the Rhondda in narratives of the British Empire. The narrative at the RHP is at pains to point out that the Rhondda was *not* peripheral in relation to 'Great Britain', but, on the contrary, was at the hub of the vast network of empire that depended on its coal:

> If you want to know what put the 'Great' in Great Britain, you don't have to look much further than Rhondda coal. In those days you couldn't do anything, from crossing the Atlantic to running a railway or a factory without coal. And Rhondda steam coal was the best in the world for that. Rhondda was world famous for it.[6]

This excess of self-aggrandizement cannot be understood outside the fact of Rhondda's essential peripherality and marginalization in the 'golden age' of empire, Great Britain *and* – as we shall see – in the traditional narratives of Welsh identity. The urge to lay claim to the spoils of 'Greatness' and centrality is part of the vigorous assertion of local community identity that the RHP is all about. It is as though the narrative is seeking to reclaim an identity for the Rhondda and an importance that has been denied to it.

In fact, the RHP's 'claiming of fame' is not based on confident and positive assertions of power, as is the case with the triumphant nation-state, through its capital-city-based national collections in grand museums (cf. Anderson, 1991). It is instead founded on an insistence on the recognition of something *lost*, something that has gone unacknowledged by the centre (whether London or Cardiff) that benefited from the Rhondda's labour and exertions. By insisting on its past fame and importance, the narrative is delivering a reproach to the centre for abandoning the Rhondda to decline and decay, and for its appropriation of the 'Greatness' all for itself. It is doing so through articulating this sense of loss, bitterness and even anger to the dominant discourse of national pride and 'Greatness'. Indeed, the RHP works hegemonically to hitch 'the Rhondda' to imperial territory/history, where Rhondda can have a long-overdue share of the 'Greatness'.

Nevertheless, these narratives only work by also acknowledging the violence, suffering and damage inflicted in the centre's usurpation of the Rhondda's resources. In admonishing the centre, the periphery's self-assertion is not the mirror-image of the violence done by empire. Again, in Bhabha's terms, the centre is present as an absence at the RHP, and the Rhondda is present as an absence in the imaginary of the British nation – but these two splittings are not equivalent. The latter implies the power of the already-constituted nation-state; the former is a counter-narrative from the margins, which nevertheless inevitably takes place within the correlates of the same integral territorial formation. Although the local heritage centre acclaims a unique *local* collective identity, it can only do so through also evoking the non-local Other – the centre against which the local is defined. Thus territorialization always involves a homogenizing place-based narrative which summons up the national in the very act of elaborating the local.

What about Wales?

There is, in fact, one mention of Wales in the three audio-visual shows at the RHP, and this instance – far from elaborating a distinctive non-British identity for Wales – actually brings the construct of 'the Welsh nation' into alignment with that of the 'British Empire'. The Rhondda is positioned as the rightful epicentre of the empire *and* of Wales – and no contradiction is asserted between these two identities:

> The Welsh Nation owes to coal the prosperity that has provided us with a university, with fine civic buildings and mighty ports. Coal has made Cardiff into a veritable Welsh Chicago. The coal bunkers of the Empire, from the Cape to Auden, from Bombay to Port Said are stocked with coal from the Rhondda – with coal that has come up, in endless streams, from this very colliery.[7]

Here, the (single) mention of Wales makes the claim that it is to coal – not to anything else – that the 'Welsh nation' owes its true identity. In doing so, it denies a distinctive identity for Wales. Indeed, the narratives assert what the two identities of empire and Wales *share*: a debt of gratitude to the miners of the Rhondda. To explain this, we need to look at how collective identity in Wales has been constructed in relation to oppositions such as industry versus agriculture, urban life versus rural life, the English versus the Welsh language.

We have suggested that the historical narratives of 'Black Gold' reproduce a historiography which is attuned to the labourist hegemony of the Valleys. This labourism has been decidedly Anglophone, based on a century-long construction of institutions to serve the needs of an industrial working class that originated both within and outside of Wales (C. Williams, 1996). Several writers on Welsh cultural identity have attested to the way in which this southern industrial, proletarian, urban identity has sat uneasily alongside a Welsh nationalist imaginary which sees the 'real Wales' as residing in the north and the west. The 'Welsh spirit' was conventionally held to reside in the traditions of rural Wales, in song and in nature (P. Morgan, 1983; Humphreys, 1995). Price (1992), for instance, describes the Valleys' identity-shift from early nineteenth-century pre-industrial rural landscape admired in the writings of B. H. Malkin, to 1930s 'landscape of degradation', in which the industrial and crowded valleys are described by different writers as a 'fallen' and defiled place:

> That Glamorgan could be viewed as the whore of the family of Wales who sold herself to English industrialism and was seduced and abandoned, is too powerful an image to be ignored. It implies . . . another Wales that was poor but pure. A Wales formed through the contemplative gaze and eternally visible as a site of unproblematic 'nature'. (Price, 1992: 99)

The social space of the Valleys, then, as the epitome of the 'Glamorgan whore', is represented by a strand of romantic Welsh writing as alien to the 'unsullied' social space of Wales. This imagination clearly hitches 'Wales' to a particular *rural* place-myth of its own, which the Welsh Nationalist Party, Plaid Cymru translated into the twin foci of Welsh identity: land and language (Kahn, 1984).[8] The place of the south Wales Valleys within these narratives of Welshness has long been a contested and politicized terrain (Humphreys, 1995).

It is clear that the question mark over the Valleys' qualification to belong to the 'true' identity of Wales has continued into the twentieth century (Giggs and Pattie, 1992b; Adamson, 1996). The question has been reactivated in recent decades with the revival of the Welsh language, and the corresponding problematic status of the English-speaking Valleys. The shifting appeals to Welsh identity made by the nationalist party, Plaid Cymru, illustrate this. Adamson's (1996) thesis is that recent inward migration to central rural Wales has contributed to a dissolution of the rural/urban, Wales/Valleys fused hybrid identity which was forged within the party through a vague and binding concept of *community*:

> The concept of community employed by Plaid Cymru has never been defined and it has retained an open meaning which allows individuals to insert their own sense of community into party rhetoric. Two dominant conceptions of community have existed. The first is a sense of rural community with an emphasis on kinship, neighbourhood and identifiable patterns of language, culture and religion. The second is a sense of industrial community, associated with coal and steel production, with networks of mutual aid, traditions of working-class politics and labourism. As long as the meaning of the term community

was not defined, all sections of the Party could feel loyalty to a concept of decentralist socialism founded in communities . . . A farmer on the Llŷn peninsula could feel as committed to the concept as a miner from Maerdy. (Adamson, 1996: 41)

It is Adamson's second kind of community identity that is foregrounded at the RHP, through its promotion of the 'Valleys version' of Welsh identity. Yet, as we have been arguing, such identities are only enunciated through their relations of difference. Thus, the construct of the 'traditional mining community' itself depends on the currency of those 'other' narratives of Welsh nationalism. If both types of collective identity appear to be losing their purchase in Welsh political culture – as Adamson suggests – we can see that the grammar of representation underlying the RHP's display of collective identity is locked in a backward-looking logic.

This is a logic which insists that identity is territorially defined. Indeed, the labourist narratives of working-class community at the RHP are in reality confined to a place-specific evocation of 'Rhondda-valleyness'. This is the contradiction on which all local heritage centres are founded: they both offer an invigorating portrayal of the unacknowledged role of local and working-class labour in the constructs of the nation, whilst also drawing a territorial boundary around this history by claiming it as the 'story of place x'. Labourist narratives of community are squeezed into the spaces of subnational territories. Thus, local heritage inevitably operates through the same territorializing modes as national heritage. Local heritage *is* – potentially – an uplifting voice from the margins reclaiming an unacknowledged local identity in the face of hegemonic national and colonial myths, but it still operates through the oppositions of territorialization: here/there; centre/periphery; nation/region; national community/local community. In the process it inevitably reproduces a grid of insider/outsider relations, which in fact underlies the whole project of 'imagining communities' – be they Valleys or nations.

Conclusion

Of all collective identity-formations that have emerged with modernity, none has been so pervasive and powerful as that of nationalism. A central factor in allowing the nation to have such powerful effects is undoubtedly its territoriality. Other representations of community – such as local community – can only work within the territorializing logic thereby ingrained in these habitual representations of community as bounded entity. Imagined communities always imply a violence of boundaries that engender the imaginative counter-positioning of Self versus Other. Homi Bhabha's (1990b) suggestion that narrating the nation is never a complete and homogeneous closure, however, forces us to consider that boundaries always imply a double-edged violence: one externally oriented as in Orientalism (the differential), the other internally oriented (the integral).

In this chapter we have focused on the second, that is, the integral identity-formation of territoriality. Following Billig, we have argued that, rather than being explicit and visible, such a formation more often takes place in seemingly banal and everyday practices of symbolic representation. The integral force of territoriality can for example be traced in the ways in which heritage presents the spatio-temporal situatedness of its objects of display. Focusing on the Rhondda Heritage Park we have explored one form of subnational collective identification, and we have shown how the representation of 'the local' is dependent on the simultaneous representation of 'the national' (and in this case, the colonial too). Two elements clearly stand out as illustrations of the integral force of territoriality in identity-formation: (1) the denial of peripherality and (2), in order to achieve this, and thereby to offer a self-important 'heritage', the dialectics of the twin imaginations of the centre (Wales and 'Great Britain'). These are two modes of territorialization which embody attempts to *ground* the spatio-temporal residue of historiography in a myth of 'Rhondda Valleyness' that is continuous with that of Britishness and 'greatness'.

In the first mode, the Rhondda Valley becomes a particular local sedimentation of (universal) 'empire'. Far from positioning the empire as Other, the RHP reclaims for the Valley a central role in its further proliferation in the late nineteenth century. The denial of peripherality implies the tacit assumption that we all know that south Wales is generally perceived as peripheral in relation to the rest of Great Britain. However, by linking the history of empire to the coal-mining industry in the Rhondda Valley, the 'community' insinuates itself into this common heritage. The geo-historical co-articulation of the local Rhondda heritage with that of empire and nation is a symbolic reclaiming of a centre, an attempt to integrate the region with the nation whilst preserving a distinct regionality (and not a Welsh nationality).

In the second mode, the RHP flags a labourist history exposing the exploitation of the miners, in relation to which the emergence of the welfare state is seen as the final culmination, and resolution, of such a struggle. The symbolic representation of the workers' struggles for decent wages, social security and safety at work provides an integrating force similar to that of empire. The tacit assumption here is that early capitalism took place under inhuman conditions of (unnecessary) exploitation. The narrative places the workers' struggle against this exploitation in a wider context of progress, which in turn is intrinsically related to that of the birth and expansion of the welfare state. The general equation between the improvement of working conditions, the emergence of a welfare state, and the nationalization of the industry clearly presents a picture in which the Rhondda Valley becomes territorially integrated with the British nation-state through a local articulation of labourism. It is significant that this is accomplished through a virtual silencing of a distinctive voice for the Welsh nation – which becomes yet another absent presence in the narrative excess of territorialization.

These two modes provide a unison and rather unproblematic continuity between the myths of 'Britishness' and 'Rhondda Valleyness' in which the very marginality of the Rhondda is denied. However, they have only become available for symbolic representation as 'heritage' when the subject-in-history is past (passed), or capable of being encoded as past (the subject in this case being the Rhondda as mining community). The myth of Rhondda Valleyness, which always bears traces of the myths of Britishness (and the silenced traces of Welshness) in the form of empire and nation, is based on a loss of the very object it attempts to articulate. Only after the mines were closed could a heritage park emerge. The decline of first empire and later welfare state have allowed for a mode of territorialization of the Rhondda Valley as itself a residue of a particular past. This also shows that the continuity between Britishness and Rhondda Valleyness remains mythical and nostalgic, as there can never be a total assimilation of the residual of 'the Valleys' (with their own myths and territorialities) into a homogeneous sense of 'the nation' – whether Welsh or British. As with the link with empire, there always remains the reminder of the local specificity of the Rhondda as a place of particular biographies, anecdotes and events.

Notes

1. For a similar argument, see Billlig (1995).
2. However, see Dicks (1997a), which offers a qualitative study of some visitor groups to the RHP, and an analysis of how these visitors interpreted the history on display, and how they defined the category of 'the Rhondda'.
3. When they do, such modes of representation are spatially and temporally confined to specific exhibitions, such as the 'Evolution of Wales' in the National Museum of Wales, which feature a high-tech, multimedia display of the evolution of Wales from the Big Bang via trilobites to the extinction of dinosaurs and the emergence of mammals (and then it stopped).
4. See Dicks (1996).
5. Interview with visitors have shown that this was the most widely and consistently remembered fact that visitors recalled at the end of their tour (Dicks, 1997a).
6. This is a quotation from one of the 'Black Gold' audio-visual presentations, in the Trefor Winding House. The narrator is Bryn Rees, a local ex-miner who narrates much of the 'Black Gold' historiography.
7. This quotation comes from the Bertie Winding House audio-visual. It is narrated by W. T. Lewis, the owner of a string of collieries in the Rhondda, including the Lewis Merthyr Colliery – the site of the RHP.
8. Whilst the rural/industrial split is a powerful 'internal' divide *within* Wales as imagined community, it needs to be remembered that this will not necessarily be visible from the 'outside'. For the non-Welsh gaze, 'Wales' may be the land of song and chapels, or the land of slag-heaps and unemployment (compare Humphreys, 1995). It is not our intention to explore the imagined community of Wales *per se*, but merely to draw a picture of the contested identities that became the focus of political struggle over the Heritage Park (see Dicks, 1997a, 1997b).

CONCLUSION
12 Nation, Identity and Social Theory

Andrew Thompson

> So people would always ask what Wales actually was. This is how I in the end came to understand the question myself, that virtually all Welshmen ask themselves what it is to be Welsh. The problematic element is characteristic. Of course on the border, it was more problematic than in North or West Wales, in the still Welsh-speaking communities. They are much further away from England. There was a curious sense in which we could speak of both Welsh and English as foreigners, as 'not us'. (R. Williams, 1979: 26)

Introduction

In the midst of growing talk of the 'end of nationalism' and the 'death of the nation-state', a volume on the nation and national identity in Wales may, in some senses, seem an untimely project. It is fast becoming something of a cliché to say that we live in a time of radical social change; the language of globalization and globalism has penetrated many spheres of our lives, from politics to advertising and from education to debates on the environment. 'Think, globally, act locally'; 'small world'; 'one world'; 'shrinking world': these are emerging as the new popular slogans of late twentieth-century societies. In advertisements for cellular phones, computers, petroleum corporations, mail-delivery services and foodstuffs, to cite but a few examples, the images we receive are of a world in which barriers of distance and space are receding. According to a growing number of scholars (Arnason, 1990; Hobsbawm, 1990; Touraine, 1995), in a world restructured according to a supranational agenda nations will become increasingly ineffectual players in a redefined global space. Against the backdrop of these changes, why should we continue to be concerned with, or concerned *about*, questions of nation and national identity?

In part, an answer to this question is self-evident, given the resurgence of nationalisms across the globe in recent years. A comprehensive analysis of the economic, political and cultural shifts during the closing decades of this millennium cannot avoid addressing the question of the attendant role of the nation and national identity. In spite of the increasingly confident claims that we are witnessing nationalism's Indian Summer – a final flourish on the road to the inexorable development of advanced capitalist globalization – it is nevertheless apparent that the sense of identity which it fosters, embedded in representations of time and space, continues to exert a significant appeal. Yet, to focus routinely on certain regions, countries or political parties (the Balkans, Northern Ireland, Le Front National) – as is so often the case with journalists, politicians and academics – serves to divert attention away from developing a rigorous critique of the role which nationalism and national identity perform in reproducing divisions between 'them' and 'us' in societies across the globe. The discourse of nation-ness and the symbolism of nationhood continue to occupy a focal position within our daily lives. Michael Billig (1995: 93) points out that the language of national identity is not solely the preserve of Bosnia, Chechnya or Rwanda, but rather is a crucial feature of language in all societies: as he writes, 'nationalism is not confined to the florid language of blood-myths . . . Small words, rather than memorable phrases, offer constant, but barely conscious, reminders of the homeland, making our national identity unforgettable.' In political rhetoric, in newspapers, in flags, emblems and ceremonies, as well as in discussions of heritage, popular music and sport (see Tomlinson, 1991; Billig, 1995; Allan and Thompson, 1998), public projections of the nation and national identity still continue to form an important element of our social milieu. Economic and political developments – such as processes of integration in western Europe (and more latterly central and eastern Europe), the formation of transnational trading blocs and the rise of, for example, global media corporations – are sponsoring changes which hold significant implications for the future of the national state, yet these changes have also served to heighten an awareness of questions of nationalism and national identity.

This concluding chapter maps some of the underlying theoretical developments in the field of studies of nationalism and national identity. My intention here is to demonstrate the evolution, within scholarly accounts, of differing ways of talking about questions of nationalism and national identity. The discussion notes that, from the work undertaken in the early twentieth century and in the aftermath of the Second World War, to the most recent studies, we have witnessed a gradual recognition of the need to explore the kinds of social and cultural processes through which a sense of national identity is reproduced. Thus while much of the early work on nationalism – even up to some of the studies of the 1970s – was directed towards analyses of the ideology of national*ism*, since the 1980s there has been a definite shift towards the need to understand how people come to acquire a sense of national identity and why this form of identity should seem so important for them. Considerations of the historical development of the ideology of nationalism still form a core debate in this area, yet this research is also complemented by investigations of how discourses of nationhood pervade our daily activities as well as studies of how individuals make sense of their national identity. I suggest that both of these modes of enquiry represent useful tools for examining the future for nationalism and national identity, as together they encourage us to consider the relationship between the kinds of structural changes which encourage greater (or lesser) sympathies with notions of national identity and the ways in which these sentiments are nurtured throughout the course of our often routine social experiences.

Nations, Nationalisms and Social Theory

Over the course of the past decade, there has developed a renewed interest in nationalism and national identity. The dramatic political changes which unfolded in eastern Europe and the former Soviet Union during the late 1980s and, more recently, the protracted negotiations over the issue of European integration, for example, have served to place questions of nation and nationalism to the fore of the political agenda in Europe. Such developments, of course, have not been restricted to Europe: from Zaire and the USA to Kashmir and Quebec, issues of ethnicity and national identity are pressing concerns, albeit with markedly differing consequences. Indeed, as the attention of scholars and policy-makers has increasingly come to focus on the matter of globalization, so the issue of the futures of the nation and nationalism has become a truly global concern. It is against the backdrop of these events that a growing number of scholars from a wide range of disciplines have sought to explore the reasons for the continued potency of national identity, and to examine the ramifications of this recent resurgence of nationalism for international relations.

The debate which has developed around these questions since the mid-1980s is not, however, without historical precedent. Fuelled by the rise of nationalism across the globe throughout the course of the nineteenth and twentieth centuries, there has emerged a burgeoning literature on the development of nationalist politics in particular countries and regions.[1] In addition, prior to this most recent period, there have also been a number of scholars, such as Carlton Hayes (1926), Hans Kohn (1944), Edward Carr (1945), Elie Kedourie (1960), Ernest Gellner (1964) and Karl Deutsch (1966), who have made important contributions to the project of documenting the rise and spread of nationalism in general. The work of historians such as Carr (1945), for example, has been significant in attempting to locate the rise of nationalism in the transition from traditional to modern, industrial society. In a different vein, the 'American' school of historians of nationalism, which includes Hayes (1926, 1931), Louis Snyder (1954, 1964) and Boyd Shafer (1955, 1972), sought to deliver an encyclopaedic survey of the differing forms of nationalism found across the world as well as throughout history.

There is much to commend the work of these early studies of nationalism, particularly – as Benedict Anderson (1996) has noted in a recent volume – given the near-absence of considerations on nationalism within the work of many of the key social theorists of the twentieth century. While scholarly interest in the issues of nationalism and the nation may have fluctuated in accordance with the undercurrents of international relations – the consequences of both World Wars, the rise of colonial and post-colonial nationalisms in the 1950s and 1960s and the 'ethnic revival' (A. D. Smith, 1981) within Western states in the 1960s and early 1970s – this earlier work opened an important conceptual debate on the meanings of 'nation' and 'nationalism' as well as producing wide-ranging empirical classificatory systems. Moreover, these earlier studies were important in stemming complacency with regard to nationalism, particularly the belief that rising affluence and 'modernization' would banish the spectre of nationalism from international relations.

Much of this work, however, has been subject to considerable criticism from more recent writers. Anthony Smith (1996a), himself one of the most prolific contributors to the current debate, has argued that within the work of Hayes, Snyder, Kohn and Shafer, although particularly in their earlier studies, the emphasis is on providing accounts of particular histories and developing classifications of nationalisms, rather than seeking to examine the kinds of general factors which give rise to the appeal of the nation and national identity. In a similar vein, James, critiquing what he calls the 'narrow empiricism' of writers such as Shafer, exclaims that 'the unimaginable complexity of the question, among other considerations, has paradoxically sent the majority of studies in the direction of sequestering the possibilities of a general social theory' (1996: 125). For others working in this field, it is the studies which have emerged since the early 1970s and, more particularly, those published since the early 1980s, which have done the most to advance the study of nationalism. Eric Hobsbawm, detailing his 'reading list' of works on nationalism, states that 'it would not . . . deserve to contain much from the age of those who have been called the "twin founding fathers" of the academic study of nationalism: Carlton B. Hayes and Hans Kohn' (1990: 3). While Benedict Anderson (1991: p. xii), introducing his revised edition of *Imagined Communities* (originally published in 1983), begins by commenting that the additions made to the literature on nationalism and the nation since the early 1980s 'have, by their historical reach and theoretical power, made largely obsolete the traditional literature on the subject' (1991: p. xii).

Certainly, Shafer's expansive tome, *Faces of Nationalism: New Realities and Old Myths* (1972), while an impressive *tour-de-horizon* of nationalisms past and present, does not take us very far in delineating a comprehensive theory of the nation or, to an even lesser extent, of national identity. For Shafer, in common with Hayes, Snyder and Kohn, the main focus of attention is on distinguishing between different forms of nationalist ideology, although principally between those of the 'developed' West, on the one hand, and those of the 'developing nations' of Africa and Asia, on the other. Within the writings of British historians like E. H. Carr (1944), Alfred Cobban (1969) and Hugh Seton-Watson (1977), the emphasis is also on the ideology of nationalism. Seton-Watson is arguably more sensitive to the need to consider the importance of factors such as geography, religion and language as mobilizing factors in the development of national consciousness than either Carr or Cobban, and indeed is more orientated towards grappling with the concepts of nation and national identity. In the case of Carr and Cobban, writing during the Second World War (and Hayes in the aftermath of the First World War), it is perhaps unsurprising that the primary concern should be with an assessment of the significance of nationalist ideologies for international relations. As Snyder, writing in the early 1950s, comments, the study of nationalism is 'of urgent concern not only for the scholar but also for statesmen and citizens dealing in international relations. For nations – with their drives, emotions and real or supposed interests – are the chief actors on the stage of present history' (1954: p. vii). Although these writers engage in discussions of the meaning of nation and nationality, their attentions are nevertheless directed towards nationalism as a specific form of ideology in which the concept of national self-determination is a central factor. By this, I mean that they are concerned with how to 'solve' the conflicts resulting from the competing territorial claims of rival national governments. The definitional problems, the issue of what kinds of processes serve to reproduce the nation and the question of how national identities are sustained in the course of daily social relations and practices, rarely figure in their analyses.

In my view, the failure of these earlier historians of nationalism to address the questions of nation and national identity in any kind of systematic manner has manifested itself in two main ways. First, there has been a tendency, evidenced in the work of historians like Hayes, Snyder, Kohn and Shafer, to construct typologies of national*ism* in the place of a sustained engagement with the issue of how and why the idea of the nation should generate such widespread appeal. Secondly, where these writers, and others such as Seton-Watson, do attempt to define the meaning of the term 'nation' and its appeal, the explanations tell us little beyond the assertion that, to take one example, 'a nation exists when a significant number of people in a community consider themselves to form a nation, or behave as if they formed one' (Seton-Watson, 1977: 5). While such a definition shifts the discussion away from the primordialist 'blood and soil' conception of the nation, it has not moved the discussion much further on from Ernest Renan's voluntaristic account of the nation, written in 1882.[2] Indeed, there is a considerable overlap between the voluntaristic theory of the nation, as advanced by writers as diverse as Renan, Kohn and Seton-Watson, and the concept of the nation as it is articulated within nationalist discourse; as James has remarked: 'despite clear transformations in thinking through the nineteenth and twentieth centuries, Renan's conception reflects a common view held by a tradition of nationalists and theorists alike' (1996: 126).

In a broad sense, however, many of these earlier writers offer a roundly critical account of nationalism. In the writings of Hayes and Kohn, for example, it is possible to discern a distinction between the 'good' nationalisms of the West and the 'bad' nationalisms of Russia and Asia (A. D. Smith, 1996a), nevertheless the underlying position in much of this historical work is that nationalism is an essentially negative, destructive phenomenon. Cobban (1969), while hopeful that the problems generated by the issue of national self-determination can be successfully resolved, points out, in a comparison between imperialism and nationalism, that the threat to a new order (post-1945) comes from an untamed nationalism: 'nationalism, not nationality or even the nation state as such, presents the danger; for the mark of nationalism is that it adds total sovereignty to the nation' (1969: 307). Shafer, in a more direct manner, states that 'I make no secret of my belief that nationalism, especially when carried to extremes, leads to war and destruction' (1972: p. xiii). Other writers, such as Kedourie (1960) and Minogue (1967), while offering theories which differ greatly from those of the historians, nevertheless share their opposition to nationalism; indeed, in the case of Kedourie we are presented with an openly hostile account.

As an undisguised, non-Marxist attack on nationalism, there are few works which surpass Kedourie's *Nationalism* (1960). For Kedourie, nationalism is a doctrine which, as he states in the opening sentence of his study, was 'invented' at the start of the nineteenth century by a group of German philosophers and which was subsequently 'transported' across Europe and across the rest of the world by like-minded intellectuals. Kedourie delivers a resoundingly critical account of what he views as the essence of the doctrine; that is, that the world is naturally divided into separate nations with their own unique cultures. Kedourie maintains that the idea of the nation was brought to life by young intellectuals, frustrated by the denial of positions of authority which they believed should be bestowed on them, and driven by the demise of some of the traditional social institutions of power, such as the church and the family. Nationalist movements attract the support of, and are led by, members of the younger generation because of an erosion of traditional social and religious values, and due to a resentment of an older generation of statesmen struggling to retain the power which is being removed from them. Nationalism, therefore, with all the reforms which it seeks to introduce, provides a platform from which they can direct their opposition towards the older, ruling authorities. Kedourie also claims that involvement in nationalist politics fulfils a more basic desire, one which would have traditionally been satisfied by those institutions from which they now feel themselves to be estranged: 'the need . . . to belong together in a coherent and stable community' (1960: 101).

Kedourie's analysis of the origins and subsequent diffusion of nationalism through Europe and, later, into Africa and Asia (Kedourie, 1971), has been subjected to critiques on a number of different fronts (A. D. Smith, 1971; Gellner, 1983). While in contrast to the historians of nationalism, he does offer a general theory of the kinds of material and intellectual conditions which underpin the attraction of the idea of the nation and national identity, given his emphasis on the young intellectual it is difficult to understand how this enthusiasm is communicated to the rest of the population. Kedourie's theory is not devoid of sociological analysis, as his consideration of the waning influence of the church and other key social institutions during the late eighteenth and early nineteenth reveals. However, as I have already suggested, Kedourie's emphasis on the realm of ideas – in particular, on the role of intellectuals – does not provide us with a satisfactory account of the kinds of cultural practices implicated in the production of the nation nor does he discuss how a sense of national identity develops within a wider set of social relations. Nevertheless, his argument that the nation and nationalism are 'invented' and his claim that this 'invention' is a product of the modern period – a view endorsed by many of the early historians of nationalism – has proved influential for many subsequent theorists.

Indeed, within the mainstream literature which has emerged since the late 1970s and early 1980s – within the work of writers such as Anthony Smith (1981, 1986), John Armstrong (1982), John Breuilly (1982), Benedict Anderson (1983), Ernest Gellner (1983), Eric Hobsbawm (1990), Josep Llobera (1995) and Liah Greenfeld (1992) to name but a few – the major division which has emerged is between, on the one hand, those who stress the modern, 'invented' character of the nation (Anderson, Gellner and Hobsbawm) and, on the other, those who seek to demonstrate that modern nations are reconstructed on the basis of pre-modern forms of ethnic community (Smith and Llobera). In spite of the considerable differences between these two approaches, and allowing for the often conflicting views between individual writers, the main aim of these studies has been to show how, since the early nineteenth century, the idea of having a national identity has come to be grounded in the social relations and material practices of modern societies. In addition, both sets of writers posit the significance of a 'historical break'; maintaining that it is the concomitant changes in the form of social, economic and political relations in the modern period which are so vital to an understanding of why the nation and national identity emerged in the late eighteenth and early nineteenth centuries.

Gellner (1994: 45), while explaining that 'the appeal of cultural ("ethnic") identity is not a delusion', nevertheless contends that any attempt to project the genealogy of the nation back beyond the modern period ignores the decisive role of industrialization in transforming the social and political terrain. For Gellner, the rise of nationalism is to be understood in terms of the context of a (modern) social order in which 'culture', rather than 'structure', determines an individual's place in a changing world.[3] An industrial economy, he notes (Gellner, 1987), is marked by a division of labour which distinguishes it from earlier, traditional forms; individuals must now be able to move to jobs, as well as between them. Such a situation is made possible by the creation of a state-organized education system, in which the medium of instruction is the official state language, a necessary prerequisite for economic growth. It is this 'generic training' (Gellner, 1983) which provides individuals with their passports to full citizenship, as it allows them to participate in economic and social life. More fundamentally, Gellner argues, the changes ushered in as a result of a programme of economic expansion, such as the creation of a 'national' culture, alter existing forms of identity and loyalty. So, while national*ism* may lay claim to timeless traditions, the reality, Gellner maintains, is that the nation could not exist outside of the modern era. He illuminates what he perceives as the inherent contradictions of nationalism when he writes that it 'preaches and defends continuity, but owes everything to a decisive and unutterably profound break in human history' (1983: 125).

For Hobsbawm, as with Gellner, the nation's imputed antiquity is a façade. While mass, public commemorations, flags, symbols and customs – the ideological trappings of the 'historic' nation – 'normally attempt to establish continuity with a suitable historic past' (Hobsbawm and Ranger, 1983: 1), such practices and 'institutions' are, he maintains, relatively recent innovations. Exploring the increase in 'invented traditions' in the period 1870–1914, Hobsbawm argues that while these 'traditions' may have been constructed 'from above' – that is, by monarchs, politicians and political movements – he also maintains that the very success of these 'traditions' in becoming established, and being accepted by the masses, indicates that they, in part, met 'a felt – not necessarily a clearly understood – need among particular bodies of people' (p. 307). Rapid social change, Hobsbawm explains, which diminishes, or destroys the social significance of old customs and traditions, generates the need for new 'invented traditions', on the part of both rulers and ruled. Yet, he maintains (p. 13) that, particularly in the case of the 'nation', the invention of 'national symbols, histories and the rest . . . all rest on exercises in social engineering which are often deliberate and always innovative, if only because historical novelty implies innovation'. Implicit, therefore, in Hobsbawm's contention that the emergence of 'invented' national traditions was directly linked to the need to forge a common, *national* solidarity in the context of a period of crisis, or social and political upheaval, is an emphasis on the present, and on achieving cohesion *in* the present.

'Ethnicists', such as Smith (1986, 1991a) and Llobera (1995), do not take issue with the issue of the modernity of national*ism*, or, indeed, the notion that modern nations differ from earlier forms of ethnic communities (or *ethnie*, to use Smith's preferred term).[4] Modern nations, Smith argues (1971: 186), are distinguished from pre-modern *ethnie* by the former's generation of 'direct membership with equal citizenship rights' and 'vertical economic integration'. However, to view this argument as echoing the claims of 'modernists' misunderstands the underlying logic of the 'ethnicist' thesis. Smith (1986) states that a key difference between members of a pre-modern *ethnie* and modern nationalists, and hence the reason why he views ethnicity as being central to his notion of the 'reconstructed' nation, lies with the methods which they use to achieve their respective, common objectives. As Smith (1986: 217) points out:

> The scale has changed, so has the context; and the means at the nationalist's disposal are much more 'scientific' and effective. But these are changes in the means, not the ends. What the nation and nationalism have done is to extend the ends and give them a larger content, by linking them to the quest for political autonomy and economic autarchy. The result is that restoring one's dignity or renewing one's culture today, are tasks of a quite different order and magnitude than in pre-modern eras.

For Smith, the emphasis is on a sense of historical 'continuity' between pre-modern *ethnie* and modern nations. Again, it is important to note that what is being argued is not that modern nations are the direct, linear descendants of pre-modern *ethnie*, but rather that surviving ethnic links to a pre-modern past represent the foundations on which the former are constructed (Smith, 1995). This point is evident in his critique of Hobsbawm's conception of 'invented traditions', where Smith explains that 'the task . . . of those who set out to forge modern nations is more one of reconstructing the traditions, customs and institutions of the ethnic community or communities which form the basis of the nation, than of inventing new traditions' (1991a: 358–9).

Llobera (1995: 214), postulating a similar account to that of Smith, argues that while all nationalisms seek to reinvigorate a sense of the past, such attempts would be fruitless unless there exists a sufficient store of 'ethnic potential' to draw on; as he writes, 'nations cannot be created or invented *ex nihilo*' (1995: 220). Llobera is in opposition to the notion that an explanation of the rise of nationalism can *only* be sought by exploring the structural conditions of industrial capitalist society. He qualifies this position, however, by arguing that while the emergence of the ideology of nationalism, as it is more commonly understood today, can be traced back to the late eighteenth and early nineteenth centuries, the origins of the ideas of 'nation', 'national identity' and 'even of an incipient patriotic nationalism' (1995: 214) are to be found in the social and political developments which took place in medieval western Europe. Llobera's analysis, then, stresses a historical continuity between medieval past and modern present, maintaining that 'if contemporary (ethno)nationalist ideologies have managed to establish themselves on a sound cultural and political basis, they are extremely resilient and can endure, albeit at times in a hibernating form, all sorts of repressive policies' (1995: p. xi).

There are, then, marked differences in the approaches developed by the 'modernists' and the 'ethnicists'. Both approaches set out to explore the origins and spread of nationalism, yet they also represent a sustained and systematic engagement with the issues of nation and national identity, in marked contrast to much of the earlier work on this subject. Unlike the historical, classifications-of-nationalisms approach, as developed in the work of Snyder and Shafer, for example, for writers as diverse as Smith and Gellner the intention is to provide explanations as to how individuals come to *think* of themselves as possessing a national identity and why this form of identity should so profoundly shape how they relate to others. To this extent then Smith and, in spite of his 'top–down' mode of analysis, Gellner seek to furnish us with accounts of national consciousness. Nevertheless, I suggest that both approaches operate at a rather abstract level. That is to say, the accounts of Gellner and Smith, for example, do not tell us enough about how national identities are sustained and reproduced throughout the course of daily social relations, nor do they provide us with any real acknowledgement that the idea of a national identity may be given any number of different inflections by different individuals.

In part, my critique stems from a dissatisfaction with the 'one culture, one nation' position which characterizes some of the current thinking on national identity. John Breuilly, in a critique of Anderson and Gellner, argues that both of these writers 'rather indiscriminately consider diverse matters such as national consciousness, nationalist doctrine, and nationalist politics. But these are very different matters and what might account for the development of one will not account for the development of another' (1985: 74). In a broader sense it may be stated that theories of nationalism do not necessarily provide the most satisfactory vantage point from which to explore questions of national identity. As I have argued elsewhere (Thompson *et al.*, 1999), nationalist discourse privileges an anonymous and undifferentiated 'people'; within such a discourse the issue of conflicting interests or experiences never features, except when it is necessary to distinguish between 'us' and 'them'. Theorists of nationalism, in an attempt to explore the emotional appeal of the nation, are themselves often guilty of reifying this conception of the culturally uniform nation. Smith (1995: 155), for example, argues that:

> By rehearsing the rites of fraternity in a political community in its homeland at periodic intervals, the nation communes with and worships itself, making its citizens feel the power and warmth of their collective identification and inducing in them a heightened self-awareness and social reflexivity.

In response it might be asked: how is possible that *all* members come to identify with the *same* culture in the *same* way? Indeed, do *all* members recognize each other as belonging to the *same* nation? One need only, for example, point to the popularly held conceptions of the cultural differences between north and south Wales to suggest that the question of a common national culture is considerably more complex than some writers have maintained. As Wollman and Spencer argue: 'under the guise of "taking nationalism seriously", there is a tendency to attribute to it on the one hand a more permanent, and more objective weight and a more automatic claim on spontaneous affections than it necessarily warrants' (1996: 22).

Within the work which has emerged since the late 1980s there is growing evidence of the need to produce a more critical approach to questions of nation and national identity (Billig, 1995; Calhoun, 1995; Guibernau, 1996; James, 1996). Central to much of this work has been an engagement with the relationship between the individual and the wider national community and, in particular, to illuminate the diversity of national experiences. Calhoun has commented on the need to establish a more critical account of nationalism along these lines, writing that, 'it is necessary to overcome the naturalizing notions of ethnicity and nation . . . and to approach the themes of peoples, publics, and nations with attention to a world of possibilities and inner tensions, not just one of static entities' (1995: 273). As Calhoun (1995: 253) correctly points out, nationalism may 'depend very much on individualism', but, as he explains, it 'establishes the nation both as a category of similar individuals and as a sort of "super-individual". As a rhetoric of categorical identity, nationalism is precisely not focused on the various particularistic relationships among members of the nation.'

At the heart of the matter is the need to move beyond theories of national*ism* in accounting for national identity. Some commentators (Schlesinger, 1987; Tomlinson, 1991; Billig, 1995) have already pointed to the attendant problems of attempting to explore national identity within the framework of theories of nationalism. Tomlinson (1991: 79), for example, notes that 'discussions of national identity are mostly found in the literature of the politics of nationalism . . . yet the specific psychological contents, the 'phenomenology', as it were, of national identity is rarely probed in detail'. Other writers, such as Billig (1995) and Jenkins (1995), have argued for the need to adopt a more 'flexible' conception of nationalism, one which, in the case of the former, allows us to comprehend the (re)production of national identity through 'banal routines' (Billig, 1995: 44), or, as in the case of the latter, is 'concerned with nationalisms rather than nationalism' (Jenkins, 1995: 385). The growth of interest within different academic disciplines as well as the import of ideas across disciplinary boundaries has generated new perspectives on questions of national identity and has offered alternative vantage points from which to consider existing contributions. Moreover, deliberations on the 'politics of identity', globalization and postmodernity, for example, have also served to highlight the attendant problems of producing general, all-embracing theoretical models within which issues of difference are subject to neglect. These developments, I would suggest, provoke us to reconsider 'nationalism' and 'national identity'. This does not mean that there is no place for the practice of constructing theoretical models around these issues;

simply, it argues that there needs to be a greater awareness of the methodological problems of such activities, particularly how such ways of talking about these issues serve to reproduce notions of 'homogeneity' at the expense of recognizing difference. It means, for example, that we need to acknowledge the operation of a vast array of differing discourses of the nation and the national – such as in the media, education, the heritage industry, political rhetoric, sports coverage and academia – and how these practices contribute to the embedding of 'national identity' in everyday experiences. Ultimately, however, it means that it is necessary to investigate how such structuring of public representations of the nation and national identity serve to demarcate, on the one hand, who is allowed to 'belong' and, on the other hand, who is not.

Conclusion

The principal aim of this chapter has been to highlight the development of debates on 'nationalism', the 'nation' and 'national identity'. This discussion does not represent a comprehensive guide to developments in the field of studies of nationalism and national identity; rather, it is an attempt to trace the shift away from some of the more traditional ways of thinking about the nation and national identity and the attendant move towards a recognition of the diversity of national experiences. To this end, I have been concerned to illustrate some of the positive changes with respect to thinking on nation and national identity. The role which ideas of nationhood occupy in everyday discourses goes largely unnoticed and, as a result, 'common-sense' assumptions about the objective differences between 'nations' are themselves rarely subject to scrutiny.

In Wales, too, we are wintering through a period of considerable social change, which is forcing us to confront the legacies of the past. Widespread processes of social and economic restructuring have contributed to the withering away of many of the traditional bases of social identity, but in their wake they have exposed alternative sites of struggle, which, in turn, have transformed the debate on Wales and Welsh identity. Thus, while there has been growing concern in Wales about the loss of a sense of community and solidarity and about the concomitant fragmentation of Wales, change has also prompted debate about the plurality of Welsh experiences. Moreover, discussion over the place of Wales within a 'Europe of the Regions' and within the wider global economy, as well as its future position in the United Kingdom, has further underscored the need to ask questions not just about the processes of change in Wales itself, but also about the impact of social, economic and political change *on* Wales.

As a result of these shifts, the 'national question' is now firmly back on the political agenda in Wales. In the context of these developments, it is important to consider the institutional bases which will, in the future, facilitate the reproduction of publicly articulated projections of Wales and Welshness. The 'problematic element' of Welsh identity, to which Raymond Williams draws our attention, is characteristic of *all* national identities. Whether one uses, as is found in the literature on nationalism, the terms 'invented' (Kedourie, 1960; Gellner, 1983), 'imagined' (Anderson, 1991) or 'reconstructed' (Smith, 1991a) to refer to the social processes which give rise to the national form, there is nevertheless a widespread acknowledgement among scholars in this field that the production and reproduction of national identities relies on a complex web of institutional and cultural practices. To paraphrase the prevailing sociological orthodoxy, then, nations are not 'natural' and we are not born possessing a sense of national identity; such 'communities' and forms of identity arise in the course of our social relations. Nevertheless, there may be those who will claim to possess a 'true' or 'pure' national identity, against which other competing claims are to be judged. As Williams explains, for some the sense of Welshness may be rendered more problematic than for others, as a consequence of the dynamics of cultural politics. As contributors elsewhere in this volume observe, issues of 'heritage', 'race', 'gender', 'community' are all implicated in differing discourses of Wales and Welshness.

Throughout the course of the development of the sociology of Wales since the mid-1970s, the fusion of wider currents in social theory and empirical research on changing social conditions in Wales has been of considerable importance. From the engagements with writers such as Hechter and Nairn in the late 1970s and early 1980s, to the more recent considerations of the current debates on nationalism and ethnicity, there has been a steady growth of scholarly interest in the processes and practices implicated in the reproduction of a variety of (often conflicting) projections of Welshness. This recent research has done much to alleviate what the editors of an earlier volume of sociological research termed a 'poverty of knowledge' (Rees and Rees, 1980) concerning aspects of social life in Wales. Now, however, with issues of Welsh nationhood once again an issue of public debate, it is an opportune time to develop a more inclusive dialogue on the national future of Wales.

Notes

1. Some of the extensive bibliographies to these studies can be found in Shafer (1955), Deutsch (1966) and Smith (1973).
2. This essay has been republished in Bhabha (1990a).
3. See Gellner (1987) for a discussion of this theme.
4. This term, *ethnie*, is perhaps the most important concept employed by A. D. Smith. A French term denoting a group which shares both peculiar cultural features and a particular sense of historical pedigree is, Smith maintains, the nearest equivalent in Western languages to the ancient Greek *ethnos*. For an introductory understanding of Smith's exact use of this term see Smith (1986).

Bibliography

Aaron, J. (1994). 'Finding a voice in two tongues: gender and colonization', in Aaron, J., Rees, T., Betts, S. and Vincentelli, M. (eds.), *Our Sisters' Land: The Changing Identities of Women in Wales*, Cardiff: University of Wales Press.
Aaron, J., Rees, T., Betts, S. and Vincentelli, M. (eds.) (1994). *Our Sisters' Land: The Changing Identities of Women in Wales*, Cardiff: University of Wales Press.
Adamson, D. L. (1984). 'Social class and ethnicity in nineteenth century rural Wales', *Sociologica Ruralis*, 24, 202–15.
Adamson, D. L. (1988). 'The new working class and political change in Wales', *Contemporary Wales*, 2, 7–28.
Adamson, D. L. (1991a). *Class, Ideology and the Nation: A Theory of Welsh Nationalism*, Cardiff: University of Wales Press.
Adamson, D. L. (1991b). 'Lived experience, social consumption and political change in Wales', in Day, G. and Rees, G. (eds.), *Nations and European Integration: Remaking the Celtic Periphery*, Cardiff: University of Wales Press.
Adamson, D. L. (1996). *Living on the Edge: Poverty and Deprivation in Wales*, Llandysul: Gomer.
Ahearne, J. (1995). *Michel de Certeau: Interpretation and its Other*, Cambridge: Polity.
Allan, S. and Thompson, A. (1999). 'The time-space of national memory', in Brehony, K. and Rassool, N. (eds.), *Nationalisms: Old and New*, London: Macmillan.
Allan, S. (1994). 'When discourse is torn from reality: Bakhtin and the principle of chronotopicity', *Time and Society*, 32, 193–218.
Anderson, B. (1983). *Imagined Communities: Reflections on the Origins and Spread of Nationalism*, 1st edn., London: Verso.
Anderson, B. (1991). *Imagined Communities: Reflections on the Origins and Spread of Nationalism*, 2nd edn., London: Verso.
Anderson, B. (1996). 'Introduction', in Balakrishnan, G. (ed.), *Mapping the Nation*, London: Verso.

Anderson, J. (1988). 'Nationalist ideology and territory', in Johnston, R. J., Knight, D. B. and Kofman, E. (eds.), *Nationalism, Self-Determination and Political Geography*, London: Croom Helm.

Anthias, F. and Yuval-Davis, N. (1993). *Racialised Boundaries*, London: Routledge.

Armstrong, J. (1982). *Nations Before Nationalism*, Chapel Hill, NC: University of North Carolina Press.

Arnason, J. (1990). 'Nationalism, globalization and modernity', in Featherstone, M. (ed.), *Global Culture: Nationalism, Globalization and Modernity*, London: Sage.

Bagley, C. and Verma, G. K. (1979). *Racial Prejudice, the Individual and Society*, Farnborough: Saxon House.

Bakhtin, M. M. (1981). *The Dialogic Imagination*, ed. M. Holquist, tr. by C. Emerson and M. Holquist, Austin, TX: University of Texas Press.

Balakrishnan, G. (ed.) (1996). *Mapping the Nation*, London: Verso.

Balibar, E. and Wallerstein, I. (1991). *Race, Nation, Class: Ambiguous Identities*, London: Verso.

Balsom, D. (1985). 'The three Wales model', in Osmond, J. (ed.), *The National Question Again*, Llandysul: Gomer.

Barker, M. (1981) *The New Racism*, London: Junction Books.

Barrios de Chungara, D. (1983). 'Women and organization', in Davies, M. (ed.) *Third World – Second Sex: Women's Struggles and National Liberation*, London: Zed.

Barthes, R. (1993) *Mythologies*, London: Vintage.

Baudrillard, J. (1983). *Simulations*. (New York: Semiotext(e)), cited in Robertson, R., 'After nostalgia? Wilful nostalgia and the phases of globalization', in Turner, B. (ed.), *Theories of Modernity and Postmodernity*, London: Sage.

Baughan, P. E. (1980), *A Regional History of the Railways of Great Britain*, Vol. 11, *North and Mid Wales*, Newton Abbot: David and Charles.

Bauman, Z. (1990). 'Modernity and ambivalence', in Featherstone, M. (ed.), *Global Culture: Nationalism, Globalization and Modernity*, London: Sage.

Bauman, Z. (1992a). 'Soil, blood and identity', *Sociological Review*, 404, 675–701.

Bauman, Z. (1992b). *Intimations of Postmodernity*, London: Routledge.

Beddoe, D. (1986). 'Images of Welsh women', in Curtis, T. (ed.), *Wales: The Imagined Nation*, Bridgend: Poetry Wales Press.

Benda, J. (1959). *The Betrayal of the Intellectuals*, Boston, MA: The Beacon Press.

Benjamin, W. (1973). 'The work of art in the age of mechanical reproduction', in Arendt, H. (ed.) *Illuminations*, tr. H. Zohn, London: Fontana.

Bennett, T. (1988). 'Museums and the people', in Lumley, R. (ed.), *The Museum Time Machine*, London: Routledge.
Betts, C. (1976). *Culture in Crisis: The Future of the Welsh Language*, Upton, Wirral: The Ffynnon Press.
Betts, S. (ed.) (1996). *Our Daughters' Land: Past and Present*, Cardiff: University of Wales Press.
Bhabha, H. K. (ed.) (1990a). *Nation and Narration*, London: Routledge.
Bhabha, H. K. (1990b). 'DissemiNation', in Bhabha, H. K. (ed.), *Nation and Narration*, London: Routledge.
Bhabha, H. K. (1994). *The Location of Culture*, London: Sage.
Billig, M. (1995). *Banal Nationalism*, London: Sage.
Borland, R., Fevre, R. and Denney, D. (1992). 'Nationalism and community in north west Wales', *Sociological Review*, 40, 49–72.
Bowen, E. G. and Fleure, H. J. (1930). 'Denmark and Wales', *Geography*, 15/6, 468–76.
Bowie, F. (1993). 'Wales from within: conflicting interpretations of Welsh identity', in MacDonald, S. (ed.), *Inside European Identities*, Oxford: Berg Publishers.
Bramwell, A. (1989). *Ecology in the 20th Century: A History*, New Haven, CT: Yale University Press.
Brecht, B. (1990). cited in Watts, M. J., 'Development 1: Power, Knowledge, Discursive Practice', *Progress in Human Geography*, 17/2 (1993), 257–72.
Brennan, T. (1990). 'The national longing for form', in Bhabha, H. K. (ed.), *Nation and Narration*, London: Routledge.
Breuilly, J. (1982). *Nationalism and the State*, 1st edn., Manchester: Manchester University Press.
Breuilly, J. (1985) 'Reflections on nationalism', *Philosophy of the Social Sciences*, 15, 65–75.
Breuilly, J. (1993). *Nationalism and the State*, 2nd edn., Manchester: Manchester University Press.
Buchanan, C. and Partners (1966) *Cardiff Development and Transportation Study: Probe Study Report*, London: Colin Buchanan and Partners.
Burke, P. (1992). 'We the people: popular culture and popular identity in modern Europe', in Lash, S. and Friedman, J. (eds.), *Modernity and Identity*, Cambridge: Polity.
Butt, Philip A. (1975). *The Welsh Question: Nationalism in Welsh Politics, 1945–1970*, Cardiff: University of Wales Press.
Calhoun, C. (1995). *Critical Social Theory*, Oxford: Blackwell.
Callaghan, J. (1987). *Time and Chance*, London: Collins.
Canovan, M. (1996). *Nationhood and Political Theory*, London: Edward Elgar.

Cardiff City Council (n.d.). *1991 Census of Population: Community Summaries*, Cardiff: Cardiff City Council.
Carr, E. H. (1945). *Nationalism and After*, London: Collins.
Cashmore, E. (1987). *The Logic of Racism*, London: Allen and Unwin.
Centre for Contemporary Cultural Studies (1982). *The Empire Strikes Back*, London: Hutchinson.
Chambers, I. (1994). *Migrancy, Culture, Identity*, London: Routledge.
Charles, N. and Davies, C. A. (1997). 'Contested communities: the refuge movement and cultural identities in Wales', *Sociological Review*, 45/3, 416–36.
Chatterjee, P. (1986). *Nationalist Thought and the Colonial World: A Derivative Discourse*, London: Zed.
Chatterjee, P. (1990). 'The nationalist resolution of the women's question', in Sangari, K. and Vaid, S. (eds.), *Recasting Women: Essays in Indian Colonial History*, Brunswick, NJ: Rutgers University Press.
Clifford, J. (1988). *The Predicament of Culture: Twentieth-Century Ethnography, Literature, and Art*, Cambridge, MA: Harvard University Press.
Cloke, P. and Milbourne, P. (1992). 'Deprivation and lifestyles in rural Wales: II. Rurality and the cultural dimension', *Journal of Rural Studies*, 8, 359–71.
Cobban, A. (1969). *The Nation State and National Self-Determination*, London: Collins.
Cohen, A. (ed.) (1982). *Belonging: Identity and Organisation in British Rural Cultures,* Manchester: Manchester University Press.
Cohen, A. (1985). *The Symbolic Construction of Community*, London: Ellis Horwood/Tavistock.
Cohen, B. G. and Jenner, P. J. (1968). 'The employment of immigrants: a case study within the wool industry', *Race,* 10/1, 41–56.
Cohen, R. (1994). *Frontiers of Identity: the British and Others*, London: Longman.
Connolly, W. E. (1994). 'Toqueville, territory and violence', *Theory, Culture and Society*, 1, 19–41.
Connor, W. (1990). 'When is a nation?', *Ethnic and Racial Studies*, 13/1, 92–103.
Cooke, P. N. (1980). 'Capital relation and state dependency: an analysis of urban development policy in Cardiff', in Rees, G. and Rees, T. (eds.), *Poverty and Social Inequality in Wales*, London: Croom Helm.
Cooke, P. (1985). 'Class practices as regional markers: a contribution to labour geography', in Gregory, D. and Urry, J. (eds.), *Social Relations and Spatial Structures,* London: Macmillan.
Crang, M. (1994). 'On the heritage trail: maps of and journeys to Old England', *Environment and Planning D: Society and Space,* 12, 341–55.

Crwydren, R. (1994). 'Welsh lesbian feminist: a contradiction in terms?', in Aaron, J., Rees, T., Betts, S. and Vincentelli, M. (eds.), *Our Sisters' Land: The Changing Identities of Women in Wales*, Cardiff: University of Wales Press.

Curtis, T. (ed.) (1986). *Wales: The Imagined Nation. Essays in Cultural and National Identity*, Bridgend: Poetry Wales Press.

Daniels, S. (1993). *Fields of Vision: Landscape Imagery and National Identity in England and the United States*, Cambridge: Polity.

Daunton, M. J. (1977). *Coal Metropolis: Cardiff, 1870–1914*, Leicester: Leicester University Press.

Davies, C. A. (1983). 'Welsh Nationalism and the British state', in Williams, G. (ed.), *Crisis of Economy and Ideology: Essays on Welsh Society, 1840–1980*, London: SSRC/BSA Sociology of Wales Study Group.

Davies, C. A. (1989). *Welsh Nationalism in the Twentieth Century: The Ethnic Option and the Modern State*, New York: Praeger.

Davies, C. A. (1994). 'Women, nationalism and feminism', in Aaron, J., Rees, T., Betts, S. and Vincentelli, M. (eds.), *Our Sisters' Land: The Changing Identities of Women in Wales*, Cardiff: University of Wales Press.

Davies, C. A. (1996). 'Nationalism – discourse and practice', in Charles, N. and Freeland, F. H. (eds.), *Practising Feminism: Identity, Difference, Power*, London: Routledge.

Davies, D. H. (1983). *The Welsh Nationalist Party 1925–1945: A Call to Nationhood*, Cardiff: University of Wales Press.

Davies, E. and Rees, A. D. (eds.) (1960). *Welsh Rural Communities*, Cardiff: University of Wales Press.

Davies, J. (1988). 'Aristocratic town-makers and the coal metropolis: the Marquess of Bute and the growth of Cardiff, 1776 to 1947', in Cannadine, D. (ed.), *Patricians, Power and Politics in Nineteenth Century Towns*, Leicester: Leicester University Press.

Davies, J. (1993). *A History of Wales*, London: Penguin.

Davis, H. H. (1979). *Beyond Class Images,* London, Croom Helm.

Day, G. (1979). 'The sociology of Wales: issues and prospects', *Sociological Review*, 27, 447–74.

Day, G. (1980). 'Wales, the regional problem and development', in Rees, G. and Rees, T. (eds.), *Poverty and Social Inequality in Wales*, London: Croom Helm.

Day, G. (1984). 'Development and national consciousness: the Welsh case', in Vermeulen, H. and Boissevain, J. (eds.), *Ethnic Challenge: The Politics of Ethnicity in Europe*, Gottingen: Edition Heredot.

Day, G. (1998). 'A community of communities? Similarity and difference in Welsh rural community studies', *Economic and Social Review*, 3 (July), 233–57.

Day, G. and Murdoch, J. (1993). 'Locality and community: coming to terms with place', *Sociological Review*, 41, 82–111.

Day, G. and Suggett, R. (1985). 'Conceptions of Wales and Welshness: aspects of nationalism in nineteenth century Wales', in Rees, G. et al. (eds.), *Political Action and Social Identity*, London: Macmillan.

Delaney, J. (1992). 'Ritual space in the Canadian museum of civilization: consuming Canadian identity', in Shields, R. (ed.), *Life Style Shopping*, London: Routledge.

Delanty, G. (1996). 'Beyond the nation state: national identity and citizenship in a multicultural society – a response to Rex', *Sociological Research On Line*, 1/3, <http:www.socresonline.org.uk/socresonline/1/3/1/html>

Denney, D., Borland, J. and Fevre, R. (1991). 'Racism, nationalism and conflict in Wales', *Contemporary Wales*, 4, 150–65.

Deutsch, K. (1966). *Nationalism and Social Communication*, New York: John Wiley.

Deutsch, K. (1969). *Nationalism and its Alternatives*, New York: Knopf.

Devine, F. (1992). 'Social identities, class identity and political perspectives', *Sociological Review*, 40/2, 229–52.

Dicks, B. (1996). 'Regeneration v. representation in the Rhondda: the story of the Rhondda Heritage Park', *Contemporary Wales*, 9, 56–73.

Dicks, B. (1997a). 'The View of Our Town from the Hill: An Enquiry into the Representation of Community at the Rhondda Heritage Park', unpublished Ph.D. thesis, University of Cardiff, Wales.

Dicks, B. (1997b). 'The life and times of community: spectacles of collective identity at the Rhondda Heritage Park', *Time and Society*, 6/2–3, 196–212.

Duffield, M. (1984). 'New racism . . . new realism: two sides of the same coin', *Radical Philosophy*, 37, 29–34.

Dumbleton, B. (n.d.). *The Second Blitz*, Cardiff: Dumbleton.

Ehrentraut, A.W. (1991). 'Heritage without history: the open-air museums of Austria in comparative perspective', *Canadian Review of Sociology and Anthropology*, 28, 46–66.

Elfyn, M. (1994). 'Writing is a bird in hand', in Aaron, J., Rees, T., Betts, S. and Vincentelli, M. (eds.), *Our Sisters' Land: The Changing Identities of Women in Wales*, Cardiff: University of Wales Press.

Emmett, I. (1964). *A North Wales Village: A Social Anthropological Study*, London: Routledge and Kegan Paul.

Emmett, I. (1982). '*Fe godwn ni eto:* stasis and change in a Welsh industrial town', in Cohen, A. (ed.), *Belonging: Identity and Organisation in British Rural Cultures,* Manchester: Manchester University Press.

Estates Gazette (1988). 'Focus on the M4 West', *Estates Gazette*, 8812, 69–93.

Evans, G. (1988). *Welsh Nation Builders,* Llandysul: Gomer.
Evans, N. (1980). 'The south Wales race riots of 1919', *Llafur: Journal of Welsh Labour History,* 3/1, 5–29.
Evans, N. (1985a). 'The Welsh Victorian city: the middle class and civic and national consciousness, Cardiff 1850–1914', *Welsh History Review,* 12, 350–87.
Evans, N. (1985b). 'Cardiff's labour traditions', *Llafur: Journal of Welsh Labour History,* 4/2, 77–90.
Evans, N. (1991). 'Immigrants and minorities in Wales 1840–1990: a comparative perspective', *Llafur: Journal of Welsh Labour History,* 4/5, 5–26.
Evans, N. (1996). 'Community, memory and history: Senghenydd and the Valleys', *Planet,* 115, 47–55.
Evans, S. (1995). 'What is to be done about Welsh racism?', *Planet,* 110, 114–16.
Eyles, J. and Evans, M. (1987). 'Popular consciousness, moral ideology, and locality', *Society and Space,* 5, 39–71.
Femia, J. V. (1981). *Gramsci's Political Thought: Hegemony, Consciousness and the Revolutionary Process,* Oxford: Clarendon Press.
Feminist Review (1993) Nationalism and national identity, 44 (Summer).
Fevre, R., Denney, D. and Borland, J. (1997) 'Class, status and party in the analysis of nationalism: lessons from Max Weber', *Nations and Nationalism,* 3/4, 559–77.
Fleure, H. J. (1921). 'Countries as personalities', *Nature,* 108/2722, 573-5.
Fleure, H. J. (1922). 'The land of Wales', in Muirhead F. (ed.), *Wales: The Blue Guides,* London: Macmillan & Co.
Fleure, H. J. (1926). *Wales and her People,* Wrexham: Hughes & Son.
Fleure, H. J. (1940). 'The Celtic west', *Journal of the Royal Society of Arts* (4 Oct.), 882–4.
Fleure, H. J. (1943). 'Peasants in Europe', *Geography,* 28/2, 55–61.
Fogelsong, R. (1996). 'Planning the capitalist city', in Campbell, S. and Farnstein, S (eds.), *Readings in Planning Theory,* Oxford: Blackwell.
Foucault, M. (1986). 'Of other spaces', *Diacritics,* 16/1, 22–7.
Foulkes, D., Jones, J. B. and Wilford, R. A. (1986). 'Wales: a separate administrative unit', in Hume, I. and Pryce, W. T. R. (eds.), *The Welsh and their Country,* Llandysul: Gomer.
Francis, H. (1985) 'The law, oral tradition and the mining community', *Journal of Law and Society,* 12/3 (Winter), 267–71.
Francis, H. and Smith, D. (1980) *The Fed,* London: Lawrence & Wishart.
Francis, R. (1983) 'Symbols, images and social organisation in urban sociology', in Pons, V. and Francis, R. (eds.), *Urban Social Research: Problems and Prospects,* London: RKP.

Frankenberg, R. (1957) *Village on the Border: A Sociological Study of Religion, Politics and Football*, London: Cohen & West.
Garfinkel, H. (1984). *Studies in Ethnomethodology*, Cambridge: Polity.
Gellner, E. (1964). *Thought and Change*, London: Weidenfeld & Nicolson.
Gellner, E. (1983). *Nations and Nationalism*, Oxford: Basil Blackwell.
Gellner, E. (1987). *Culture, Identity and Politics*, Cambridge: Cambridge University Press.
Gellner, E. (1994). *Encounters with Nationalism*, Oxford: Blackwell.
Gerth, H. H. and Mills, C. W. (eds.) (1948). *From Max Weber*, London: Routledge and Kegan Paul.
Giddens, A. (1984). *The Constitution of Society*, Cambridge: Polity.
Giddens, A. (1985). *The Nation-State and Violence*, Vol. 2 of *A Contemporary Critique of Historical Materialism*, Cambridge: Polity.
Giggs, J. and Pattie, C. (1992a). 'Croeso i Gymru – welcome to Wales: but welcome to whose Wales?', *Area*, 24/3, 268–82.
Giggs, J. and Pattie, C. (1992b). 'Wales as a plural society', *Contemporary Wales*, 5, 25–63.
Gilliam, A. (1991). 'Women's equality and national liberation', in Mohanty, C. Russo, A. and Torres, L. (ed.), *Third World Women and the Politics of Feminism*, Bloomington, IN: Indiana University Press.
Gilroy, P. (1987). *There Ain't No Black in the Union Jack*, London: Hutchinson.
Golwg (1996). 'Nid Du a Gwyn', Dylan Iorwerth (7 Feb).
Gould, P. C. (1988). *Early Green Politics: Back to Nature, Back to the Land, and Socialism in Britain 1880–1900*, Brighton: Harvester Press.
Gramsci, A. (1971). *Selection from the Prison Notebooks*, London: Lawrence & Wishart.
Greenfeld, L. (1992). *Nationalism: Five Roads to Modernity*, Cambridge, MA: Harvard University Press.
Gregory, D. (1994). *Geographical Imaginations*, Oxford: Blackwell.
Griffiths, D. (1996). *Thatcherism and Territorial Politics*, Aldershot: Avebury.
Gruffudd, P. (1994). 'Back to the land: historiography, rurality and the nation in inter-war Wales', *Transactions of the Institute of British Geographers*, 19/1, 61–77.
Gruffudd, P. (1995a). 'Remaking Wales: nation-building and the geographical imagination', *Political Geography*, 14/3, 219–39.
Gruffudd, P. (1995b). 'Heritage as national identity: histories and prospects of the national pasts', in Herbert, D. T. (ed.), *Heritage, Tourism and Society*, London: Mansell.
Guibernau, M. (1996). *Nationalisms: The Nation-State and Nationalism in the Twentieth Century*, Cambridge: Polity.

Gwent Health Authority (1990). *Gwent Profile of Illness and Health*, Pontypool: GHA.
Hague, C. and Thomas, H. (1997). 'Planning capital cities: Edinburgh and Cardiff compared', in Macdonald, R. and Thomas, H. (eds.), *Nationality and Planning in Scotland and Wales*, Cardiff: University of Wales Press.
Hall, S. (1980). 'Encoding/Decoding', in Hall, S., Hobson, D., Lowe, A. and Willis, P. (eds.), *Culture, Media, Language*, London: Hutchinson.
Hambleton, R. and Mills, L. (1993). 'Local government reform in Wales', *Local Government Policy Making*, 19/4, 45–55.
Hamilton, N. (1988). 'The City Centre', in Evans, E. and Thomas, H. (eds.), *Cardiff Capital Development*, Cardiff: Cardiff City Council.
Harris, J. (1996). 'Glass waves and crystal necklaces', *Planet*, 115, 6–13.
Harvey, D. (1989). 'Monument and myth: the building of the Basilica of the Sacred Heart', in Harvey, D., *The Urban Experience*, Oxford: Blackwell.
Harvie, C. (1994). *The Rise of Regional Europe*, London: Routledge.
Haugeland, J (1992). 'Dasein's disclosedness', in Dreyfus, H. and Hall, H. (eds.), *Heidegger: A Critical Reader*, Cambridge, MA: Basil Blackwell.
Hayes, C. (1926). *Essays on Nationalism*, New York: Macmillan.
Hayes, C. (1931). *The Historical Evolution of Modern Nationalism*, New York: Richard Smith.
Hechter, M. (1975). *Internal Colonialism: The Celtic Fringe in British National Development 1536–1966*, London: Routledge & Kegan Paul.
Hechter, M. (1985). 'Internal colonialism revisited', in E. A. Tiryakin and E. A. Rogowski (eds.), *New Nationalisms of the Developed West*, London: Allen and Unwin.
Henderson, J. and Karn, V. (1987). *Race, Class and State Housing: Inequality and the Allocation of Public Housing in Britain*, Aldershot: Gower.
Hester, S. (1991). 'The social facts of deviance in schools', *British Journal of Sociology*, 42/3, 443–63
Hetherington, K. (1996). 'The utopics of social ordering: Stonehenge as a museum without walls', in Macdonald, S. and Fyfe, G. (eds.), *Theorising Museums*, Oxford: Basil Blackwell.
Hewison, R. (1987). *The Heritage Industry: Britain in a Climate of Decline*, London: Methuen.
Hewison, R. (1989). 'Heritage: an interpretation', in Uzzell, D. L. (ed.) *Heritage Interpretation*, London: Bellhaven Press.
Hill, R. S. (1974). 'Planning, Decision-Making and Democracy: A Case Study of the Planning Process in Cardiff', M.Sc. dissertation, Department of Town Planning, UWIST, Cardiff.
Hobsbawm, E. (1990). *Nations and Nationalism since 1780*, Cambridge: Cambridge University Press.

Hobsbawm, E. and Ranger, T. (1983). *The Invention of Tradition*, Cambridge: Cambridge University Press.
Hooge, L. (1992). 'Nationalist movements and social factors: a theoretical perspective', in Coakley, J. (ed.), *The Social Origins of National Movements: The Contemporary West European Experience*, London: Sage.
Hosking, G. and Schopflin, G. (eds.) (1997). *Myths and Nationhood*, London: Hurst and Co.
Hroch, M. (1985). *Social Preconditions of National Revival in Europe: A Comparative Analysis of the Social Composition of Patriotic Groups among Smaller European Nations*, Cambridge: Cambridge University Press.
Humphreys, R. (1995). 'Images of Wales', in Herbert, T. and Elwyn Jones, G. (eds.), *Post-War Wales*, Cardiff: University of Wales Press.
Hutchinson, J. (1987). *The Dynamics of Cultural Nationalism*, London: Allen and Unwin.
Huyssen, A. (1995). *Twilight Memories: Marking Time in a Culture of Amnesia*, London: Routledge.
Ignatieff, M. (1993). *Blood and Belonging: Journeys into the New Nationalisms*, London: BBC Books/Chatto & Windus.
Imrie, R. and Thomas, H. (1993). 'The limits of property-led regeneration', *Environment and Planning C: Government and Policy*, 11, 87–102.
Jackson, P. (1989). *Maps of Meaning*, London: Unwin Hyman.
James, P. (1996). *Nation Formation: Towards a Theory of Abstract Community*, London: Sage.
Jameson, F. (1991). *Postmodernism or the Cultural Logic of Late Capitalism*, London: Verso.
Jenkins, G. A. (1992). *Getting Yesterday Right: Interpreting the Heritage of Wales*, Cardiff: University of Wales Press.
Jenkins, R. (1995). 'Nations and nationalisms: towards more open models', *Nations and Nationalism*, 1/3, pp. 369–90.
Jenkins, R. (1996). *Social Identity*, London: Longman.
Johnson, N. (1995). 'Cast in stone: monuments, geography and nationalism', *Environment and Planning D: Society and Space*, 13, 51–65.
Jones, Bobi (1974). 'The roots of Welsh inferiority', *Planet*, 22, 53–72.
Jones, G. (1948). *A Prospect of Wales*, London: Penguin.
Jones, R. Merfyn (1982). *The North Wales Quarrymen 1874–1922*, Cardiff: University of Wales Press.
Jordan, G. (1988). 'Images of Tiger Bay: did Howard Spring tell the truth?', *Llafur: Journal of Welsh Labour History*, 5/1, 53–7.
Kahn, K. (1984). 'Land, language and community: a symbolic analysis of Welsh nationalism', *Michigan Discussions in Anthropology*, 7, 11–32.
Kedourie, E. (1960). *Nationalism*, London: Hutchinson.

Kedourie, E. (ed.) (1971). *Nationalism in Africa and Asia*, London: Weidenfeld & Nicolson.
Kellas, J. G. (1991). *The Politics of Nationalism and Identity*, Basingstoke: Macmillan.
Khleif, B. B. (1978). 'Ethnic awakening in the first world: the case of Wales', in Williams, G. (ed.), *Social and Cultural Change in Contemporary Wales*, London: Routledge.
Khleif, B. B. (1980). *Language, Ethnicity and Education in Wales*, The Hague: Mouton Publishers.
King, A. D. (1993). 'Cultural hegemony and capital cities', in Taylor, J. et al. (eds.), *Capital Cities*, Ottawa: Carleton University Press.
Kohn, H (1944). *The Idea of Nationalism: A Study in its Origins and Background*, New York: Macmillan.
Kristeva, J. (1988). *Étrangers à nous-mêmes*, Paris: Fayard.
Laponce, J. A. (1993). 'Ottawa, Christaller, Horowitz and Parsons', in Taylor, J. et al. (eds.), *Capital Cities*, Ottawa: Carleton University Press.
Lash, S. and Urry, J. (1987) *The End of Organized Capitalism*, Cambridge: Polity.
Lewis, E. and P. (1949). *The Land of Wales*, London: B. T. Batsford.
Lewis, R. (1949). 'This is Not What We Want', *The Welsh Nationalist*, 18/8, 1 and 8.
Lewis, S. (1936a). 'The case for Welsh nationalism', *The Listener* (13 May), 915–16.
Lewis, S. (1936b). 'Paham y gwrthwynebwn yr ysgol fomio', Y *Ddraig Goch*, 10/3, 6–7.
Lewis, S. (1975). *Egwyddorion Cenedlaetholdeb, Principles of Nationalism*, Cardiff: Plaid Cymru.
Lewis, S. (1985). 'Deg Pwynt Polisi', in *Canlyn Arthur: Ysgrifau Gwleidyddol*, Llandysul: Gwasg Gomer.
Llobera, J. (1995). *The God of Modernity: The Development of Nationalism in Western Europe*, Oxford: Berg.
Lockwood, D. (1966). 'Sources of variation in working class images of society', *Sociological Review*, 21/1, 55–73.
Lord, P. (1992). *The Aesthetics of Relevance*, Llandysul: Gomer.
Lord, P. (1994). *Gwenllian: Essays on Visual Culture*, Llandysul: Gomer.
Lovering, J. (1978). 'The theory of the internal colony and the political economy of Wales', *Review of Radical Political Economics*, 10, 55–67.
Luckin, B. (1990). *Questions of Power: Electricity and Environment in Inter-War Britain*, Manchester: Manchester University Press.
MacDonald, S. (1993). 'Identity complexes in western Europe', in MacDonald, S. (ed.), *Inside European Identities*, Oxford: Berg.

Marks, D. (1996). 'Slate heritage – the history of a Welsh industry or a trip down the light fantastic?' unpublished conference paper.
Marshall, G., Vogler, C., Rose, D. and Newby, H. (1987). 'Distributional struggle and moral order in a market society', *Sociology*, 21/1, 55–73.
Marshall, T. H. (1950). *Citizenship and Social Class*, Cambridge: Cambridge University Press.
Massey, D. (1995). 'Places and their pasts', *History Workshop Journal*, 39 (Spring).
Massey, P. (1937). 'A portrait of a mining town', *Fact*, 8 (15 Nov.), 7–78.
Matless, D. (1998). *Landscape and Englishness*, London: Reaktion Books.
Matthews, C. F. (1949). *Wales Can Prosper the TVA Way*, Caernarfon: Welsh Economic Development Association.
Mellor, D. (ed.) (1987). *A Paradise Lost: The Neo-Romantic Imagination in Britain 1935–55*, London: Lund Humphries/Barbican.
Miles, R. (1987a). 'Recent Marxist theories of nationalism and the issue of racism', *British Journal of Sociology*, 38, 24–43.
Miles, R. (1987b). 'Racism and nationalism in Britain', in Husband, C. (ed.), *'Race' in Britain: Continuity and Change*, London: Hutchinson.
Miles, R. (1993). *Racism after Race Relations*, London: Routledge.
Miles, R. and Dunlop, A. (1986). 'The racialisation of politics in Britain: why Scotland is different', *Patterns of Prejudice*, 20/1, 23–32.
Miles, R. and Phizacklea, A. (1984). *White Man's Country: Racism in British Politics,* London: Pluto Press.
Minogue, K. (1967). *Nationalism*, London: Methuen.
Moore, H. (1994). *A Passion for Difference*, Cambridge: Polity.
Moore, R. (1975). *Racism and Black Resistance in Britain*, London: Pluto Press.
Morgan E. (1996) 'Changing a stagnant and bitter system', *Where Wales? The Nationhood Debate, The Western Mail* (June).
Morgan, K. O. (1963). *Wales in British Politics*, Cardiff: University of Wales Press.
Morgan, K. O. (1981). *Rebirth of a Nation, 1880–1980*, Oxford and Cardiff: Clarendon Press and University of Wales Press.
Morgan, K.O. (1995). *Modern Wales: Politics, Places and People*, Cardiff: University of Wales Press.
Morgan, P. (1983). 'From a death to a view: the hunt for the Welsh past in the romantic period', in Hobsbawm, E. and Ranger, T. (eds.), *The Invention of Tradition*, Cambridge: Cambridge University Press.
Morgan, P. (1986a). 'Keeping the legends alive', in Curtis, T. (ed.), *Wales: The Imagined Nation. Essays in Cultural and National Identity*, Bridgend: Poetry Wales Press.
Morgan, P. (1986b) 'The gwerin of Wales: myth and reality', in Hume, I.

and Pryce, W. T. R. (eds.), *The Welsh and their Country*, Llandysul: Gomer.

Morgan, R. (1994). *Cardiff: Half and Half a Capital*, Llandysul: Gomer.

Morris, D. and Williams, G. (1994). 'Language and social work practice: the Welsh case', in *Social Work and the Welsh Language*, Cardiff: CCETSW/University of Wales Press.

Morris, J. and Wilkinson, B. (1989). *Divided Wales: Local Prosperity in the 1980s*, Cardiff: Cardiff Business School.

Morris, P. (1996). 'Community beyond tradition', in Heelas, P., Lash, S. and Morris, P. (eds.), *Detraditionalization: Critical Reflections on Authority and Identity*, Oxford: Blackwell.

Morton, H. V. (1932). *In Search of Wales*, London: Methuen.

Mosse, G. L. (1985). *Nationalism and Sexuality: Middle-Class Morality and Sexual Norms in Modern Europe*, Madison, WI: University of Wisconsin Press.

Nairn, T. (1977). *The Break up of Britain: Crisis and Neo-Colonialism*, London: New Left Books.

Nairn, T. (1986). 'Culture and politics in Wales', in Hume, I. and Pryce, W. T. R. (eds.), *The Welsh and their Country*, Llandysul: Gomer.

Nash, C. (1993). 'Remapping and renaming: new cartographies of identity, gender and landscape in Ireland', *Feminist Review*, 44, 39–57.

National Museum of Wales (1974). *Welsh Folk Museum, St Fagans – Handbook*, St Fagans: National Museum of Wales.

Neuwirth, G. (1969). 'A Weberian outline of a theory of community: its application to the "Dark Ghetto"', *British Journal of Sociology*, 20/2, 148–63.

Palmer, A. (ed.) (1948). *Recording Britain*, vol. 3, Oxford: Oxford University Press/Pilgrim Trust.

Parkin, F. (1979). *Marxism and Class Analysis*, London: Tavistock.

Peach, C. (1968). *West Indian Migration to Britain*, Oxford: Oxford University Press for the Institute of Race Relations.

Peate, I. C. (1929). 'Y crefftwr yng Nghymru', *Y Ddraig Goch*, 4/1, 4 and 8.

Peate, I. C. (1935a). 'Letter to Clough Williams-Ellis', 31 May. CPRW Papers 9/19. National Library of Wales, Aberystwyth.

Peate, I. C. (1935b). *The Llŷn Peninsula: Some Cultural Considerations*. Memo in CPRW Papers 9/19. National Library of Wales, Aberystwyth.

Peate, I. C. (1941). 'Mynydd Epynt', *Y Llenor*, 20/4, 183–8.

Peate, I. C. (1943). 'Yr ardaloedd gwledig a'u dyfodol', *Y Llenor*, 22/1–2, 10–18.

Penrose, J. (1993). 'Reification in the name of change', in Jackson, P. and Penrose, J. (eds.), *Constructions of Race, Place and Nation*, London: UCL Press.

Plaid Cymru (1998). *The Best for Wales: Plaid Cymru's Programme for the New Millennium*, Cardiff: Plaid Cymru.

Pollner, M. (1987). *Mundane Reason: Reality in Everyday and Sociological Discourses*, Cambridge: Cambridge University Press.

Pratt, M. L. (1992). *Imperial Eyes: Travel Writing and Transculturation*, London: Routledge.

Price, D. (1992). 'Gazing at the Valleys: Representation and the Cultural Construction of South Wales', unpublished Ph.D. thesis, University of Birmingham.

Pryce, W. T. R. (1986). 'Wales as a culture region: patterns of change 1780–1971', in Hume, I. and Pryce, W. T. R. (eds.), *The Welsh and their Country*, Llandysul: Gomer.

Rabinow, P. (1996). 'On the archaeology of late modernity', in *Essays on the Anthropology of Reason*, Princeton, NJ: Princeton University Press.

Race and Class (1991). Special Issue, *Europe: Variations on the Theme of Racism*, 32/3.

Rawkins, P. M. (1979). 'An approach to the political sociology of the Welsh nationalist movement', *Political Studies*, 27, 440–57.

Rawkins, P. M. (1983). 'Uneven development and the politics of culture', in Williams, G. (ed.), *Crisis of Economy and Ideology: Essays on Welsh Society, 1840–1980*, London: SSRC/BSA Sociology of Wales Study Group.

Rees, A. D. (1950). *Life in a Welsh Countryside*, Cardiff: University of Wales Press.

Rees, G. (1993). 'Book reviews', *Sociology*, 27/2, 307–12.

Rees, G. (1997). 'The politics of regional development strategy: the programme for the Valleys', in Macdonald, R. and Thomas, H. (eds.), *Nationality and Planning in Scotland and Wales*, Cardiff: University of Wales Press.

Rees, G. and Lambert, J. (1981). 'Nationalism as legitimation? Notes towards a political economy of regional development in south Wales', in Harlowe, M. (ed.), *New Perspectives in Urban Change and Conflict*, London: Heinemann.

Rees, G. and Rees, T. (eds.). (1980) *Poverty and Social Inequality in Wales*, London: Croom Helm.

Rees, G. and Rees, T. (1983). 'Migration, industrial restructuring and class relations: an analysis of south Wales', in Williams, G. (ed.), *Crisis of Economy and Ideology: Essays on Welsh Society, 1840–1980*, London: SSRC/BSA.

Rees, J. F. (1963). *The Problem of Wales and Other Essays*, Cardiff: University of Wales Press.

Rex, J. (1996). 'National identity in the democratic multi cultural state',

Sociological Research Online, 1/2, <http://www.socresonline.org.uk/socresonline1/2/1.html>

Rex, J. and Moore, R. (1967). *Race, Community and Conflict – a Study of Sparkbrook*, Oxford: Oxford University Press for the Institute of Race Relations.

Roberts, B. (1992). 'A mining town in wartime: the fears for the future', *Llafur*, 6, 1, 82–95.

Roberts, B. (1994). 'Welsh identity in a former mining valley: social images and imagined communities', *Contemporary Wales*, 7, 77–93, and this volume.

Roberts, D. (1981). 'The Welsh Slate Quarrying Communities 1911–1939', unpublished Ph.D. thesis, University of Wales, Aberystwyth.

Roberts, D. (1984). *'Dros Ryddid a Thros Ymerodraeth': Ymatebion yn Nyffryn Ogwen 1914–1918*, Dinbych: Argraffwyd gan Wasg Gee.

Robertson, R. (1990). 'After nostalgia? Wilful nostalgia and the phases of globalisation', in Turner, B. S. (ed.), *Theories of Modernity and Postmodernity*, London: Sage.

Robins, K. (1997). 'Tradition and translation: national culture in its global context', in McDowell, L. (ed.), *Undoing Place?*, London: Arnold.

Rodger, J. (1992). 'The welfare state and social closure: social division and the "underclass"', *Critical Social Policy*, 12/2, 45–63.

Rosaldo, M. (1987). 'Moral/analytic dilemmas posed by the intersection of feminism and social science', in Rabinow, P. and Sullivan, W. M. (eds.), *Interpretive Social Science: A Second Look*, Berkeley, CA: University of California Press.

Rowbotham, S. (1992). *Women in Movement: Feminism and Social Action*, London: Routledge.

Said, E. W. (1978). *Orientalism*, London: Routledge and Kegan Paul.

Said, E. W. (1994). *Representations of the Intellectual: The 1993 Reith Lectures*, London: Vintage.

Samuel, R. (1994). *Theatres of Memory*, London: Verso.

Samuel, R. (1995). 'Theme parks – why not?', *Independent on Sunday*, 12 February.

Schama, S. (1996). *Landscape and Memory*, London: Fontana Press.

Schirmer, J. G. (1989). '"Those who die for life cannot be called dead": women and human rights protest in Latin America', *Feminist Review*, 32, 3–29.

Schlesinger, P. (1987). 'On national identity: some conceptions and misconceptions criticized', *Social Science Information*, 26/2, 219–64.

Schwarzmantel, J. (1987). 'Class and nation: problems of socialist nationalism', *Political Studies*, 35, 239–55.

Schwarzmantel, J. (1992). 'Nation versus class: nationalism and socialism in theory and practice', in Coakley, J. (ed.), *The Social Origins of*

National Movements: The Contemporary West European Experience, London: Sage.
Searle, G. R. (1979). 'Eugenics and politics in Britain in the 1930s', *Annals of Science*, 36, 159–69.
Seton-Watson, H. (1977). *Nations and States: An Enquiry into the Origins and Politics of Nationalism*, London: Methuen.
Shafer, B. C. (1955). *Nationalism: Myth and Reality*, New York: Harcourt, Brace and World.
Shafer, B. C. (1972). *Faces of Nationalism*, New York: Harcourt Brace Jovanovich.
Sherwood, M. (1991). 'Racism and resistance: Cardiff in the 1930s and 1940s', *Llafur: Journal of Welsh Labour History*, 5/4, 51–70.
Shields, R. (1991). *Places on the Margin: Alternative Geographies of Modernity*, London: Routledge.
Sibley, D. (1995). *Geographies of Exclusion*, London: Routledge.
Sivanandan, A. (1978). 'From immigration control to "induced repatriation"', *Race and Class*, 20, 75–82.
Smith, A. D. (1971). *Theories of Nationalism*, London: Duckworth.
Smith, A. D. (1973). 'Nationalism: trend report and bibliography', *Current Sociology*, 21, 3.
Smith, A. D. (1979). *Nationalism in the Twentieth Century*, Oxford: Martin Robertson.
Smith, A. D. (1981). *The Ethnic Revival in the Modern World*, Cambridge: Cambridge University Press.
Smith, A. D. (1986). *The Ethnic Origins of Nations*, Oxford: Blackwell.
Smith, A. D. (1991a). 'The nation – invented, imagined, reconstructed', *Millennium*, 20/3, 353–68.
Smith, A. D. (1991b). *National Identity*, Harmondsworth: Penguin.
Smith, A. D. (1992). 'Chosen peoples: why ethnic groups survive', *Ethnic and Racial Studies*, 15/3.
Smith, A. D. (1995). *Nations and Nationalism in a Global Era*, Cambridge: Polity.
Smith, A. D. (1996a). 'Nationalism and the historians', in Balakrishnan, G. (ed.), *Mapping the Nation*, London: Verso.
Smith, A. D. (1996b). 'Culture, community and territory: the politics of ethnicity and nationalism', *International Affairs*, 72/3, 445–58.
Smith, D. (1984). *Wales! Wales?*, London: Allen and Unwin.
Smith, D. (1996). 'Progress or prozac?', *Where Wales? The Nationhood Debate, The Western Mail* (June).
Smith, D. and Williams, G. (1980). *Fields of Praise*, Cardiff, University of Wales Press.
Smith, D. E. (1987). 'Women's perspective as a radical critique of

sociology', in Harding, S. (ed.), *Feminism and Methodology*, Bloomington, IN: Indiana University Press.
Snyder, L. (1954). *The Meaning of Nationalism*, New Brunswick, NJ: Rutgers University Press.
Snyder, L. (1964). *The Dynamics of Nationalism*, Princeton, NJ: Van Nostrand.
Stacey, M. (1969). 'The myth of community studies', *British Journal of Sociology*, 20/2, 134–47.
Stapledon, R. G. (1943). *The Way of the Land*, London: Faber & Faber.
Stapledon, R. G. (1944). *The Land Now and Tomorrow*, London: Faber & Faber.
Stoker, G. and Mossberger, K. (1994). 'Urban regime theory in comparative perspective', *Environment and Planning C: Government and Policy*, 12, 195–212.
Sutherland in Wales/Sutherland yng Nghymru (1976). London: Alistair McAlpine.
Tarrant, M. (1942). 'Mining Town – 1942', File Report 1498, in the Tom Harrison Mass-Observation Archive, The Library, University of Sussex, Brighton. This study has been edited (in book form) as Roberts, B. and Tarrant, M., 'A Mining Town in Wartime: A Mass-Observation Study' (unpublished).
Taylor, J., Lengellé, J. and Andrew, C. (eds.) (1993). *Capital Cities*, Ottawa: Carleton University Press.
Thomas, D. (1989). 'Wales in 1988: an economic survey', *Contemporary Wales*, 3, 199–233.
Thomas, E. (1983). *Wales*, Oxford: Oxford University Press.
Thomas, H. and Imrie, R. (1993a). 'Cardiff Bay and the project of modernisation', in Imrie, R. and Thomas, H. (eds.), *British Urban Policy and the Urban Development Corporations*, London: PCP.
Thomas, H. and Imrie, R. (1993b). 'What's in a name? Realignment in the politics of urban redevelopment in Cardiff', *Planet*, 101, 8–13.
Thomas, H. (1989). 'Cardiff – City Profile', *Cities*, 91–101.
Thomas, H. (1994). 'The local press and urban renewal', *International Journal of Urban and Regional Research*, 18, 315–33.
Thomas, H. (1995). 'A model in planning consultation', *Surveyor* (1 June), 14–15.
Thomas, H., Stirling, T., Brownhill, S. and Razzaque, K. (1996). 'Locality, urban governance and contested meanings of place', *Area*, 28, 186–98.
Thomas, N. (1998). 'Now the party is over', *Planet*, 127, 27–30.
Thompson, A. (1994). 'The Social Construction of Welsh Identity', unpublished Ph.D. thesis, University of Wales, Bangor.

Thompson, A., Adamson, D. and Day, G. (1999) 'Bringing the local back: the production of Welsh identity', in Brah, A., Hickman, M. and Mac an Ghaill, M. (eds.), *Thinking Identities: Ethnicity, Racism and Culture*, London: Macmillan.

Tomlinson, J. (1991). *Cultural Imperialism*, London: Pinter.

Tomos, A. (1994). 'A Welsh lady' in Aaron, J., Rees, T., Betts, S. and Vincentelli, M. (eds.), *Our Sisters' Land: The Changing Identities of Women in Wales*, Cardiff: University of Wales Press.

Touraine, A. (1995). *Critique of Modernity*, Oxford: Blackwell.

Turner, B. S. (1990) cited in Robertson, R. 'After Nostalgia? Wilful nostalgia and the phases of globalization', in Turner, B. S. (ed.), *Theories of Modernity and Postmodernity*, London: Sage.

Urry, J. (1981). *The Anatomy of Industrial Societies*, London: Macmillan.

Urry, J. (1990). *The Tourist Gaze*, London: Sage.

Urry, J. (1996). 'How societies remember the past', in Macdonald, S. and Fyfe, G. (eds.), *Theorizing Museums*, Cambridge: Blackwell/The Sociological Review.

Uzzell, D. L. (1989). 'Introduction: the natural and built environment', in Uzzell, D. L. (ed.), *The Natural and Built Environment*, London: Bellhaven Press.

Vale, E. (1935a). *The World of Wales*, London: J. M. Dent & Sons.

Vale, E. (1935b). 'Wales: the spirit and the face', *The Beauty of Britain*, London: B. T. Batsford.

Valentine, G. (1995). 'Creating transgressive space: the music of KD Lang', *Transactions of the Institute of British Geographers*, NS20, 474–85.

Van Loon, J. (1996). 'A cultural exploration of time: some implications of temporality and mediation', *Time and Society*, 5/1, 61–84.

Van Loon, J. (1997). 'Chronotopes of/in the televisualization of the 1992 L.A. riots', *Theory, Culture and Society*, 89–104.

Vergo, P. (1989). *The New Museology*, London: Reaktion Books.

Waller, R. (1962). *Prophet of the New Age: The Life and Thought of Sir George Stapledon*, London: Faber & Faber.

Walsh, K. (1992). *The Representation of the Past: Museums and Heritage in the Postmodern World*, London: Routledge.

Ward, M. (1983). *Unmanageable Revolutionaries: Women and Irish Nationalism*, London: Pluto Press.

Weber, M. (1946, reprinted 1973). 'The nation', in Gerth, H. H. and Wright-Mills, C. (trs. and eds.) *From Max Weber: Essays in Sociology*, New York: Oxford University Press.

Weber, M. (1968). *Economy and Society*, ed. G. Roth and C. Wittich, New York: Bedminster Press.

Welsh Nationalist Party (London branch) (1944). *Plan Electricity for Wales*, London: Welsh Nationalist Party.

West, B. (1988). 'The making of the English working past', in Lumley, R. (ed.), *The Museum Time Machine,* London: Routledge.

Western Mail (1998). 'Anti Welsh statements go to the Commission for Racial Equality' (2 Jan.).

Western Mail (1998). 'Racist groups target Wales for recruits' (7 May).

Willener, A. (1975). 'Images, action, "Us" and "Them" ', in Bulmer, M. (ed.), *Working Class Images of Society,* London: RKP/SSRC.

Williams, C. (1995). 'Race and racism: some reflections on the Welsh context', *Contemporary Wales*, 8, 113–31.

Williams, C. (1996). *Democratic Rhondda*, Cardiff: University of Wales Press.

Williams, C. (1998). 'European Year Against Racism: The Torfaen Project', unpublished report, Torfaen County Borough Council.

Williams, C. H. and Smith, A. D. (1983). 'The national construction of social space', *Progress in Human Geography*, 7/4, 502–18.

Williams, D. (1955). *The Rebecca Riots*, Cardiff: University of Wales Press.

Williams, D. T. (1936). 'Linguistic divides in north Wales: a study in historical geography', *Archaeologia Cambrensis*, 91, 194–209.

Williams, G. (1966). *Merthyr Politics: The Making of a Working Class Tradition*, Cardiff: University of Wales Press.

Williams, G. (1978). *Social and Cultural Change in Contemporary Wales*, London: Routledge and Kegan Paul.

Williams, G. (1980). 'Industrialisation, inequality and deprivation in rural Wales', in Rees, G. and Rees, T. (eds.), *Poverty and Social Inequality in Wales*, London: Croom Helm.

Williams, G. (1981). 'Economic development, social structure and contemporary nationalism in Wales', *Review*, 2, 275–310.

Williams, G. (1983). *Crisis of Economy and Ideology: Essays on Welsh Society, 1840–1980*, London: SSRC/BSA Sociology of Wales Study Group.

Williams, G. (1985). 'The political economy of contemporary nationalism in Wales', in Tiryakin, E. and Rogowski, R. (eds.), *New Nationalisms of the Developed West*, New York: Allen and Unwin.

Williams, G. (1986). 'Recent trends in the sociology of Wales', in Hume, I. and Pryce, W. T. R. (eds.), *The Welsh and their Country*, Llandysul: Gomer.

Williams, G. (1994). 'Discourses on "nation" and "race": a response to Denney *et al.*', *Contemporary Wales*, 6, 87–103.

Williams, G. A. (1980). 'Locating a Welsh working class: the frontier years', in Smith, D. (ed.), *A People and a Proletariat: Essays in the History of Wales, 1780–1980*, London: Pluto Press.

Williams, G. A. (1982). *The Welsh in their History*, London: Croom Helm.

Williams, G. A. (1985). *When Was Wales? A History of the Welsh*, London: Black Raven Press.

Williams, R. (1979). *Politics and Letters: Interviews with New Left Review*, London: New Left Books.

Williams, S. R. (1991). 'The true "Cymraes": images of women in women's nineteenth-century Welsh periodicals', in John, A. V. (ed.), *Our Mothers' Land: Chapters in Welsh Women's History, 1830–1939*, Cardiff: University of Wales Press.

Williams, T. (1996). 'Pobl Pontcanna chatter away democracy', *Where Wales? The Nationhood Debate*, *The Western Mail* (June).

Wilson, J. (1996) 'The Chicago of Wales: Cardiff in the nineteenth century', *Planet*, 115, 14–25.

Wollman, H. and Spencer, P. (1996). 'Blood and sacrifice: politics versus culture in the construction of nationalism', paper delivered to the British Sociological Association Annual Conference, University of Reading, April.

Woolf, S. (1996). *Nationalism in Europe 1815 to the Present: A Reader*, London: Routledge.

Wright, P. (1995). 'Heritage clubs slug it out', *Guardian* (4 Feb.).

Wright, P. (1985). *Living in an Old Country*, London: Verso.

Yuval-Davis, N. (1997). *Gender and Nation*, London: Sage.

Zolberg, V. L. (1996). 'Museums as contested sites of remembrance', in Macdonald, S. and Fyfe, G. (eds.), *Theorizing Museums*, Oxford: Blackwell/The Sociological Review.

Index

A55 203
Aaron, J. 17, 105–7
Aberystwyth 156–7, 160
Act of Union 160
Adamson, D. 6–8, 12, 15–16, 20, 48–68, 70, 78, 112, 115, 132–3, 174, 228–9
Adamsdown 182
Adfer 136
aesthetics 150–1
African National Congress 143
agriculture 159, 162–6
Ahearne, J. 214
Allan, S. 235
Anderson, B. 10, 12–14, 34, 48, 58, 70–2, 76–7, 82, 92, 94, 111–12, 133, 138, 149, 208–11, 223, 224, 236, 237, 248
Anderson, J. 150
androcentrism 92, 95, 205
Anglesey 140, 161
Anglicization 55, 59, 151, 161–2
Anglo-Welsh 65, 66
Anthias, F. 71–2
anthropology 14, 157, 216
anti-English sentiment 81
anti-immigration 129–48
anti-imperialism 80
anti-racism 83
Armstrong, J. 240
arson 131–2, 147
art 16, 150–3, 167, 192
Arthurian legend 152
Arts and Crafts Movement 162
audio-visual presentations 217–27
Austria 62, 63

Bagley, C. 143–4
Balibar, E. 45–6
Balsom, D. 112

banal nationalism 30–1, 79, 82, 214–15
Bangor 32, 37, 40, 46
Barker, M. 145
Barrios de Chugara, D. 94
Baudrillard, J. 197
Baughan, P. E. 204
Bauman, Z. 128, 213, 224
Beamish 200
Bebb, A. 162
Beddgelert 204
Beddoe, D. 171
belonging 46–7, 77, 213
Benda, J. 48, 67
Benjamin, W. 218
Bennett, T. 192, 197
Bergson, H. 157
Betts, C. 98
Betts, S. 17
Bhabha, H. 14, 84, 208, 211, 213, 225–6, 230
Biffen, J. 148n
bilingualism 28, 103, 175
Billig, M. 14, 30–1, 77, 214–15, 234, 245
black and ethnic minorities 83, 86
black communities 82, 83, 84
black population 15, 17
black Welsh identity 87
Blaenau Ffestiniog 194, 198–204
borders 3, 14, 86, 139, 233
Borland, J. 13, 18–19, 72–6, 112, 129–48
Borrow, G. 153
boundaries 133, 135, 150, 207–18, 230
bourgeoisie 7–8, 10, 55–6, 206
Bowie, F. 39, 86
Bramwell, A. 162
Brecht, B. 194, 197
Brennan, T. 211
Breuilly, J. 241, 244
Bristol 178

INDEX   271

British Broadcasting Corporation 87, 159
British empire 9, 19, 22, 209, 225–7, 230–2
British National Party 147, 85
British nationalism 69, 70, 88
British racism 84, 88
British sociology 5
British state 6, 69–70, 117, 149, 231
Britishness 9, 21–2, 29, 39, 70, 77, 144, 149, 151, 165, 209, 225, 230–2
Buchanan, C. 176–7, 225–6
British Wales 112, 113–14, 124
Buchanan, C. 176–7, 225–6
built environment 171, 187, 188
Butetown 182
Butt Philip, A. 56

Caernarfon 37, 81, 196, 203
Calhoun, C. 30, 245–6
Callaghan, J. 175
Campaign for the Preservation of Rural Wales 160
Canovan, M. 30–1
Capel y Ffin 152
capital cities 169, 171
capitalism 7, 163–4, 192, 211, 222, 231, 244
Cardiff 20, 82–3, 168–90, 201, 218, 225–6
Cardiff Bay Development Corporation 181–7
Cardiff Bay 20, 170
Cardiff Rugby Club 180
Caribbean 142
Carr, E. H. 236, 238
Cashmore, E. 144
categorization 34–8
Cathays Park 168, 171, 174
Cefn 132, 141
Celtic Fringe 9, 69, 79, 153, 157–8
Centreplan 177–8
chapels 118, 120, 153, 157
Charles, N. 106
Chartism 63
Chatterjee, P. 93, 95
childcare 102
Chechnya 184
children 99, 101–2
citizenship 17, 77, 83, 243
city boosterism 178, 184

civic leaders 172
civic nationalism 96–7
civil society 54, 98
class 6–7, 59, 63, 65–7, 91, 93–5, 114–16, 126–7, 171, 191–206
Clifford, J. 213
Cloke, P. 13, 112, 121
coal industry 21, 219–25
coal-owners 220
Cobban, A. 239
Cohen, A. 133–5, 140–1, 148n
Cohen, B. G. 145
collective identity 207–9, 221–4
Cohen, R. 39, 40, 41, 46
collective memory 61, 67, 111
colonialism 79, 95, 104, 143, 172, 210, 212, 229
commodification 66, 158, 192, 206
common knowledge 36–7
common sense 17, 247
Communist Party 220
community 6, 12, 13, 16, 18, 77–8, 111, 113–14, 133–9, 149–50, 158–62, 194, 207–11, 216, 218–19, 221–4, 241, 247, 248
conflict 15, 17–19, 22–3, 116, 131, 136, 142, 144–8, 210
Connolly, W. 212
Connor, W. 128
Conservative Party 112, 129, 140, 143–4, 176
Constable, J. 150
consumption 170, 179
contested identity 23, 38–40, 45–7, 73–7, 208, 225–32
Conwy Valley 203
Cook, A. J. 220
Cooke, P. 180
copper industry 203
council housing 131, 140, 147, 175
counter-hegemony 60
Crang, M. 219
Crwydren, R. 106
cultural imperialism 79
culture 3, 8, 31, 38, 45, 49, 51, 53, 54, 57, 58, 64, 67, 73, 78, 86, 94, 96, 98, 111, 112, 124, 138–9, 143–4, 159–62, 167, 192, 227, 241, 243
Curtis, T. 39, 149
Cymdeithas yr Iaith Gymraeg 72, 80, 101–2, 106, 132, 136, 140, 141, 143

Cymru Fydd 55–60, 68

Daniels, S. 150
Davies, C. A. 11, 13, 15–18, 70, 88, 90–108
Davies, D. H. 60, 65, 99, 159, 163
Davies, E. 6
Davies, J. 172
Day, G. 6, 7, 8, 11–17, 27–47, 78, 111
de Tocqueville, A. 212
de-industrialization 18, 159, 162
Delaney, J. 216
Delanty, G. 69, 76–7
democracy 30
Denmark 158–9, 162
Denney, D. 18, 72–6, 129–48
Depression 63
Deutsch, K. 235
devolution 4, 6, 9, 29, 88
diaspora 70, 83
Dicks, B. 15, 19, 21–2, 207–32
discourse analysis 11
disestablishment 56
domestic sphere 93, 98, 102, 104
Duffield, M. 145
Durkheim, E. 38, 51
Dwyfor 132

economic development 7, 12, 141, 191
economic policy 60
economic restructuring 5, 12–13, 111–28
Edinburgh 172
education 3, 16, 61, 64, 67, 68, 93–4, 98, 159, 212, 241
Edwards, O. M. 58, 61
Ehrentraut, A. W. 62–3
eisteddfodau 60, 65, 120, 130, 157
Eldridge, M. 153
electricity 164–6
Elfyn, M. 106
élites 7–8, 55, 56, 59, 61, 63, 66, 67, 78, 87, 92, 94, 117, 170
Ellis, T. E. 56
Emmet, I. 46–7
empire see British empire
England 19, 75, 112, 130, 140, 142–8, 150, 153, 157–9, 163, 172, 191, 193, 202, 235
English language 198–206, 227
English nationalism 80

English identity 29, 32, 33, 36, 37, 40, 85, 124
Englishness 70, 80, 191
enhabitation 215
epistemology 17, 90, 95, 103, 107
Epynt 161–2
estate agents 131
ethnic absolutism 74, 78
ethnic communities 114
ethnic identity 8, 83, 111, 116, 117, 122, 186, 193, 241
ethnic minorities 104
ethnic revival 236
ethnicists 242, 243
ethnicity 7, 16, 193–4, 206, 235, 246
ethnie 243, 249n
ethnocentrism 74
ethnography 160, 216
ethnomethodology 47
Europe 4, 57, 93, 104, 218, 234, 235, 248
European integration 235
European Union 173
Europeanization 173
Evans, G. 61
Evans, N. 77, 80, 172, 173
exploitation 7, 10, 95, 135, 224, 231
extremism 123

family 92–4, 100
farmers 163–6
femininity 105, 171
feminism 13, 15,17, 88, 90–108
Fevre, R. 15, 18–19, 72–6, 129–48
Ffestiniog Railway 192, 198–200, 204
fictive ethnicity 45
flagging 215
Fleure, H. 156–9, 160, 164, 167
folk culture 158–62
folk museums 62–3
forgetting 212–13, 215, 223
Foucault, M. 216
Frankenberg, R. 6
Free Wales Covenanters 131, 142–3
fund-raising 100
functionalism 63

Gaeltacht 158
Gellner, E. 8, 10, 27, 48, 51–2, 92, 94, 133, 136, 212, 240, 241–2, 248, 249
gender 90–108, 114, 171, 221, 248
geographical imagination 150–1, 160, 162

geography 11, 93, 137–8, 145, 149–50, 156, 160, 167, 207–18
German philosophy 239
Germany 93
Giddens, A. 126, 212
Giggs, J. 198, 228
Gilroy, P. 87, 145, 183, 211
Glamorgan 228
Glasgow 172
Gilliam, A. 94
globalism 233
globalization 3, 23, 211, 246
Golwg 75
Gould, P. C. 162
Gramsci, A. 16, 53–5, 60, 67, 197
Greenfeld, L. 96, 241
Gregory, D. 150
Gruffudd, P. 13, 16, 19–20, 149–67
Guibernau, M. 38, 245
gwerin 19, 59, 63–4, 66–7, 77–8, 151, 159–62
Gwynedd 129–48, 155, 193–206
Gwynedd County Council 130, 196

Hall, S. 129, 217
Harvey, D. 170
Harvie, C. 173
Hayes, C. 235, 237
Healey, D. 148n
Hechter, M. 5–12, 79, 112, 248
hegemony 16, 50–3, 59, 72, 76, 82, 88, 113, 169, 229
Henderson, J. 148n
heritage industry 15, 20–2, 49, 60, 66, 117, 125, 191–206, 247
hermeneutics 217
heterotopia 216
Hetherington, K. 216
Hewison, R. 192, 194, 218, 220
historiography 4, 16, 151, 213, 219–24
history 4, 21, 91, 150, 156, 192–3, 198, 202, 204, 207–18
Hobsbawm, E. 61, 233, 237, 242, 243
Home Rule 57, 87, 125
house prices 130, 140
housing 129
housing policy 18, 129–48
Hroch, M. 50
Humphreys, R. 227–8
Huyssen, A. 222
hybridity 81, 84, 88

iconography 217
ideological state apparatuses 63
ideology 9, 12, 90–108, 149, 163–4, 193, 209–10, 212
Ignatieff, M. 96
imaginative geography 213
imagined community 12, 70–2, 84, 111–28, 135–6, 194, 209–11, 213–14, 229–30
immigration 15, 18–19, 81, 85, 129–48, 228
imperialism 80, 205, 211, 239
independence 124–5
Indian nationalism 93
individualism 246
industrial revolution 58, 59, 62, 65–6, 236, 241
industrialization 7, 18, 21, 62, 64, 156, 241
industrialism 62, 65, 123, 157, 159, 164–5, 194, 228
intellectuals 16, 20, 48–68, 91, 239–41
intelligentsia 48, 49, 52, 58, 64, 66, 151
internal colonialism 6–10, 162
invented traditions 242, 243
Ireland 6
Irish nationalism 102, 104, 158
Ironbridge Gorge Trust 202

James, P. 51, 237, 245
Jameson, F. 192, 197, 200
Jenkins, G. A. 197
Jenkins, R. 40, 246
Jenner, P. J. 145
jobs 141, 145–6, 194
Jones, D. 152
Jones, G. 153
Jones, R. M. 198, 205
Jones, T. 136
Jordan, G. 183

Kahn, K. 228
Karn, V. 148n
Kashmir 235
Kedourie, E. 50–2, 239–41, 248
Khleif, B. 9–11
King, A. 169–70
Kinnock, N. 222
Kohn, H. 96, 235, 237
Kristeva, J. 213

Labour government 222

labour movement 66, 173–4, 220–3
Labour Party 3, 112, 124, 220
labourism 18, 220–1, 227–9, 231
Laclau, E. 11
Lambert, J. 11–12
land 19, 150, 221, 228
landscape 19–20, 149–67, 195–200, 228
language 16, 91, 96, 144, 147, 221, 228
Lash, S. 200
Latin America 102
legislation 97, 147, 212
legitimacy 169
legitimation 52, 91
Lewis, E. 156
Lewis, R. 165
Lewis, S. 60, 103, 159–61
Lewis, W. T. 220
Liberal Party 7, 55–60
Llafur 65
Llanberis 141, 195, 198
Llanberis Lake Railway 192, 196, 198, 201
Llechwedd slate caverns 198, 202–4
Llobera, J. 241, 243–4
Lloyd George, D. 56
Llŷn Peninsula 159–60, 161
local government 130, 147, 148n, 175–81, 196, 203
local identity 14, 27–47, 111–28, 207–8, 218, 225, 229
Lockwood, D. 111
London 172
Lord, P. 151
Lovering, J. 7

M4 corridor 116, 178
Malkin, B. H. 228
maps 209–10
marginality 208, 218, 226, 229, 231
Marks, D. 15, 21, 191–206
marquess of Bute 171, 172
Marxism 7–10, 53–5, 59, 79
masculinity 171, 205
Massey, D. 155, 196, 206
Matless, D. 155
Meibion Glyndŵr 79, 132, 143, 147
Mellor, D. 151
Merched y Wawr 100
Merthyr Rising 63
middle class 28, 43, 91, 93–4, 99–100, 173

Milbourne, P. 13, 112, 121
Miles, R. 70, 143, 145
Millennium Commission 203
Miners' Federation 220
miners' strike 115, 222
mining disasters 220
mining identity 115, 127
Minogue, K. 239
modernism 154
modernists 64–5, 67, 154–5, 164, 167, 229, 243
modernity 242
modernization 7, 50–3, 179, 181, 182
Montgomeryshire 156
Moore, R. 145, 148n
moral geography 149–61
Morgan, E. 27
Morgan, K. O. 56, 59, 61
Morgan, P. 58, 151, 221, 227
Morris, D. 86
Morris, P. 223
Morris-Jones, J. 58
Morton, H. V. 155–6
Mosse, G. 93
multiculturalism 17, 76, 83, 84, 87, 88
mundane reason 47
Murdoch, J. 13, 111
museography 214–18
museums 49, 191–232
music 16
Mussolini, B. 158
myth 12, 97, 104, 153, 192, 207–8, 215, 217, 223, 229, 231–2

Nairn, T. 5–12, 69, 70, 248
nation, 27, 29–30, 31, 32, 45, 49, 71, 73, 74, 76, 88, 114, 171, 208–14, 234, 238, 242, 245–7, 248
  reification 245–7
National Front 144, 147
National Assembly of Wales 4, 20, 27, 83, 88, 99, 101, 124
national identity 27, 29, 32, 38, 48, 49, 50, 51, 60, 66, 85, 171, 233, 235, 237, 244, 246
national memory 16, 55–6, 151–3
National Museum of Wales 60, 61, 161, 170, 172, 177, 209, 218
national parks 158
national self-determination 237
National Stadium 170, 171

National Theatre 177
nationalization 221–2, 231
nationalism 6–9, 17–19, 23, 27, 30, 34, 46, 47, 48, 64, 66, 69, 73, 84, 90–108, 117, 123, 129–48, 212–14, 235, 236, 240, 242, 245, 246
  British *see* British nationalism
  civic 87, 88, 96–7
  and common sense 17
  cultural 64, 117, 124
  discourses 12, 16, 24–5, 30, 84, 91–4, 107, 146–8, 210–11, 223, 245
  English *see* English nationalism
  ethnic 96–7, 107
  fortress 64
  and intellectuals 16, 91, 48–68
  theories 10–11, 22, 50–5, 95, 208–16, 236–47
  United Kingdom 4–5, 6–10, 29
nation-building 62
nation-state 3, 45, 50, 70, 88, 91, 103, 226, 235, 239
neo-colonialism 74
neo-Marxist, theories of nationalism 8–11
neo-Romantics 151, 167
Neurwirth, G. 113
New Commonwealth 19, 70, 75, 85, 144–5
new racism 73
new working class 115
newspapers 27, 29, 39, 69, 85, 181, 234
nomadism 83
Nonconformism 7, 55–7, 65, 66, 151, 153
Northern Ireland 96–7, 234
Norwegian church 186
nostalgia 194, 196–7, 200, 222, 231
Nottingham 178
novels 209

Oakwood Miners' Institute 62
oppression 17, 80, 95–9, 103–5, 107, 143
organic intellectuals 54, 60, 67
orientalism 213

Padarn 141, 196–8
Pakistan 19, 85, 144–5
Palmer, A. 153
Paris 172
Pattie, C. 198, 228

Peach, C. 145
peasants 153, 155, 157, 159–60, 163
Peate, I. 160–1, 164, 166–7
Pembrokeshire 152, 155, 161
Penclawdd 155
Penrose, J. 171
peripherality 225–7
periphery 6–10, 79, 166, 225–7, 229–30
phenomenology 33, 246
Phizacklea, A. 143
Picturesque movement 151
Piper, J. 153
pit closures 222
Plaid Cymru 6, 12, 17, 57, 59–60, 65–6, 76, 80, 87–8, 99–101, 103, 105, 124, 131–2, 136, 158–66, 228
planning policy 162–6, 168–90
poets, poetry 106, 157–8, 192
planning policy 162–6, 168–90
political science 39
politicians 129–32, 143–8, 175, 215
politics 4, 11–20, 22, 55–7, 64–6, 76, 91, 95, 98, 105–6, 129–48, 172, 175, 176–81, 184
Porth Neigwl 159–60
Porthmadog 200, 203–4
positive discrimination 100
post-colonialism 212, 236
postmodernity 3, 14, 194, 246
Powell, E. 129, 144–6
Pratt, M. L. 151
pre-industrial 57, 63
pre-modern 241, 243
Preseli hills 161
Price, D. 228
primordialism 239
progress 157, 231
proletariat 10, 54, 58, 227
Pryce, W. T. R. 199
Public Works and Town Planning Committee 176

Rabinow, P. 164, 167
race 17–18, 69–89, 94, 147, 157, 248
Race Relations Act 85
racial 69, 70, 72, 78, 114
racialization 7, 78, 85–8, 129, 148, 171, 183, 185–7
racism 13, 15, 17, 69–89, 129, 142–3, 145–6, 211
  British *see* British racism

radicalism 56, 59, 164
railways 15, 21, 155–7, 191–206
Ranger, T. 61, 242
Rawkins, P. 8, 64–5, 67
Rees, A. D. 6
Rees, G. 11, 24, 111, 113, 117, 173, 223, 249
Rees, T. 24, 249
regeneration 20, 175–7, 206, 218
religion 16, 91, 96–7, 104, 136, 144, 153, 157, 212
regional consensus 113, 116
regional identity 116
religion 31, 52, 55, 58, 240
remembering 212
Renan, E. 239
Report into the State of Education in Wales (1847) 104
residency qualifications 147, 148n
restructuring 116
Rex, J. 69, 71, 148n
Rhondda 209, 214–15, 220–32
Rhondda Heritage Park 19, 21, 209, 214–32
riots 83
roads 183–5
Roberts, B. 13, 18, 21, 66, 86, 111–28
Robertson, R. 197
Robins, K. 186
Rosaldo, M. 95
Romantic movement 150–1
Rowbotham, S. 94
Rowntree, K. 153
rugby football 118, 119, 180
rural industry 164–6
rural society 6, 13, 157
ruralism 151, 157–62, 228
rurality 13, 19–20, 21, 226

Said, E. 48, 208, 213, 225
St David's Centre 179, 180
St David's Day 119, 120
St Ives 151
Samuel, R. 192–3
Schama, S. 150
Schirmer, J. G. 102
Schlesinger, P. 246
Schopflin, G. 77
Scotch Cattle 59, 68
Scotland 4–6, 9, 70, 96–7
Scott Report 164, 166

Scottish identity 29, 32
Schwarzmantel, J. 53
Searle, G. R. 157
secularization 53, 55, 59
semiotics 217
servants 94
Seton-Watson, H. 237
sexuality 93
Shafer, B. 237–8, 239, 243
shipyards 204
shopping centres 170, 179
Sianel Pedwar Cymru (S4C) 6, 123
Sibley, D. 170
singing 119, 221, 227
Sivanandan, A. 146
slate industry 141, 191–206
slave trade 84
Smith, A. D. 52–3, 96, 111, 138, 149–50, 236, 240–3, 245, 248
Smith, D. 27, 39
Smith, D. E. 95
Snowdon Mountain Railway 197
Snowdonia National Park 195, 200
Snyder, L. 236, 237, 243
social anthropology 39
social boundaries 40, 112–16, 127
social closure 7, 51, 73–4, 87, 113–14, 137–47
social constructionism 38–45, 136, 171
social exclusion 113
social housing 185
social identity 39, 40, 126, 127
social image 66, 111–12, 126
social movement 90–108, 136
Socialism 53, 59, 88, 99, 221
socialization 6, 40
sociology 39, 111, 126, 240, 248
    of Wales 5–6
sovereignty 4, 91, 239
space/spatial 15, 46, 83, 84, 151, 206, 207–32, 235
sport 28, 29, 168, 171, 180, 234
Stanbrook, I. 144
Stapledon, G. 157–8
state 52, 241
status groups 148n
steam engines 197–8, 204
stereotypes 29–30, 66
strikes 115
Suggett, R. 6, 12
Sutherland, G. 152–3